Albert Camus.

DATE			

Bloom's Modern Critical Views

Bloom's Modern Critical Views

Modern Critical Views

ALBERT CAMUS

Edited and with an introduction by
Harold Bloom
Sterling Professor of the Humanities
Yale University

CHELSEA HOUSE PUBLISHERS
New York ◊ Philadelphia

Library of Congress Cataloging-in-Publication Data
Albert Camus.
  (Modern critical views)
  Bibliography: p.
  Includes index.
  1. Camus, Albert, 1913–1960—Criticism and
interpretation.   I. Bloom, Harold.   II. Series.
PQ2605.A3734Z546   1988   848'.91409   87–25696
ISBN 1–55546–313–4

Contents

Editor's Note

This book gathers together a representative selection of the best criticism devoted to the writings of Albert Camus. The critical essays are reprinted here in the chronological order of their original publication. I am grateful to Olga Popov and Henry Finder for their aid in editing this volume.

My introduction makes a critical estimate of the two famous novels *The Stranger* and *The Plague*, finding each to be severely limited as fiction by their essayistic tendentiousness. Victor Brombert, analyzing the story "The Renegade," finds in it a preoccupation with the modern intellectual's death drive. In a study of the cross-play of guilt and innocence, Roger Shattuck compares *The Stranger* to Melville's *Billy Budd*. The notebooks of Camus are reviewed by Paul de Man, who shows us a figure that is "attractive in its candor, but not authoritative in its thought." Jacques Guicharnaud writes on the theater of Camus and Sartre, dramatists of ideas, while E. Freeman contributes a specific study of *Caligula*, Camus's major play.

The major extended essays *The Myth of Sisyphus* and *The Rebel*, are seen by Donald Lazere as difficult, problematic works, though he assigns lasting value to the *Myth*. René Girard, formidable polemicist and Jansenist moralist, challenges Camus's own conviction that in *The Stranger* Meursault is somehow innocent and the judges essentially guilty. Reading *The Plague*, Patrick McCarthy traces in it the transition from Camus as tragic writer to Camus as apostle of brotherhood.

David R. Ellison, analyzing the rhetoric of *The Fall* sees it as an instance of Blanchot's "metaphorical scheme of dizziness." In a reading of the story "The Growing Stone," English Showalter, Jr., tries to define something close to Camus's final moral vision. A more political emphasis is brought to the stories in *Exile and the Kingdom* by Susan Tarrow, who reveals how they record "the impasse in which Camus found himself with regard to the Algerian situation," so much at variance with his moralized dreams.

Introduction

Sartre remains the classic commentator upon Camus, whom he assimilated to Pascal, to Rousseau, and to other French moralists, "the precursors of Nietzsche." To Sartre, Camus was "very much at peace within disorder," and so *The Stranger* was "a classical work, an orderly work, composed about the absurd and against the absurd." Shrewdly, Sartre finally assigned *The Stranger* not to the company of Heidegger or Hemingway, but to that of *Zadig* and *Candide,* the tales of Voltaire. Rereading Camus's short novel after forty years, I marvel at Sartre's keen judgment, and find it very difficult to connect my present impression of the book with my memory of how it seemed then. What Germaine Brée termed its heroic and humanistic hedonism seems, with the years, to have dwindled into an evasive hedonism, uncertain of its own gestures. The bleak narrative retains its Hemingwayesque aura, but the narrator, Meursault, seems even smaller now than he did four decades ago, when his dry disengagement had a certain novelty. Time, merciless critic, has worn *The Stranger* rather smooth, without however quite obliterating the tale.

René Girard, the most Jansenist of contemporary critics, "retried" *The Stranger,* and dissented from the verdict of "innocent" pronounced by Camus upon Meursault:

> If supernatural necessity is present in *L'Etranger,* why should Meursault alone come under its power? Why should the various characters in the same novel be judged by different yardsticks? If the murderer is not held responsible for his actions, why should the judges be held responsible for theirs?

Girard is reacting to an unfortunate comment by Camus himself: "A man who does not cry at the funeral of his mother is likely to be sentenced to death." In Girard's judgment, the quest of Camus was to convince us

1

that judgment of guilt is always wrong. Girard calls this an "egotistical Manichaeism" and convicts Camus of "literary solipsism," particularly in one devastating sentence: "Camus betrays solipsism when he writes *L'Etranger* just as Meursault betrays it when he murders the Arab." On this reading, the "innocent murder" is a metaphor for the creative process. Meursault is a bad child and Camus becomes as a child again when he writes Meursault's novel. Girard considers the novel an aesthetic success, but a morally immature work, since Meursault himself is guilty of judgment, though Camus wishes his protagonist not to be judged. "The world in which we live is one of perpetual judgment," Girard reminds us, in Pascalian vein. For Girard, the figures comparable to Meursault are Dostoevsky's Raskolnikov and Dimitri Karamazov. For Camus, those figures presumably were Kafka's Joseph K, and K the land surveyor. Either comparison destroys *The Stranger*, which has trouble enough competing with Malraux and Hemingway. Against Girard, I enter my own dissent. *The Stranger* is barely able to sustain an aesthetic dignity and certainly is much slighter than we thought it to be. But it is not morally flawed or inconsistent. In its cosmos, guilt and innocence are indistinguishable, and Jewish or Christian judgments are hopelessly irrelevant. Meursault is not, as Girard says, a juvenile delinquent, but an inadequate consciousness dazed by the sun, overwhelmed by a context that is too strong for him:

> On seeing me, the Arab raised himself a little, and his hand went to his pocket. Naturally, I gripped Raymond's revolver in the pocket of my coat. Then the Arab let himself sink back again, but without taking his hand from his pocket. I was some distance off, at least ten yards, and most of the time I saw him as a blurred dark form wobbling in the heat haze. Sometimes, however, I had glimpses of his eyes glowing between the half-closed lids. The sound of the waves was even lazier, feebler, than at noon. But the light hadn't changed; it was pounding as fiercely as ever on the long stretch of sand that ended at the rock. For two hours the sun seemed to have made no progress; becalmed in a sea of molten steel. Far out on the horizon a steamer was passing; I could just make out from the corner of an eye the small black moving patch, while I kept my gaze fixed on the Arab.
>
> It struck me that all I had to do was to turn, walk away, and think no more about it. But the whole beach, pulsing with heat, was pressing on my back. I took some steps toward the stream. The Arab didn't move. After all, there was still some distance

between us. Perhaps because of the shadow on his face, he seemed to be grinning at me.

I waited. The heat was beginning to scorch my cheeks; beads of sweat were gathering in my eyebrows. It was just the same sort of heat as at my mother's funeral, and I had the same disagreeable sensations—especially in my forehead, where all the veins seemed to be bursting through the skin. I couldn't stand it any longer, and took another step forward. I knew it was a fool thing to do; I wouldn't get out of the sun by moving on a yard or so. But I took that step, just one step, forward. And then the Arab drew his knife and held it up toward me, athwart the sunlight.

A shaft of light shot upward from the steel, and I felt as if a long, thin blade transfixed my forehead. At the same moment all the sweat that had accumulated in my eyebrows splashed down on my eyelids, covering them with a warm film of moisture. Beneath a veil of brine and tears my eyes were blinded; I was conscious only of the cymbals of the sun clashing on my skull, and, less distinctly, of the keen blade of light flashing up from the knife, scarring my eyelashes, and gouging into my eyeballs.

Then everything began to reel before my eyes, a fiery gust came from the sea, while the sky cracked in two, from end to end, and a great sheet of flame poured down through the rift. Every nerve in my body was a steel spring, and my grip closed on the revolver. The trigger gave, and the smooth underbelly of the butt jogged my palm. And so, with that crisp, whipcrack sound, it all began. I shook off my sweat and the clinging veil of light. I knew I'd shattered the balance of the day, the spacious calm of this beach on which I had been happy. But I fired four shots more into the inert body, on which they left no visible trace. And each successive shot was another loud, fateful rap on the door of my undoing.

The "absurd" and the "gratuitous" seem wrong categories to apply here. We have a vision of possession by the sun, an inferno that fuses consciousness and will into a single negation, and burns through it to purposes that may exist, but are not human. Gide's Lafcadio, a true absurdist, said he was not curious about events but about himself, while Meursault is not curious about either. What Meursault at the end calls "the benign indifference of the universe" is belied by the pragmatic malevolence of the sun. The true influence upon *The Stranger* seems to me Melville's *Moby-Dick*, and for the whiteness of the whale Camus substitutes the whiteness of the sun. Meursault is no quester, no Ahab, and Ahab would not have allowed him aboard the *Pequod*. But the cosmos of *The Stranger* is essentially the cosmos of *Moby-Dick;* though in many of its visible aspects Meursault's world might seem to have been formed in love, its invisible spheres were formed in fright. The Jansenist Girard is accurate in finding Gnostic hints in the world of Camus, but not so accurate in judging Camus to possess only a bad child's sense of innocence. Judging Meursault is as wasteful as judging his judges; that blinding light of the sun burns away all judgment.

II

Forty years after its initial publication, Camus's *The Plague* (1947) has taken on a peculiar poignance in the era of our new plague, the ambiguously named AIDS. *The Plague* is a tendentious novel, more so even than *The Stranger*. A novelist requires enormous exuberance to sustain tendentiousness; Dostoevsky had such exuberance, Camus did not. Or a master of evasions, like Kafka, can evade his own compulsions, but Camus is all too interpretable. The darkest comparison would be to Beckett, whose trilogy of *Molloy, Malone Dies,* and *The Unnamable* conveys a sense of menace and anguish, metaphysical and psychological, that dwarfs *The Plague*.

Oran, spiritually rejecting the healthy air of the Mediterranean, in some sense brings the Plague upon itself; indeed Oran *is* the Plague, before the actual infection arrives. That may sound impressive, but constitutes a novelistic blunder, because Camus wants it both ways and cannot make it work either way. Either the relatively innocent suffer an affliction from outside, or the at least somewhat culpable are compelled to suffer the outward sign of their inward lack of grace. Truth doubtless lies in between, in our lives, but to *represent* so mixed a truth in your novel you must be an accomplished novelist, and not an essayist, or writer of quasi-philosophical tales. Dostoevsky dramatized the inwound textures of transcendence and material decay in nearly every event and every personage, while *The Plague* is curiously bland whenever it confronts the necessity of dramatizing anything.

I am unfair in comparing Camus to Beckett, Kafka, Dostoevsky, titanic authors, and it is even more unfair to contrast *The Plague* with Dickens's *A Tale of Two Cities*, since Dickens is very nearly the Shakespeare of novelists. Yet the two books are surprisingly close in vision, structure, theme, and in the relation of language to a reality of overwhelming menace. Camus's Plague is a version of Dickens's Terror, and Dr. Rieux, Rambert, Father Paneloux, Tarrou, and the volunteer sanitary workers all follow in the path

of the noble Carton, since all could proclaim: "It is a far, far better thing
that I do, than I have ever done." One can think of the Plague as AIDS,
Revolutionary Terror, the Nazi occupation, or what one will, but one still
requires persuasive representations of persons, whether in the aggregate or
in single individuals.

"Indifference," properly cultivated, can be a stoic virtue, even a mode
of heroism, but it is very difficult to represent. Here also Camus fails the
contest with Melville or Dostoevsky. Consider a crucial dialogue between
Tarrou and Dr. Rieux, both of them authentic heroes, by the standards of
measurement of any morality, religion, or societal culture:

> "My question's this," said Tarrou. "Why do you yourself show
> such devotion, considering you don't believe in God? I suspect
> your answer may help me to mine."
>
> His face still in shadow, Rieux said that he'd already answered:
> that if he believed in an all-powerful God he would cease curing
> the sick and leave that to Him. But no one in the world believed
> in a God of that sort; no, not even Paneloux, who believed that
> he believed in such a God. And this was proved by the fact that
> no one ever threw himself on Providence completely. Anyhow, in
> this respect Rieux believed himself to be on the right road—in
> fighting against creation as he found it.
>
> "Ah," Tarrou remarked. "So that's the idea you have of your
> profession?"
>
> "More or less." The doctor came back into the light.
>
> Tarrou made a faint whistling noise with his lips, and the doc-
> tor gazed at him.
>
> "Yes, you're thinking it calls for pride to feel that way. But I
> assure you I've no more than the pride that's needed to keep me
> going. I have no idea what's awaiting me, or what will happen
> when all this ends. For the moment I know this; there are sick
> people and they need curing. Later on, perhaps, they'll think
> things over; and so shall I. But what's wanted now is to make
> them well. I defend them as best I can, that's all."
>
> "Against whom?"
>
> Rieux turned to the window. A shadow-line on the horizon
> told of the presence of the sea. He was conscious only of his ex-
> haustion, and at the same time was struggling against a sudden,
> irrational impulse to unburden himself a little more to his com-
> panion; an eccentric, perhaps, but who, he guessed, was one of
> his own kind.

"I haven't a notion, Tarrou; I assure you I haven't a notion. When I entered this profession, I did it 'abstractedly,' so to speak; because I had a desire for it, because it meant a career like another, one that young men often aspire to. Perhaps, too, because it was particularly difficult for a workman's son, like myself. And then I had to see people die. Do you know that there are some who *refuse* to die? Have you ever heard a woman scream 'Never!' with her last gasp? Well, I have. And then I saw that I could never get hardened to it. I was young then, and I was outraged by the whole scheme of things, or so I thought. Subsequently I grew more modest. Only, I've never managed to get used to seeing people die. That's all I know. Yet after all—"

Rieux fell silent and sat down. He felt his mouth dry.

"After all—?" Tarrou prompted softly.

"After all," the doctor repeated, then hesitated again, fixing his eyes on Tarrou, "it's something that a man of your sort can understand most likely, but, since the order of the world is shaped by death, mightn't it be better for God if we refuse to believe in Him and struggle with all our might against death, without raising our eyes toward the heaven where He sits in silence?"

Tarrou nodded.

"Yes. But your victories will never be lasting; that's all."

Rieux's face darkened.

"Yes, I know that. But it's no reason for giving up the struggle."

"No reason, I agree. Only, I now can picture what this plague must mean for you."

"Yes. A never ending defeat."

Tarrou stared at the doctor for a moment, then turned and tramped heavily toward the door. Rieux followed him and was almost at his side when Tarrou, who was staring at the floor, suddenly said:

"Who taught you all this, Doctor?"

The reply came promptly:

"Suffering."

"Indifference" to transcendence here is a humanistic protest "in fighting against creation as he found it," a defense of the dying against death. It is a stoicism because Rieux is no longer "outraged by the whole scheme of things," even though he continues to know that "the order of the world is shaped by death." The best aesthetic touch here is the moment when Tarrou and Rieux come to understand one another, each finding the meaning of the Plague to be "a never ending defeat." But this is wasted when, at the conclusion of the passage I have quoted, Rieux utters the banality that "suffering" has taught him his pragmatic wisdom. Repeated rereadings will dim the passage further. "A shadow-line on the horizon told of the presence of the sea." Conrad would have known how to integrate that into his complex Impressionism, but in Camus it constitutes another mechanical manifestation of symbolism, reminding us that Oran opened itself to the Plague by turning its back upon the sea.

Camus was an admirable if confused moralist and the legitimate heir of a long tradition of rational lucidity. He did not write a *Candide* or even a *Zadig;* I cannot recall one humorous moment anywhere in his fiction. *The Stranger* and *The Plague,* like his other fictions, are grand period pieces, crucial reflectors of the morale and concerns of France and the Western world in the 1940s, both before and after the Liberation from the Nazis. Powerful representations of an era have their own use and justification and offer values not in themselves aesthetic.

VICTOR BROMBERT

"Le Renégat,"
or the Terror of the Absolute

Future generations may well admire, above all the rest of Camus's work, the nightmarish perfection of this parable, with its incantatory rhythms and blinding images of pain. It is, however, a disturbing text. Brutality assumes hysterical proportions. Feverish, convulsive images build up to an apocalypse of cruelty.

"*Quelle bouillie, quelle bouillie!*" The opening words refer to the pulp-like state of the narrator's mind. But it is his body which was first literally beaten to a pulp. In an unlivable, "maddening" landscape, under the rays of a savage sun, the human flesh is exposed to the worst indignities. In the white heat of an African summer, the victim is whipped and salt is lavishly sprinkled on his wounds. Beaten about the head with wet ropes until his ears bleed, he is left moaning under the eyes of a bloodthirsty Fetish. Sadistic women assist his torturers, while he in turn is forced to witness the torture and rape of others. Inhuman cries, bestial matings, orgiastic rituals culminate in scenes of mutilation. His tongue is cut out, his mouth filled with salt. But nothing seems to satisfy this lust for pain. The victim himself—willing collaborator of his tormentors—yearns for more punishment.

Punctuated by onomatopoeic effects (the submissive interjection ô, the guttural râ, râ, the haunting rattle of thirst, hate and death), this frenzied tale offers no respite. But what is all this violence about? Why does the narrator accept it with gratitude, even with relish? On the surface, the story appears simple enough. A student in a theological seminary is consumed with the

From *The Intellectual Hero: Studies in the French Novel 1880–1955.* © 1960, 1961 by Victor Brombert. J. B. Lippincott, 1961.

desire to convert heathens, to force upon others the truth of his faith. He decides to set out as a missionary to the African "city of salt," Taghâsa—a "closed city" which few have entered, and from which even fewer have returned. Having heard of the spectacular cruelty of its inhabitants, he feels attracted by the glorious possibility of converting them to the God of Love. Although warned by his superiors that he is not ready, not "ripe," he dreams of penetrating into the very sanctuary of the Fetish, of subjugating the savages through the sheer power of the Word.

Events take, however, an unexpected turn. He discovers that evil is stronger than he thought, and soon accepts this strength as the only truth. The tortured missionary is thus, ironically, converted by the very Fetish he set out to destroy. He discovers the joy and the power of hatred. His new masters teach him how to despise love. He adores, as he has never adored before, the axlike face of the Fetish who "possesses" him. At the end of the story, as though to outdo his new masters and to avenge himself on his old ones, he savagely kills the new missionary, while calling for the eternal Reign of Hatred.

The virtuosity of these pages is remarkable. Nowhere else has Camus revealed himself so accomplished a master of images, sounds and rhythms. The fulgurating whiteness of the landscape, the piercing sun-fire of this white hell, the liquefaction of time under the burning refraction of a thousand mirrors—all this is suggested in the hallucinating interior monologue which presses forward as though indeed the only speech left the tongueless narrator were the metaphorical "tongue" of his feverish brain. In this "cold torrid city" Taghâsa, with its iron name and the steel-like ridges of its landscape, a defiant race has built a surrealistic city of salt.

The salt and the sun—these are indeed the basic images in "Le Renégat." The word "sun," in itself symbol of absolute violence, appears up to four times in the same paragraph. "Savage" and "irresistible," it is the sun of death and of flies. It "beats," it "pierces," making holes in the overheated metal of the sky. Visual images, as well as images of sound and touch, are relentless reminders of the theme of hardness. The narrator hears in his own mouth the sound of rough pebbles. He fondles the barrel of his gun, while the stones and rocks all around him crackle from the heat. There is hardly a transition between the ice-coldness of the night and the crystal-like dazzlement of the day. But it is the very rhythm of the speech—panting, harsh, elliptical yet smooth—which marks the greatest achievement of this text. Audacious, yet pure in a Racinian manner, the language and the syntax swiftly glide from affirmation to negation.

Virtuosity is, however, not Camus's purpose. Even when originally inspired by vivid personal impulses and sensations (surrender to air, sun, water; love of nature; pagan sensuality), most of Camus's writing seems irresistibly drawn toward an allegorical meaning. The very titles of his work which so often suggest a loss, a fall, an exile or a spiritual disease, point to a parabolic tendency and at times even seem to come close to Christian theological concerns. He may be, like Jean-Baptiste Clamence in *La Chute*, an *ailing* prophet, sick with the very illusions and weakness he feels compelled to denounce. But this solidarity with illness only makes the diagnosis more urgent.

The missionary in "Le Renégat," who discovers that only guns have souls, is very sick indeed. His sickness, a particularly dangerous one: the obsessive quest for the absolute. His superiors at the seminary are perfectly right: he does not know "who he is." This ignorance of his true self sets the stage for the most shocking discoveries. But, on the symbolic level, it also points to the transcendental urges which bring about self-negation and self-destruction.

Who, indeed, is the narrator? Who is this missionary-renegade with his desire for "order" and his dream of absolute power? "Dirty slave," he calls himself with characteristic self-hatred. Intelligent, but hard-headed (*"mulet," "tête de vache"*), he is from his youth on attracted to cruelty, finding the very idea of barbarians exciting. A hunter of pain, he imagines that the very girls in the street will strike at him and spit in his face. He dreams of teeth that tear, and enjoys the voluptuous image of his imagined pain.

This masochistic eroticism which instinctively leads him to Taghâsa is clearly of a symbolic nature. The rape by the evil Fetish is perpetrated not so much on his body as on his mind. The missionary surrenders to the Fetish in a quasi-sexual ecstasy of pain. But this surrender is of an intellectual nature: the allegory deals with the drama of the mind. In a climate whose extreme heat precludes contact between human beings, his new masters, these "lords" of the salt mines, succeed in brainwashing the absolutist, or rather in converting him. *Absolute* dedication to good is transmuted into *absolute* dedication to evil.

The allegorical identity of the Renegade thus emerges. He is the modern intellectual, heir to a Humanist culture, but now impatient with the "seminary" coziness of his tradition and with its sham, and who, in search of systems and ideologies, espouses totalitarian values that have long ago declared war (and he knows it!) on the thinker and his thought. Thus amorous hate and amorous surrender are the logical consequence of a denial of life in favor of abstraction. The missionary-intellectual believes he is out to convert the barbarians; in fact he seeks tyranny in order to submit to it.

This betrayal, however, remains ambivalent. On the one hand, it shows up the poison of ideological absolutes; on the other, it reveals the deep-rooted suicidal impulses of the intelligentsia. The missionary-renegade, bitter against his former teachers and ashamed of his cultural heritage, seeks not only the destruction of what he is, but of what he represents. He has "an account to settle" with his entire culture. That is, one must assume, the meaning of his murdering the missionary. By killing him, he attempts to kill what he himself stands for, as well as the spiritual guild to which he belongs. The betrayal is a vengeance, but this vengeance is also self-punishment!

The terror of the absolute, so powerfully conveyed by this story, is one of Camus's permanent themes. The missionary who reneges his mission does so because his thirst for a despotic ideal can only find satisfaction in evil. For evil, unlike good, can be absolute in human terms. The Renegade, seeing that good is a constantly postponed and tiring project, refuses to pursue any further an ever receding boundary. He knows that the Reign of Goodness is impossible. So he turns to the Reign of Evil as to the only abstraction that can be translated into a flawless truth. For only the square truth, the "heavy" and "dense" truth, can be acceptable to the seeker of the absolute. "Only evil can go to its own limit and reign absolutely." The conversion, to be sure, leads to a denial of all values. "Down with Europe, down with reason, honor and the cross." But this is the price to pay: the militant need for absolute affirmation implies absolute negation. Ideology replaces life. The missionary-intellectual becomes a grave-digger who prepares his own burial. No problem of our time has preoccupied Camus more than this disastrous temptation of the absolute and the death wish of the modern intellectual.

ROGER SHATTUCK

Two Inside Narratives: Billy Budd *and* L'Etranger

Like two mineral specimens different in color and texture yet remarkably similar in structure, Melville's last novel and Camus's first seem designed for comparison. A few scholars have remarked the kinship without analyzing it at length. Direct influence can be ruled out, since Camus read *Billy Budd* after having written *L'Etranger*. Thus we are left very much in the clear with something suggestive to assay. The evident value of comparing the independent approach of two major authors to a similar theme is here augmented by the fact that the significance of both works remains in dispute.

The two narratives turn on the same, essentially equivocal situation. From one point of view, a real crime, not of passion or premeditation, but of impulse, is described as an innocent action. From an opposing point of view, a spiritually innocent man discovers and ultimately affirms his guilt. "Innocence and guilt . . . in effect changed places," writes Melville just before Billy's trial. In both books this ambivalent situation arises through the rigid application of a system of justice to a murder that follows a series of fortuitous misdemeanors. Billy, for example, spills soup in Claggart's path. Two days after his mother's funeral Meursault goes to a Fernandel movie with his new girlfriend. In each case a lengthy trial scene leading to the death sentence reveals the narrowness and distortion of the "justice" defined respectively by the British Articles of War in 1797 and by the Napoleonic Criminal Code. Yet neither man defends himself against the charges, nor does he show any remorse. Thus the two crimes remain inwardly unjudged and produce no moral anguish, even though both Billy and Meursault accept

From *Texas Studies in Literature and Language* 4, no. 3 (Autumn 1962). © 1962 by the University of Texas Press.

their guilt. In his final moment Billy cries out, "God bless Captain Vere!" and dies peacefully. Meursault finds the prosecutor's case against him "plausible" and faces the facts in the middle of his trial: "J'ai senti alors quelque chose qui soulevait toute la salle et, pour la première fois, j'ai compris que j'étais coupable." The statement turns on the fact that at this point Meursault still cannot disengage what he inwardly knows himself to be from what society judges him to be.

This cross-play of innocence and guilt leads directly into the characters of the two heroes. Though given very different backgrounds and temperaments, they immediately reveal that something has already dislocated their entire mode of existence, and has produced their unlikely but alluring innocence. Of Billy, Melville states that in moments of strong feeling he was "apt to develop an organic hesitancy, in fact more or less of a stutter or even worse." This single flaw suffices to signify a mysterious imbalance in his character. And here we strike upon the first real illumination afforded by the comparison of these two novels. Meursault's inability to reply to any question that demands a choice or a preference, his habitual response of "Cela m'est égal," amounts to a metaphysical stutter more serious than Billy's. Their inarticulateness, the impediment between their consciousness and the world, is not accidental but essential. It defines Billy and Meursault as truncated men whose actions must necessarily appear ambivalent.

Under longer scrutiny these similarities of theme yield to extensive differences in the narrative style employed. Billy's story comes to us through the eyes and mind of a shadowy narrator who speaks alternately as a keen witness (who nevertheless misses many of the crucial scenes), and as a singularly obtuse and tendentious commentator on the events. His refracting presence has been neglected by all but one critic, Lawrance Thompson, who makes it the basis for interpreting the story as essentially ironic, a masked quarrel with God. From behind this further ambiguity of style, however, one fact emerges clearly: none of the principal characters changes in the course of the action, Billy least of all. "The handsome sailor" as Melville repeatedly calls him, is born to his status of "natural" election, learns nothing from experience, and maintains to the end his upright character and resignation to misfortune. We learn that, though a foundling, he is "evidently no ignoble one." Though many critics have proposed a major shift in Billy's attitude toward life and death during the off-stage interview in which Captain Vere tells him the sentence, nothing in the text supports this hypothesis. Even with allowances for irony, Billy remains the "noble barbarian," a second Adam with no taint of the serpent but a stutter, an angel of God. Accordingly, his punishment is imposed solely on the basis of his deed, without consideration for his innocence of character and lack of evil intent.

The exact opposite holds for Meursault. The trial focuses not on his deed but on the purported insensitivity and moral depravity of every part of his life. And, unlike Billy, he changes. The unpremeditated and fateful shooting, plus the ritualized trial, conspire to capsize Meursault's inner equilibrium.

The change in his state of being can be detected in the narrative style which, totally unlike that of *Billy Budd,* appears at first to be restricted to the hero's immediate sensations recorded without the categories of civilized living. From the outset, however, one stumbles over sentences which protrude above the flatness of the prose. Very early in the story, for instance, during the scene of the wake, Meursault breaks through the surface of his monotone: "J'ai eu un moment l'impression ridicule qu'ils étaient là pour me juger." One barely notices the shift in point of view. Some sixty pages later, after the much discussed explosion of metaphors in the passage on the shooting on the beach, Meursault finds himself oddly afraid of the examining magistrate and makes this highly sophisticated observation about his fear: "Je reconnaissais en même temps que c'était ridicule parce que, somme toute, c'était moi le criminel." This is no transparent sensibility. He is beginning to catch sight of himself. The primitive first person singular of passive sensation has gradually secreted beside itself another, highly penetrating person of reflection. And this bifurcation of sensibility asserts itself in the style in the shape of a double *je,* which functions simultaneously as first person and as third person looking back astonished. It is the reverse of Diderot's or Stendhal's mimetic and enthusiastic *il,* which they frequently brandish as if it were a first person. In *L'Etranger* Camus displays a consciousness discovering itself in a crucial process, recollection of which is usually irretrievable from the hinterland of childhood.

This emergence of self, first seen stirring in the syntax, is brought out further by an equally subtle device which raises the events of the story out of the dead level of meaninglessness. There is an innocent-looking passage at the end of the second chapter that seems to close us out of Meursault's life by closing the whole dreary incident of his mother's death and burial. But not so:

> J'ai fermé mes fenêtres et en revenant j'ai vu dans la glace un bout de table où ma lampe à alcool voisinait avec des morceaux de pain. J'ai pensé que c'était toujours un dimanche de tiré, que maman était maintenant enterrée, que j'allais reprendre mon travail et que, somme toute, il n'y avait rien de changé.

This instant, in which Meursault glimpses just a corner of his existence in the mirror, this little still-life image of his surroundings, is the first of a series of happenings that force Meursault to see himself, to reflect on his life. And we are carried back into the story instead of being sealed out of it. The instances of Meursault's self-beholding become increasingly explicit: the bizarre "automatic" woman in the restaurant, the newspaper clipping in his cell, the "sad, severe" face he sees reflected in his mess bowl, the startling sound of his own voice when he finds he is talking to himself, the journalist staring fixedly at him in the courtroom, and the testimony of the witnesses talking on and on about him. Finally Meursault's lawyer reviews all the events of the case, using the first person, a convention that turns Meursault into a fascinated and helpless spectator of his own life: "Moi j'ai pensé que c'était m'écarter encore de l'affaire, me réduire à zéro et, en un certain sens, se substituer à moi." This series of disturbing self-confrontations leaves Meursault divided and weakened at a time when he wants for the first time to be *comme tout le monde,* a normal human being. He never has his wish. The chaplain's visit and offer of absolution and intercession provoke from Meursault violent self-affirmation as a criminal outcast. Thus at the end he strives to reassemble his divided sensibility. He strikes out not so much at the "absurdity" of his life, as we are frequently told, as at a threat to the one role left to him: that of embittered but courageous victim who wants people's hate and not their help.

The contrast in action is, therefore, pronounced. Billy's fate is virtually given in his birth with its obscure defect. Self-sacrifice leaves him unchanged. Meursault, still an uncomprehending sleepwalker in the murder scene on the beach, finally calls fate down on his head when he grasps the meaning of his act. Self-sacrifice makes him a man.

At this point a change of method is required to search beyond the set of similarities and differences examined up to now. The science of crystal-lography discovered over a century ago insists that in comparing mineral specimens one must not be content with looking at them but must go on to examine a beam of light that has passed through them. The discovery of plane-polarized light led to major revelations about the internal molecu-lar structure of crystals. The final stage of the comparative method applied to related works like *Billy Budd* and *L'Etranger* may be to regard them in series, seeking the clearest meaning they transmit together.

It is here that Melville's cryptic and cautionary subtitle, *An Inside Nar-rative,* takes on significance for both novels. Applied in the present context to Camus's novel, it appropriately calls attention to the deepest movement of the book's action: a human consciousness undergoing mitosis, an inner division experienced very late by a physically mature man. We witness the process from inside through the ambiguous and shifting use of a double *je.*

Meursault's final self-affirmation as a condemned man is a truly heroic effort to bring the parts back together in defiance of society's judgment and of Christian forgiveness.

Meursault's separation from himself and return, sighted through Melville's complementary action, allows fresh insight into the character structure of *Billy Budd*. Billy never comes unstuck from himself because he already belongs to a larger division. In Melville's story we are symbolically carried inside the microcosm of one individual broken into three parts: Captain Vere standing for the pride of both reason and authority, Claggart, who represents "depravity according to nature," and Billy, who embodies ingenuous goodness. None of the three is pure, and none is a whole man. *The Indomitable* puts to sea less as the ship of state or society than as the ship of a complex individual. Under the stress of social and political upheaval lengthily described in the opening chapters, this living unit, this multiple man sacrifices one part of himself in order to maintain discipline. The whole pulse of the novel implies that such a sacrifice must be lethal. *Billy Budd* is anything but a "testament of acceptance," as it has often been described since E. L. G. Watson's article in 1933. Nor is it (as it has been labelled by an eloquent lecturer for a society working to abolish the institution) the only novel ever written in defense of capital punishment. In unmistakable allegory Melville presents the possibility of man's inward division and the accompanying dangers of self-destruction.

Held up together to the light, these two novels have an iridescent quality, a flickering of implied meanings ranging from Christian atonement, to the embodiment of fate in social situations, to the sinfulness of God himself. Despite flaws of artificial style and some labored symbolism in both books, they are true gems with the capacity to refract light in multiple ways. But the clearest beam they transmit when set in the proper alignment emanates from a single area of experience. These two inside narratives reveal man's consciousness deadlocked with its own most awe-inspiring work—civilization—here in the form of "justice" under law. The particular natures of Billy and Meursault lead to exceptional treatments of this theme, faced less squarely and less often in fiction than we should like to believe.

We have come to think of the novel as the exhibiting of a hero constantly testing, risking, and extending himself in some form of play-acting inspired by the realization of being alive: Robinson Crusoe to Rastignac to Proust's Marcel. Stendhal's most characteristic creations prove themselves in moments of intense crisis by their ability to improvise both action and emotion. In novels so markedly different as those of D. H. Lawrence and Virginia Woolf, the heroes, after first acertaining the strictures of life around them, begin to recast their inner being in response to glimpsed possibilities of experience. But the two heroes we have been examining refuse to engage in this energetic psychological prospecting in the face of the "forms" of civilized existence. Billy never deviates from his given character and has no qualms about himself. True, he fears a flogging and is stunned by his impulsive violence; but he sleeps soundly the night before his execution. Meursault, just a few degrees more sophisticated than Billy, begins in a comparable state of mind, is then wrenched far enough out of this restricted sensibility to see himself as others see him, goes on to refuse that knowledge in the scene with the chaplain, and at the end reasserts his original "simple" consciousness of himself as a man. Thus they both stubbornly remain on a level with the *mécanique* of justice that condemns them and do not evade it by any subtle psychological contortion.

In an era of post-Freudian plastic surgery of the soul, it is this flat-footedness of character that gives the two books their archaic tone and haunting appeal. Billy's final blessing and Meursault's final curse grow out of the same primitive moral awareness of how man has constructed around himself the potential instrument of his own destruction. Melville and Camus do not squander their distress on the future of civilization. They know that in the struggle to live with it and ahead of it, it is the self that suffers and the self that may perish. Save him.

PAUL DE MAN

The Mask of Albert Camus:
Notebooks 1942–1951

The subtle but radical change that separates the intellectual atmosphere of the fifties from that of the sixties could well be measured by one's attitude towards the work and the person of Albert Camus. During his lifetime he was for many an exemplary figure; his work bears many traces of the doubts and agonies that such an exalted position inevitably carries with it. He has not ceased to be so: In several recent literary essays, written by men whose formative years coincided with the period of Camus's strongest influence, the impact of his presence can still be strongly felt. On the other hand, one can well imagine how he might prove disappointing to a new generation, not because this generation lacks the experience that shaped Camus's world, but because the interpretation he gave of his own experience lacks clarity and insight. That Sartre and Merleau-Ponty, different from each other as they are, seem more closely attuned to the modern temper is by itself no proof of their superiority. Nor indeed does this make Camus necessarily the defender of permanent values. Before we can blame our times for moving away from him, we must clarify our notion of what he represents.

The publication of the *Notebooks* is a useful addition to the understanding of a writer who, in his fiction, always chose to hide behind the mask of a deliberate, controlled style or behind a pseudo-confessional tone that serves to obscure, rather than to reveal, his true self. The "I" that addresses the reader in *The Stranger* and in *The Fall*, and the collective "we" of *The Plague*, are never to be directly identified with the voice of Camus; in accor-

From *The New York Review of Books* 5, no. 10 (23 December 1965). © 1965 by NYREV, Inc.

dance with the tradition of the novel, the author reserves the right to keep his interpretations of characters and events implicit and ambivalent. The genre of the novel is, by definition, oblique, and no one thinks of blaming Cervantes for the fact that, up to this very day, critics cannot agree whether he was for or against Don Quixote. More contemporary figures, however, are not allowed the same immunity especially if, like Camus, they openly intervene in public and political matters and claim to experience personal conflicts that are typical of the historical situation in general. In such cases, one is certainly entitled to look for utterances in which the true commitment (or the true uncertainty) of the writer is revealed.

Camus's *Notebooks* do not offer an easy key to the understanding of an irresolute man. In this second volume of his private notes—the first volume of the *Notebooks,* covering the period from May 1935 to February 1942, has also been published in English—Camus's personal reserve has increased rather than diminished, and the lack of intimacy or of self-display is both admirable and unusual. There is nothing here of the abandon, the indiscretion of many intimate journals, very little self-justification or, for that matter, self-analysis. The second volume of the *Notebooks* deals with the period from January 1942 till March 1951, during which the main events in Camus's personal, public, and literary life took place: his forced stay in occupied France after the Allied landing in North Africa, his participation in the Resistance and subsequent political activity as editor of *Combat,* the considerable success of his novels and plays, which made him one of the most influential writers of the post-war era. It is during this period that he wrote *The Plague* and the ambitious essay *Man in Revolt (The Rebel* in its American edition), which interprets the modern predicament as a historical conflict of values. It was also during this period that Camus's inner conflicts and hesitations gained in intensity, leading to a growing retreat from public action, the eventual break with Sartre, and the combination of bitterness and lucidity that one finds in *The Fall.*

Obviously it was a very rich and complex period—but only the remotest echoes filter through to the pages of these notebooks. Readers who expect revelations, strong opinions, anecdotes, and the like will be disappointed. Even the most unsettling personal episodes in Camus's life appear in remote and indirect perspectives. For instance, when he suffered an unexpected recurrence of his early tuberculosis in 1949, his reaction to the event appears in the *Notebooks* only in the form of a poignant note quoted from one of Keats's last letters, written while he was dying in Rome of the same disease. The example, one among many, shows how remote the notebooks are from a personal journal. They are essentially workbooks, comparable to the sketchpads that certain painters carry with them, in which reactions to the outside world are recorded only insofar as they are relevant to the work in progress.

The *Notebooks* consist primarily of outlines for future plays or novels, notes on current reading, early versions of passages, records of situations or remarks observed at the time and stored away for later reference. Camus made considerable use of these notes: many key passages from later books first appear here, frequently as brief notations without further comment or reflections. For a student of Camus's work, the *Notebooks* thus contain much important information. The present collection will prove indispensable, especially to interpreting *The Plague* and *The Rebel*. Together with the notes and variants established by Roger Quilliot for the *Pléiade* edition of the novels and plays, the *Notebooks* give us the kind of information about the genesis of Camus's writing that is ordinarily made available only many decades after an author's death.

But the *Notebooks* can also serve a less specialized function, and help towards a general consideration of Camus's development. No matter how rigorous the reserve, how decorous the self-restraint, a fuller image nevertheless shines through these pages, though more by what they leave unsaid than by what they bring to light. One is struck, for instance, by the considerable difference in tone between the later pages of the *Notebooks* and those contained in the previous volume. The earlier remarks frequently had the spontaneous, lyrical quality of ideas and impressions revealed for their own sake. No deep gulf separates the actual person from the writer, and what is of interest to the one also serves the other. When, in 1940, Camus describes his reactions to the city of Oran he does so with a vivacity of perception that brings the city to life even more effectively than in the opening pages of *The Plague*. The pages on Oran in the 1940 notebook are felicitous in themselves and useful to his later work as well. As the notebooks progress, and especially after the war, such happy conjunctions between the writer's experience and his literary work become less and less frequent: Camus deliberately tore himself away from his natural inclinations and forced upon himself a number of alien concerns. As a result, the *Notebooks* reflect an increasing feeling of estrangement and solitude. One feels an almost obsessive commitment to work, a rejection of any moment of private experience as self-indulgence. The man and the writer have less and less in common, and the writer owed it to his avocation to keep repressing his personal life:

> Only by a continual effort can I create. My tendency is to drift toward immobility. My deepest, surest inclination lies in silence and the daily routine. . . . But I know that I stand erect through

that very effort and that if I ceased to believe in it for a single moment I should roll over the precipice. This is how I avoid illness and renunciation, raising my head with all my strength to breathe and to conquer. This is my way of despairing and this is my way of curing myself.

The resolution undoubtedly has moral grandeur, but it requires the constant rejection of a personal quality which is, in fact, not just oriented towards silence and mechanical routine. Outcries of rebellion against solitude punctuate the notebooks and give them a more somber tone than is found in any of Camus's dramatic or fictional works. Optimistic assertions about the necessity of dialogue and the ultimate value of the individual are interspersed with notations of despair: "Unbearable solitude—I cannot believe it or resign myself to it"; "Utter solitude. In the urinal of a major railway station at 1 a.m." The spontaneous elation that inspires the pages on Algiers, Oran, and the cities of Italy in the early notebooks has been replaced by this note of despair and alienation: for the solitude that torments Camus is most of all an estrangement from what he considers his authentic former self. The more he gets involved with others, with social issues and public forms of thought and action, the more he feels a loss of contact with his true being.

This evolution is so frequent in modern literature that it certainly does not, by itself, warp Camus's interpretation of his times. His loneliness is genuine, not a pose; the scruples that haunted him while he was being increasingly rewarded by a society in which he participated so little are apparent in many passages of the *Notebooks*. It cannot be said of him, as of the hero of *The Fall*—who is an amalgamation of several contemporaries with certain personal traits of Camus himself—that he lived in bad faith, buying a good conscience by substituting for genuine abnegation the stance and the rhetoric of sacrifice. If one suspects that Camus was thriving on his exposure of contemporary nihilism, enjoying an intellectual position that claimed to suffer from the absurdity of the age while making this absurdity fashionable—then the note of real disarray sounded throughout the *Notebooks* should dispel such doubts. The paradox in which Camus was caught is both more interesting and more intricate: it is not his good faith but the quality of his insight that is to be questioned.

Camus very rightly made his own isolation the basis of his negative diagnosis of the present course of history. He then interpreted this isolation as a conflict between the individual and history. There never is any doubt in his mind that the source of all values resides in the individual, in his ability to resist the monstrous encroachments that history makes upon his integrity.

And for Camus this integrity, which he strove to shelter from totalitarian and deterministic forms of thought, is founded in man's capacity for personal happiness. Camus's concern for others is always protective: he wants to keep intact a potential happiness, a possible fulfillment that every individual carries within him. Socialism is for him an organization of society that safeguards this potentiality: hence his enthusiasm for Belinski's "individualistic socialism" against Hegel's claims for totality and universality. The source of this conviction, however, is to be found in Camus's own experience, and the quality of his thought depends, finally, on the intrinsic quality of his inner experience.

On this point, early works such as *Noces* and especially the earlier *Notebooks* dating from before *The Stranger*, are highly instructive. Camus's sense of personal fulfillment is perhaps most clearly revealed in the exalted pages he wrote in September 1937 during a visit to the cities of Tuscany:

> We lead a difficult life. We don't always succeed in adjusting our actions to our vision of things. . . . We have to labor and to struggle to reconquer solitude. But then, one day, the earth shows its primitive and naive smile. Then it is as if struggles and life itself were suddenly erased. Millions of eyes have contemplated this landscape before, but for me it is like the smile of the world. In the deepest sense of the term, it takes me outside myself. . . . The world is beautiful, and nothing else matters. The great truth the world patiently teaches us is that heart and mind are nothing. And that the stone warmed by the sun, or the cypress magnified by the blue of heaven are the limits of the only world in which being right has meaning: nature without man. . . . It is in that sense that I understand the word "nakedness" [*dénuement*]. "To be naked" always contains a suggestion of physical freedom and I would eagerly convert myself to this harmony between hand and flower, to this sensuous alliance between the earth and man freed of humanity if it were not already my religion.

These passages have the intensity of a writer's most personal vision. They stand behind Camus's entire work and reappear at the surface at those moments when he speaks in his own voice: when Rieux and Tarrou free themselves of the historical curse of the plague in a regenerative plunge into the sea; when the snow falls on Amsterdam at the end of Clamence's confession in *The Fall*. We can see from these passages that what Camus calls solitude in the later notebooks is not, in fact, solitude at all, but the intolerable intrusion of others upon the sacred moment when man's only bond with reality is his bond with nature. In Camus's mythology, the historical parallel to this moment is Greece and he laments at length the disappearance from our own world of Hellenic simplicity—as he laments the disappearance of landscapes from his own books. He quotes Hegel: "Only the modern city offers the mind the terrain in which it can be conscious of itself" and comments: "Significant. This is the time of big cities. The world has been amputated of a part of its truth, of what makes its permanence and its equilibrium: nature, the sea, etc. There is consciousness only in city streets!" And yet cities play an important part in Camus's novels: *The Plague* and *The Fall* are intensely urban in spirit; Amsterdam and Oran are far more than a mere backdrop; they play as central a part as any of the characters. But in Camus's cities a man does not come to know himself by contact with others even by experiencing the impossibility of such contact. In their inhuman anonymity, they are the nostalgic equivalent of the unspoiled nature that has departed from this earth. They have become the haven of our solitude, the link with a lost Arcadia. When city and nature unite in a landscape of nostalgia at the end of *The Fall,* his hero's outcry seems natural enough: "Oh sun, beaches and the isles under the seawind, memories of youth that cause one to despair!" Baudelaire knew a similar nostalgia in the midst of the modern city, but he set himself sharply apart from those who gave in to it, extending to them only pity. The *Notebooks* make it clear that, on this point, there is no distance between Camus and his fictional characters. And whereas the nostalgic figures in Baudelaire feel the attraction of a homeland that has really been theirs, Camus feels nostalgia for a moment that is ambivalent from the outset.

For if one considers this moment, to use his own words, as an instant of "physical freedom" when the body fits within the balance of the elements, then it would be a legitimate assertion of natural beauty on a rather primitive level. "The world is beautiful and nothing else matters." The sentence expresses an idyllic state that does not involve other people and stands outside time—Adam not only before the Fall but before the birth of Eve. In this condition "love is innocent and knows no object." Solitude is no burden since so little consciousness is present; on the contrary, it protects us from alien intrusions. One could compare the feeling with passages in D. H. Lawrence or understand in its terms Camus's affinity with certain aspects of the early Gide. It could be the basis for an amoral and asocial anarchism: Camus explicitly stresses that this encounter can only take place between nature "without man" and man "freed of humanity." This "nakedness" is an athletic freedom of the body, an Arcadian myth that the romantic neo-Hellenists could only have treated in an ironic mode. Camus's use of irony and ironic narrative devices never put this fundamental vision in doubt; in the privacy of his *Notebooks,* it asserts itself even more powerfully as an act of indestructible faith. Camus protests against history as a destroyer of nature and a threat to the body. History is a diabolical invention of German philosophers, a modern curse: "The whole effort of German thought has been to substitute for the notion of human nature that of human situation and hence to substitute history for God and modern tragedy for ancient equilibrium. . . . But like the Greeks I believe in nature." In this respect, Camus is indeed as remote as possible from existential modes of thought, and one can understand his irritation at being so frequently associated in people's minds with Sartre. In a remark that anticipates their future quarrel, Camus accuses Sartre of wanting to believe in a "universal idyll"—apparently unaware that he is himself the prisoner of an idyllic dream that differs from the one he attributes to Sartre only in the respect that it is personal rather than universal. There is no evidence that he ever woke up from this dream.

Camus's work, however, does not display a consistent development of this single vision. Even in the quoted passage from his earlier notebooks, when his naive Hellenism asserts itself in its purest form, a word play on the term *dénuement* introduces the other aspect of his thought. The "nakedness" implied by the *nu* in *dénuement* suggests the barrenness of a human condition that is essentially unsheltered and fragile—not man's "physical freedom" but his subservience to the laws of time and mortality. Camus has a sense of human contingency. The *Notebooks* record many brief episodes, imagined or observed, in which the frailty of the human condition is suddenly revealed when everyday routine is interrupted by an unexpected confrontation with death or suffering—as when he records his mother's horror at the thought of having to face the War years in the dark because of the blackout, or notes the expression on people's faces in a doctor's office, or tells of the death of an old actor. On a larger scale, the nightmarish aspects of the last War have the same effect, but several notebook entries reveal Camus's sensitivity to this kind of experience well before the war.

His best essay, *The Myth of Sisyphus,* develops from observations of this kind. His particular moral sense, one of protectiveness, is rooted in this awareness of man's "nakedness." But this nakedness has nothing in common with "physical freedom." A reconciliation of the two notions is not easily achieved; it comes about only in the highest manifestations of art or thought. And the first step in such a reconciliation always involves the renunciation of the naive belief in a harmony at the beginning of things. When Camus characterizes Greek art as a "benign barrenness" (*un dénuement souriant*), he does not seem to realize that this equilibrium is the final outcome, and not the starting point, of a development that is anything but "natural." Rooted in a literal and physical notion of unity, his own thought falls apart, on the one hand, in a seductive but irresponsible dream of physical well-being and, on the other, in a protective moralism that fails to understand the nature of evil. Camus never ceased to believe that he could shelter mankind from its own contingency merely by asserting the beauty of his own memories. He made this assertion first with proud defiance in *The Stranger,* and later, with more humility but no essential change, in *The Fall.* He always considered himself exemplary, the privileged possessor of a happiness the intrinsic quality of which he overestimated. Others, whose sense of happiness was deeper and clearer than his own, had long since understood that this gave them no increased power over their own destiny, let alone over that of others. His work contains some beautiful flights of lyrical elation along with some astute observations on the incongruity of the human condition. It is lacking however, in ethical profundity despite its recurrent claims to high moral seriousness. And it is entirely lacking in historical insight: ten years after its publication *The Rebel* now seems a very dated book. The *Notebooks* make the reasons for this failure clearer. Without the unifying surface of a controlled style to hide them, the contradictions are much more apparent than in the novels or the essays. The figure that emerges is attractive in its candor, but not authoritative in its thought.

When Camus was a young man, he used to be a goalkeeper for a student soccer team and he wrote articles, in the club paper, extolling the joys of victory or, even more eloquently, the melancholy of defeat. The goalkeeper of a soccer team is, to some extent, a favored figure: the color of his shirt differs from that of his teammates, he enjoys the privilege of touching the ball with his hands, etc. All this sets him apart from the others. But he has to pay for this by accepting severe restrictions: his function is purely defensive and protective, and his greatest glory to avoid defeat. He can never be the agent of real victory and, although he can display style and elegance, he is rarely in the thick of things. He is a man of flashy moments, not of sustained effort. And there is no sadder sight than that of a defeated goalkeeper stretched out on the field or rising to retrieve the ball from the nets, while the opposing attackers celebrate their triumph. The melancholy that reigns in the *Notebooks* reminds one of Camus's youthful sadness on the soccer field: too solitary to join the others up front, but not solitary enough to forego being a member of the team, he chose to be the goalkeeper of a society that was in the process of suffering a particularly painful historical defeat. One could hardly expect someone in that difficult position to give a lucid account of the game.

JACQUES GUICHARNAUD

Man and His Acts:
Jean-Paul Sartre
and Albert Camus

During the forties, with Anouilh becoming ever more involved in his the-atrical game, Salacrou continuing his variations on a Pascalian theme, and Montherlant trying to express deep confusion in clear terms, Sartre and Camus were successfully giving both a modern and an intelligible form to this return to man. Their originality consisted in achieving it without re-verting to a scientific viewpoint, a vision limited to psycho-physiological determinism. What might have resulted in a neopositivism—considering the collapse of our supposedly transcendent and absolute values—appears, on the contrary, as an affirmation of man's privileged metaphysical position. With the added notion that philosophy is more an object of action than of speculation, more a part of life than a play of ideas, the medium for existen-tialist thought became quite naturally a work of fiction: the novel or theatre.

Starting from the principle that man is alone before man and from the fact that such a situation is understandable or conceivable only in terms of action, Sartre and Camus have tried to create a type of theatre in which the concrete representation of life and their own philosophical concepts are absolutely inseparable. Given their basic philosophical positions, the dia-logue is indissolubly bound up with physical *acts*. Whether the plays take the form of historical drama (Sartre's *Le Diable et le Bon Dieu*), allegory (Camus's *L'Etat de siège*), a kind of semi-detective story (Sartre's *Les Mains sales* and even *Nekrassov*, Camus's *Le Malentendu*), or a series of debates (Sartre's *Huis Clos*, Camus's *Les Justes*), the spectator is held by the expec-tation of rebounds, the promise of extreme and definitive acts, the surprise

From *Modern French Theatre from Giraudoux to Genet.* © 1967 by Yale University. Yale University Press, 1967.

of certain dramatic effects, and the double question: What is going to happen? How will it turn out? Sometimes both writers do end by creating a rush of physical happenings that border on the unreal (Camus's *Caligula*, for instance, might seem like an arbitrary catalogue of acts of cruelty and madness), causing some critics to describe their plays as "melodramatic."

Physical action, generally violent, takes on a new value as treated by Sartre and Camus, since their basic philosophy consists in destroying the importance traditionally accorded to motives. What really counts are not the reasons for an act but the act itself, its present significance, and the significance it gives to the characters and the world. In other words, the search for the psychological causality of an act is either shown to be vain or replaced by an investigation of the act's significance. This does not mean that motives are altogether eliminated. Although explanations may be reduced to a minimum, they are indeed necessary, for the acts are not gratuitous. Caligula himself, in Camus's play, does not gratuitously experiment with the gratuitous: he is impelled by a "need for the impossible," the "need for something that is not of this world." Yet the motive is presented very briefly and in such terms that it seems more metaphysical than psychological. In certain cases the spectator, accustomed to long verbal explanations, may be baffled. This is especially true in the case of *Le Malentendu*, in which Martha's need for escape, leading to her murdering the wealthy clientele of the Inn in order to get money, is explained rather sketchily and always in the same terms. While a traditional writer of "psychological theatre" would have devoted most of the play to long digressions on the psychology of suffocation, the misery and dismal mediocrity of Martha's life, and so on, Camus merely sums up those digressions in an image of the sun and the sea. For the true subject of his play lies rather in the absurd and fatal conjuncture of Martha's acts and her brother's almost unexplained behavior.

Even in a retrospective work such as Sartre's *Huis Clos,* in which the acts are in the past and the characters try to evaluate them, no emphasis is put on discovering why, through what determinism of the world and men, the characters happened to commit their crimes. Indeed, when they try, as Garcin occasionally does, they fail to reach any conclusion. Since the play is chiefly a study of the different ways in which men "bear" their acts, when any psychological causality is introduced, it is only as an a posteriori rationalization of the characters themselves and is no more than a present state of consciousness. Similarly, in *Les Mains sales* the long flashback that makes up the greater part of the play contributes nothing but plain facts, with no explanation: the meaning of Hoederer's murder is given only in the present and by way of Hugo's decision. As for *Les Séquestrés d'Altona,* the hero is so tortured by the possible historical *significance* of his monstrous war crimes that he takes refuge in madness.

It has often been pointed out that Giraudoux's characters have hardly any pasts and are completely open to their futures. With a very different vision of the world, Sartre and Camus present much the same attitude. What counts for them is the project an act represents or its meaning in the present—a meaning that changes according to the agent's choices and the interpretation of other people. Of course, for the existentialists a concrete situation requires that a certain *nature* be taken into account. No existentialist ever dreamed of denying given elements such as a man's body, sex, age, social class, and temperament. In fact, the weight of those elements, along with a consciousness of it and the effort made to objectify it or reject it, is inseparable from the subject matter of *Les Mains sales, Le Diable et le Bon Dieu,* and *Les Séquestrés d'Altona.* To use the existentialist vocabulary, all freedom is *en situation;* but since Sartre and Camus want to bring out the irreducible element that distinguishes man from the rest of the world, their interest lies more in its manifestations and creations than in the mechanism of "natures" or "essences," which are considered as secondary.

Such emphasis in theatre means a complete reversal of the treatment of action: acts are presented not as products but as inventions. An act is therefore seen as a creation, almost as unique and irreplaceable as a signed work of art, and at the same time as both a source of drama and drama itself, not only at the moment it is committed—when it implies a struggle and a choice—but even afterward, in man's effort to clarify the relationship between it and himself. Sartre's characters' frequent use of the expression "my act" emphasizes the idea of its being both an outer object and a reciprocal bond between man and what he does. His plays are investigations of the different relations of man to his acts, whether he tries to rid himself of them (which is impossible, hence Estelle's painful tragedy of bad faith in *Huis Clos,* Franz's escape into madness in *Les Séquestrés d'Altona,* and Heinrich's devil in *Le Diable et le Bon Dieu)* or completely assumes them. Without denying all the excuses that science gives for his behavior, man is considered in the perspective of the formula: in any case, whatever I do, *I* am the one who does it.

Taking this formula as a central point, the existentialist theatre opens out around it and examines the ethical and political extensions it implies. Men are considered as having no excuses, since from the start it has been accepted that man is thus distinguished from the rest of the world. As a result, the play's intensity depends largely on the seriousness of the acts committed. Everyday acts, taken one after another, can be successfully used in the novel, as in Sartre's *La Nausée*. However, since dramatic economy demands that the weight of dilution be replaced by the shock of concentration, the effect must be produced through a violent or monstrous act—a point of view very similar indeed to the Greek, Shakespearean, or classical concept of exemplary and extreme acts. If it is true that every act brings man's very being into question, what better means is there than murder, where even an illusion of reparation is impossible. Moreover Sartre and Camus, in the belief that great violence is a sign of the times, use murder in all its forms.

The more horrible the act, the more the individual, who always acts *alone*, begins to "question." While the solitude and anguish involved in murder had already been described by Malraux in *La Condition humaine*, Sartre and Camus combine the greatest violence and the deepest solitude in their situations. For them solitude is what separates the would-be murderer from the arguments in favor of the murder. In *Les Mains sales*, for example, Hugo begins to like Hoederer, whom he wants to kill for political reasons, just as Kaliayev, in *Les Justes*, had decided to throw a bomb at the Grand Duke until he saw children in the carriage. Emphasis is put on the isolation of each individual in his action or his suffering, in a vision of the world where, to use Roquentin's terms in *La Nausée*, there is obviously no "communion of souls"; for, as he says, "I have not fallen so low." My suffering is *my* suffering just as my murder, even in the case of collective action, is *my* murder.

The isolation of man in action is often symbolized by the choice of heroes whose basic situations are exceptional. Orestes' background has made him a stranger to all the cities in Greece (*Les Mouches*), Hugo is a young bourgeois in the Communist party (*Les Mains sales*), Goetz is a military leader and a bastard born of a nobleman and a peasant (*Le Diable et le Bon Dieu*), Lizzie is a prostitute on the fringe of American society (*La Putain respectueuse*), Nekrassov is an adventurer (*Nekrassov*), Kean is a great actor (*Kean*), Caligula is an emperor (*Caligula*), and Kaliayev is a poet (*Les Justes*). Sometimes, of course, there are more specific reasons for the choice of certain characters: in *Les Mains sales*, for example, Sartre was speaking directly to the young bourgeois Frenchmen attracted by communism at the time. In general, however, the characters' exceptional situations are meant not to imply that humanity is naturally divided into heroes and the superfluous rest of mankind but to express, in the form of a hyperbolic metaphor, the similar agony of any man faced with himself.

The agony here is metaphysical. Although the hero may be acting out of passion or in the name of some value, what suddenly strikes him is the bare fact of his own existence and the dizzying vacuum of the nothingness it implies. Whether the hero be Camus's Caligula or Sartre's Garcin, Goetz,

or Hugo, his hopeless discovery is that the world is absurd and his acts the
unjustified creations of his freedom.

"You are no more than the sum of your acts," says Inez to Garcin
in *Huis Clos*. The traditional idea that man commits some particular act
because he is thus-and-so is replaced with its opposite: by committing some
particular act, man makes himself thus and so. Nothingness to start with,
man spends his life giving himself an essence made up of all his acts, and
it is through acting that he becomes conscious of original nothingness. The
anguish that grips him is provoked by that nothingness, the absence of justification, and the metaphysical responsibility which makes him the creator of
his own essence.

The idea is alien to many minds. First of all, it is uncomfortable. More
importantly, however, it eliminates the notion of human nature, a fundamental concept in Western thought, and treats human destiny in itself as meaningless and useless agitation—in other words, as absurd. Since the dramatic
hero also finds the idea difficult to accept, the conflict between his awareness
of the absurd and his need for justification constitutes the strongest dramatic
tension in Sartre's and Camus's works.

Once the hero accepts the idea—if he does—a second dramatic conflict
is created: What is he to do now? The choice is simple. Either he can fall
back into blindness and bad faith—that is, into a belief in reasons, eternal
essences, and the value of established orders, human or divine, with a meaning given in advance—or he can assume his acts and his life, fully aware of
the world's absurdity, and accept the crushing responsibility of giving the
world a meaning that comes from himself alone.

In his first play, *Les Mouches*, Sartre showed the transition from frivolous freedom to the discovery of terrifying metaphysical freedom. He also
showed that the discovery is unbearable (Electra's collapse) and at the same
time how, unbearable as it may be, man can save himself and others when
he assumes his act, as Orestes did.

Orestes is an apprentice, as Caligula is to a certain extent in Camus's
play and Goetz in *Le Diable et le Bon Dieu*, except that Orestes is in the
privileged position of not being from anywhere and participating in nothing. When Jupiter tells him about the crimes of Clytemnestra and Aegisthus,
he answers: "I couldn't care less. I'm not from here." A bit later, when he
begins to dream about the lives of men who are anchored in one place, with
their possessions and their worries, he feels a touch of regret but continues all the same to congratulate himself on what he calls his "freedom":
"Thank God I am free. Oh! How free I am. And what a superb absence is
my soul." There Sartre, with the help of the Greek myth, skipped a certain

number of stages. His hero is already outside the blind conformity of collective behavior. Having begun life with the illusion of disengagement taught him by his cosmopolitan pedagogue, Orestes, at the cost of a great struggle and a double murder, succeeds in creating the "royal way" that leads him to assume his own acts. In addition to his pedagogue's impossible frivolity, he has to avoid two temptations: the attitude of those who belong to the oppressed social group, convinced that their oppression is in the order of things, and its correlative, the alliance with a divine order, symbolized by the terrifying and grotesque figure of Jupiter. In other words, Orestes must avoid the freedom of the "spider's web that floats ten feet above the earth at the mercy of the wind," as well as the human and divine traps that transform man into something determined, into "stone." By murdering his mother and her lover, he discovers that an act is nothing more than an enormous and obscene presence, a parasite of man, both exterior and possessive, and he understands that the act is his and only his. He also understands that it has objective consequences: a tyrant's death frees the oppressed people, whose bondage stemmed only from the tyrant. But as far as the act itself is concerned, only the agent can determine its weight, only the agent bears the burden. *Les Mouches* is thus a sumptuous metaphor intended to show men that responsibility is not synonymous with guilt and that the world of men is made up of the impact of actions, whose meaning comes only from the men who committed or suffered them. The play also indicates that the plague (and here we partially rejoin Camus) exists only to the degree that men accept it. Since the plague is in fact no more than the imposition of responsibility on others from the outside, man has the power to counter that act with a contrary act.

This point of view has brought true overtones of tragedy to the theatre of Sartre and Camus. Their heroes love life. They have no particular desire to die, nor do they seek any glorification in death. But they prefer death to a degradation of the man within them. They fall from a high state in that, whether emperors or proud terrorists, they are reduced to suicide, prison, and physical or moral torture. Furthermore, the catastrophe is always accompanied by an awareness which makes them superior to that which crushes them. Their awareness, however, implies not the recognition of a superior order but rather a recognition of man as the one and only value.

On this level Sartre's and Camus's plays can be divided into two categories: those in which emphasis is put on the agony itself (*Le Malentendu, Huis Clos*) and those in which both writers, succumbing to a kind of proselytism, seem to want to prove that the only way of really being a man among men is to assert one's freedom by rebelling against established orders, mere masks of the absurd (*L'Etat de siège, Les Mouches*). In the second category the theme of the efficacy of action prevails over that of its absurdity. In *L'Etat de siège* the hero dies, but his revolt continues and sea air purifies the pest-ridden city, whereas in *Le Malentendu* Martha's suicide leaves the spectator with a bitter impression. Not that her death is useless, for it has the ultimate value of a protest, but at the end of the play the world closes in on Martha's testimony, just as the heavy, blind earth will cover her body. Yet in both categories, whether the action is effective or only a desperate protest, the basic tragedy and heroism are the same, and the writers' intentions were the same: to bring out, from behind the false face of humanity, man's true condition

Here the return to man excludes a tableau of daily life and mediocrity. Men are truly men not in their petty and niggardly daily acts but rather at the moment when the idea of man is heroically brought into question through themselves. Consequently, when everyday banalities are suggested, it is only to emphasize their *inauthenticité*—that is, their power to dehumanize the individual by blinding him to his own freedom. In the belief that the portrayal of beings and situations at their most ordinary and average constitutes a misunderstanding of humanism, Sartre and Camus make a distinction between a false humanity—which doubtless merits being portrayed, but not as the true definition of man—and a true humanity, which in the world today can be found in any individual at moments of great crisis or in extreme situations. At such times man really wonders what he is. What counts is the portrayal of man stripped of his pettiness and "the most man possible"—that is, not positively defined but rather suspended between possible definitions—for man can be defined as being outside any definition and at the same time bewilderingly in search of one. The best means of concretely expressing this point of view is the portrayal of characters caught in a paroxysm of situations and acts.

While both the existentialists' and Camus's way of considering the relation between man and his acts is profoundly dramatic in itself, the addition of a supplementary element, bearing also on the basic philosophy, makes the plays of Sartre and Camus not only dramatic but theatrical as well.

In the three chapters devoted to Albert Camus's theatre in her book *Camus,* Germaine Brée comes back time and again to the theme of the play within the play and the characters' own staging of it. The "play" that Caligula deliberately puts on as an answer to the blind performance of the Roman patricians and humanity in general is the most striking example. In *Le Malentendu* the action is made up of two opposed scenarios: Ian's return to his homeland—both written and played by him—and the scenario

of melodramatic murders enacted by Martha and his mother. The Plague
in *L'Etat de siège* stages his own arrival by sending a comet into the skies
of Cadiz as a Prologue; he then transforms the decor and forces the people
to play parts, stipulated in advance, in a vast allegory of oppression and
dehumanization. Even the heroes of *Les Justes* are cast as actors who are
conscious of the roles assigned to them, wear disguises, and devise the staging for a political assassination. Thus Camus's characters are made up of
those who write their own dramas and play the parts of their own choosing
and those who are subjected to a scenario written by others.

Sartre also seems to have had a similar theatrical vision in most of his
plays: the characters in *Huis Clos* act out precisely the drama expected of
them by the powers of hell; Goetz is the stage director of Good and Evil
in *Le Diable et le Bon Dieu;* Jupiter and Aegisthus organize the collective
spectacle of men and the universe in *Les Mouches;* the leading characters
in *Nekrassov* and *La Putain respectueuse* are made to play parts written in
advance by the powers of this world; and the problems of the actor himself
are portrayed in *Kean,* an adaptation of Alexandre Dumas's play.

On the whole, such references to a theatre of life give an especially theatrical savor to the works of Sartre and Camus. Their devices are somewhat
comparable to those of Cocteau and Anouilh, but the implications and significance are different. The use of an imposed scenario or a play within the
play is meant to furnish a means for action rather than provide a solution
to life. The job of the stage director consists in assigning a place and a function to everyone and everything in relation to a given end and a plan of the
whole. Defined as part of a whole, things and individual beings must sacrifice their spontaneity and freedom. The tension thus created generally results
in an explosion of the elements outside the game or of anyone who freely
refuses to enter in. Sometimes the stage director's order wins (*La Putain
respectueuse*); most often the unpredictability of the absurd (*Le Malentendu*)
or of freedom (*Les Mouches, Les Mains sales, Le Diable et le Bon Dieu,
L'Etat de siège*) reduces man's scenarios and the metaphoric scenarios of the
gods to nothing; and on occasion the individual or private self, the person
who answers for his own fears, loves, and so on, stands out at the height of
the action as isolated and separated from the overall plan (*Les Justes, Morts
sans sépulture*).

The great directors are the oppressors, the liberators, and the experi-
menters. Jupiter and Aegisthus, the Plague, the American senator, and in
certain respects the Communist party belong to the first category; the revolutionaries and Martha, in relation to herself, to the second; Caligula and
Goetz to the third. In other words, this particular form of second degree

theatre, as compared to that found in other works, is presented not as an aesthetic solution of the absurd but as a metaphor of the oppressive order as well as the necessary means to explode its lies and injustices. Whether mask or antimask, it takes the form of a scenario written in advance and, through a necessary antithesis, evokes the themes of freedom and contingency. Anouilh also used the device in *Antigone, L'Alouette,* and other plays in which the heroes refuse to play the game of a scenario written in advance, but his solution lies in the play itself, in the very theatricalism of the conflict, whereas in Sartre and Camus theatrical creation is always a means, never a reconciliatory end.

In *Le Diable et le Bon Dieu* Goetz is an extraordinary actor who identifies with the roles of his choice. Several times during the play he is called "buffoon." He acts for an audience—God—but finally discovers that his "play" has been no more than a bloody farce and that the spectator he counted on was missing: from the balcony of the sky only a gaping emptiness looks down upon him. Just as in Camus's play Caligula tried to be pure Evil, Goetz tried to be one hundred per cent Good. While both are inventors and challenge the order of the world, their social experiments leave them with emptiness and negation, since a desire for the absolute in the name of man leads to the destruction of man and the loss of humanity. As Germaine Brée points out, such imposition of the absolute is much the same as the Plague's absolute and abstract order in *L'Etat de siège.*

Having brought their heroes to the experience of nothingness and the consciousness of a universe without hope and without illusion, both writers found it necessary to reintegrate life. In *Caligula* Cherea, who "lives within the truth, without hope and without delusion . . . recognizes the relative human order in which reign 'those truths of the flesh' that are lived and not demonstrated." Others return to life through the concrete tasks imposed by urgent problems: Goetz finally agrees to use his talents as a military leader by helping the peasant rebellion; Diego, in *L'Etat de siège,* succeeds in convincing his fellow citizens to open the doors of the city and let in the sea air.

The basic conflict, then, is threefold: the comedy of a world of illusions (false justifications) as opposed to the theatre or anti-theatre of those who seek the absolute, and both opposed to the plain fact of existence as it is lived or to be lived, individually and collectively. In Camus existence as such is expressed more or less allegorically in the character Cherea in *Caligula* and the Mediterranean richness of certain images in *L'Etat de siège* and *Le Malentendu.* Sartre expresses it less poetically in Hoederer's vitality and relation to objects in *Les Mains sales,* Hilda's love in *Le Diable et le Bon*

Dieu, and *Nekrassov*'s gaiety. But since it is most often outside the play, it can only be alluded to. Man's unchanging tragedy lies both in the search for it and in the tension between the first two elements of the conflict.

Despite great similarities in basic philosophy and theatrical vision, Sartre and Camus differ profoundly on the aesthetic level, just as in a comparable way *La Nausée* differs from *L'Etranger,* or *La Peste* from *Les Chemins de la liberté.*

Sartre's dramatic universe is nearer to realism or traditional naturalism. Eric Bentley points out the fact that *Huis Clos* is essentially Strindbergian in tone and a drawing-room comedy in form. Indeed, three Boulevard melodramas can easily be made out of each of the three characters' lives: a frivolous young lady who killed her child, a rather nasty lesbian who led her friend to suicide, a pacifistic journalist who deserted in time of war—all psychological dramas with social implications and perfect material for a "well-made" play. Even the setting for each drama is suggested: the lesbian's room with its gas stove, the newspaper office with the editors in shirt sleeves, and the elegant room in Switzerland with its windows giving onto the lake. Sartre deliberately chose three rather typical news items and kept certain "true" details—that is, their naturalist color.

When Camus chooses a news item (*Le Malentendu*), he chooses an exceptional one and then strips it of anything that might evoke everyday life. Moreover, he eliminates any familiarity or banality from language. Actually, Camus's characters all speak the same language—a kind of stylized and intense common denominator which wipes out any naturalist implications behind their purified intentions and feelings—whereas Sartre, although he brands his characters with his own images and syntax, fills their dialogue with expressions and devices that closely copy naturalist "reality." One has only to compare the hangman's lines in the fourth act of *Les Justes* with those of Hoederer's bodyguards in *Les Mains sales* or the guards of Apollo's temple in *Les Mouches.* In the case of characters who would normally use slang, Camus keeps it to a minimum, while Sartre deliberately uses it as much as possible, along with syntactical ellipses.

Much the same may be said in regard to form. In Sartre there are frequent references to traditional or familiar genres: vaudeville, drama, historical drama. The decors themselves are conventional: real rooms, real garrets, and real German countryside. Even a fantastic setting like the Second Empire drawing room in *Huis Clos* is fantastic because of its realism: the Barbedienne bronze statue, the Louis Philippe couch, and the bricks that obstruct the window are scenically effective only if they look real and are not artistically suggested. In that respect, Sartre has contributed considerably less to the development of theatre than Camus, who avoided most references to familiar genres, aimed at a very special economy in his settings as well as language, and launched out into experiments of highly stylized total theatre.

Yet Sartre had reasons for what he did. He wanted first to get the spectator on familiar ground and then gradually bring him into existentialist drama, far from that familiar ground. In *Huis Clos,* for example, the naturalism of each character's "case" and the realism of language and decor create an image of the beyond that is acceptable to audiences accustomed by films and theatre to seeing death represented in very earthly forms. The true subject of the play, however, is revealed on a third level. Beyond the anecdotal interest of a few adventures or perversions and the modernist pathos of the allegory of hell, it concerns the relation of one consciousness to another, the search for a definition of the self with the help of others, and the realization that the presence and judgment of others is necessary and yet leads to an impasse. On that level the whole takes on all its meaning, and we discover that the play is not a metaphor of hell but that the image of hell is a metaphor of the hopeless suffering of individuals in search of their definitions in the eyes of others, yet constantly brought back to themselves.

Garcin's reticence in telling how he deserted and especially how he physically fell apart at the time of his execution is an excellent subject for a naturalistic psychological drama (the pacifist has a shameful secret: he acted out of cowardice), and part of the dialogue is directed toward that drama but at one point turns away from it and moves toward an existentialist perspective. Once it has been established that an inquiry into the motives for an act does not reveal the act's meaning, Garcin's hopeless tragedy lies in the fact that he is unable to determine the meaning of his life by himself and is condemned to live between two women—one totally indifferent to the question and the other who, needing "the suffering of others in order to exist," decides that he has been cowardly and is thus satisfied with the spectacle of his shame.

Sartre's plays lead the spectator from the universe of perception, common sense, and psychological or aesthetic habits to an existentialist conclusion, often difficult in its newness. What he shows essentially is that his vision of the world is inherent in the normal universe. His method consists in bringing it out progressively, and often the progression itself makes up the greater part of the play.

Les Mains sales is presented as a politico-detective drama in the form of an investigation and a trial, based on a simple question comparable to the suspense-provoking questions in melodrama: Why did Hugo kill Hoederer? The suspense is all the more acute in that the spectator knows that Hugo's life depends on the answer. The investigation itself, which takes up six of the seven tableaux, is in the form of a flashback concerned only with the simple fact of Hoederer's death, leaving the murder committed by Hugo in all its ambiguity. Sartre played the game of detective-story melodrama according to the rules, but he stopped short of melodramatic satisfaction. The "secret" one is supposed to uncover is not uncovered and it becomes increasingly clear that it is impossible to uncover it. In a sense the naturalistic melodrama destroys itself under one's very eyes, leaving hero and spectator open to whatever lies ahead. Having finished his long demonstration and created the necessary vacuum, Sartre can then go on to lead both hero and spectator into the true subject of his play: in the last fifteen minutes one discovers that the meaning of Hoederer's murder does not lie in Hugo's reasons for it, which in any case remain ambiguous; his true motive is the one he chooses *afterward*, when, fully aware of the situation, he determines—through his own death—the meaning of the situation and the value of Hoederer's life and his own. Somewhat the same gradual transition takes place within Goetz and the spectator in *Le Diable et le Bon Dieu*, although its dialectic is not as clear because of the play's vast proportions.

In Camus's plays also, spectator and hero are led to make a common discovery, and the element of detective-story suspense—the interest in what will happen next—is one dimension of his theatre. But the level of the play's true subject is given straight away. There is almost no transition from one vision of the universe to another. *Caligula* begins with the Emperor having just discovered the world of freedom and the absurd. Had Sartre written *Caligula*, he would doubtless have shown the hero making his decisive discovery in the first act, beginning with Drusilla's death, and would go on to show how Caligula was shocked by it and how it led up to his final experiment. In Camus's play the curtain goes up on an imaginary world whose dimensions are given from the very beginning and once and for all—hence the dual impression of classical economy and intransigence.

Camus's uncompromising aesthetics is based on a symbolic vision, far indeed from Sartre's. The Germany of *Le Diable et le Bon Dieu*, deformed and stylized as it may be, *is* Germany during the period of the peasant revolts, whereas the Rome of *Caligula* has as little reality as the Naples of certain of Molière's comedies or the Poland of *Ubu Roi*. Sartre takes a historic event and brings out its significance. Camus starts with a general dramatic conflict and then embodies it fictionally. In other words, symbol prevails over locality. Thus, despite a few clear allusions to the present state of Spain, the Cadiz of *L'Etat de siège* represents as imaginary a locality as the North African city in his novel *La Peste*. It is quite simply a city in a dry, sun-scorched country near the sea, which enables Camus to make use of his familiar myths.

While Sartre generally first tells a story, rich enough in realistic elements to be self-contained, Camus constructs a poetic allegory based on a conflict. In her book on Camus, Germaine Brée points out that Camus's most obviously anecdotal play, *Le Malentendu*, "is entirely symbolical." In *Caligula*, *Les Justes*, and *L'Etat de siège* the traditional creation of characters is replaced by the symbolic embodiment of possible attitudes to a dramatic conflict. Consequently, Camus lays himself open to the traditional criticism of allegorical literature—the contrived embodiment of ideas or entities. But in all aesthetic sincerity and by means of an immediate stylization of dialogue and characters, Camus does present his plays as intellectual creations from the moment the curtain goes up.

Less popular than his other plays but more ambitious and perhaps closer to the "modern tragedy" he sought, *L'Etat de siège* represents a synthesis of Camus's aesthetics and general ideas, combining the philosophy of acts and extreme situations with a certain form of symbolism. In his preface Camus explains how Jean-Louis Barrault, inspired by Artaud, was haunted by the meaning and symbol of the plague and wanted to create a play around it. Camus, having just published his novel *La Peste*, was the obvious man to write the script. In this case the symbol was given first. Since he had already worked with it on several levels in his novel, Camus's job consisted in making the maledictions that crush man coincide with the physical ravages of the plague. Moreover, the metaphor is not spontaneous; it is the result of the collective effort of Artaud, Barrault, and Camus. *L'Etat de siège* is thus characteristic of Camus's art in that it is the development and extension of a simile he had already worked out; it is a theatrical exercise on a given subject: organized totalitarianism as the plague of the modern world.

The plague itself is embodied in a rather portly man in uniform, who takes over the government in Cadiz with the help of his secretary, Death. The symbol is obvious and becomes increasingly so at the beginning of the second act, when the Kafkaesque satire on bureaucracy starts to sound like Courteline-become-metaphysical. In addition, every character in the play, when confronted with the Plague, embodies a simple attitude, a commonplace opinion or way of behaving—the most important, next to the rebellious hero's, being that of Nada, who by his very name represents man at the level of nihilistic despair. Allegorical as it may be, however, the play is no less "existentialist" in its general philosophy: the hero successfully counters the established order with the refusal of a free being—a refusal which, ironically enough, almost seduces Death but for which the hero finally does pay with his life. Moreover, the play contains symbols of all the necessary existentialist stages: *inauthenticité,* rebellion, confidence in life despite everything.

A "total" play in its themes, Camus and Barrault wanted also to make it a total play on a scenic level: abstract dialogue, lyrical tirades, individual and collective pantomime, spectacular effects. Both totalities are meant to correspond in the alternation between the comments of the real people (lovers, fishermen, and so on) and the speeches of personified abstractions (the Plague and Death). While the play fails in part because of the fact that the whole is more an intellectual allegory than a living synthesis, it is one of the rare attempts at uniting modern philosophy and modern theatre.

Camus's and Sartre's aesthetics are as different as their general ideologies are similar. Where in Sartre innovations in form are secondary to content, in Camus aesthetic consciousness is inseparable from the substance. Yet their intentions are much alike in that both have tried to give French audiences theatre that is neither an agreeable repetition of past masterpieces, even recent ones, nor a purely modernist aesthetic thrill. They have also agreed on the idea of an art that is completely concerned with and conceived in terms of our times. Their common purpose has been both to describe the man of today and to write for the man of today. Such is doubtless the intention of all writers, but in Sartre and Camus it takes the form of a conscious rule, affirmed and reaffirmed as a writer's first duty. An acute consciousness of the modern world and a true identification with its problems and demands have determined the themes and aesthetics of both. And although Camus had time and again refused to be labeled "existentialist," he *can* be considered committed or *engagé,* if literary *engagement* is taken in its broadest sense, as writing for one's time, directly or indirectly about one's time, with man's freedom as an ultimate goal.

In the light of such an attitude many literary positions must be rejected as survivals of a dead past. Psychological analyses in classical terms, reducing man to a determinism which is now thought to be precisely not man; historical and picturesque reconstruction for itself; freezing man in the ice of dead essences; the exclusive cult of beauty; placing the meaning of the world outside man—all are eliminated, not absolutely but relatively: the present and man's tragedy at this moment of history are considered more important and rich enough to take precedence over any other concern.

Thus the central problem of Malraux's novels has been brought to the theatre by Sartre and Camus. They chose their subjects among the most burning issues of our times: wars, oppression, rebellions, revolutions, and through them reached the so-called universal themes—but stated them in new terms. Instead of traditional psychologism, the entire human being is called into question.

Camus's allegorization and his refusal to emphasize, as does Sartre, the topical aspect of his dramas show that he aimed at a nonhistoric universality. He does, however, keep today's problems always in the foreground. His choice of the plague as a symbol was determined less by its timeless universality than by its particularly violent activity at the present time. "Today the technique is perfected," says the Plague in *L'Etat de siège,* after having gone over the plagues of the past "when the idea was there. But not the whole idea." In other words, although the plague is doubtless continuous and permanent, it is at its height in the modern world. "Codified" to perfection, it is close to an absolute victory over subjugated man. Yet today is also a time of hope among men who have understood that they are free.

In trying to make this clear in their plays and to reach the largest possible public, Sartre in his works as a whole and Camus in *L'Etat de siège* were often forced, given the difficulty of their philosophies, into simplifications and sometimes even concessions. Sartre compromised by using Boulevard details and facile naturalist techniques, especially flagrant in *Les Séquestrés d'Altona.* He also spelled out certain of his arguments in easily assimilated formulas and, by seeming intellectually clearer, sacrificed many nuances necessary to a complete understanding of his philosophy, while losing in dramatic reality as well. As for Camus, his often abstract maxims, used as articulations, are sometimes more intellectual than dramatic.

For theirs is a theatre of ideas—exactly the kind Gide had hoped to see created by Giraudoux. Neither Sartre nor Camus are primarily playwrights. Sartre is, above all, a professional philosopher. Camus is obviously more of an artist and was always active in the world of theatre, but all of his works are dominated by intellectual searching and the examination of ideas. What distinguishes their plays from other "philosophical" theatre, however, is the absolutely dramatic and concrete nature of their philosophy itself. The fundamental problem of the definition of man and the world is truly embodied in living acts.

E. FREEMAN

Caligula

La mort est là, comme l'irréfutable preuve de l'absurdité de la vie.

—MALRAUX, *La Voie royale*

Jean Grenier—quel merveilleux ami, toujours vous ramenant vers l'essentiel malgré vous! Grenier fut mon premier maître et il l'est resté.

—CAMUS

*C*aligula is Camus's first completely original play and undoubtedly his best and most enduring. Although it was not performed until 1945, *Caligula* was drafted in a fairly complete form by 1939 and was intended to be put on by the Théâtre de l'Equipe. Camus himself, since he played the lead in most of the productions of his two companies, would have taken the part of Caligula. As he was to put it later with characteristic irony: "Les acteurs débutants ont de ces ingénuités. Et puis j'avais 25 ans, âge où l'on doute de tout, sauf de soi. La guerre m'a forcé à la modestie."

The play made an immediate impact when it was first performed in 1945. It opened on 26 September at the Théâtre Hébertot, ran for nearly a year, and was revived professionally at least three times during Camus's lifetime, in 1950, 1957 and 1958. It seems clear that the initial success was due at least in part to the "creation" of the role of Caligula by the brilliant but at that time unknown Gérard Philipe, under the direction of Paul Oettly—no small stroke of luck for Camus. Yet at the same time the play possessed an intrinsic appeal for the spectators of 1945. It dealt with a

From *The Theatre of Albert Camus: A Critical Study.* © 1971 by E. Freeman. Methuen, 1971.

theme which appeared clear-cut and relevant in its political implications (if at times difficult and obscure in its metaphysical premises): the dangers of philosophical absolutism. This theme is put across in a play with a simple and linear plot which nevertheless holds a very great theatrical appeal. It combines on the one hand, particularly in those scenes in which Caligula is alone with just one of the four other leading characters, moments of very effective and legitimate pathos, and on the other hand the most powerful verbal and scenic rhetoric of the sort that is virtually inescapable in any play about Gaius Caligula. Finally for the audiences of 1945 there was the ghoulish and macabre fascination of the hero himself at a time when Europe and particularly France were emerging from the chaos created by Hitler and Mussolini, two imperial megalomaniacs whose personalities bore many superficial likenesses to that of Caligula. The legitimacy or otherwise of this interpretation is an important point in any discussion of *Caligula,* and will be examined in due course.

The play is based on the last three years in the life of Gaius Caesar— nicknamed "Caligula" in his childhood because he wore the military boot *caliga*—who was one of the maddest of the Julio-Claudian Emperors described by Suetonius in his *Lives of the Caesars.* Suetonius' sensational biography, more of a collection of lurid atrocities and murders allegedly committed by Caligula than a biography in a modern sense, is ideally suited to Camus's purpose as suggested by one of his first notes for the play in January 1937: "Caligula ou le sens de la mort." In so far as the facts set out by Suetonius are "facts" at all, Camus sticks fairly closely to the historical outlines of Caligula's life and death. Gaius Caesar "Caligula" was born on August 31, A.D. 12 and stabbed to death in January A.D. 41, the victim of a conspiracy led by two colonels of the guard, Cassius Chaerea and Sabinus. At his death Caligula had been emperor for nearly four years, a period which became increasingly a reign of terror. Suetonius' account is a colourful fabric of anecdotes about the social and political scandals, surrealistic obscenities, rape, murder, incest and miscellaneous lunacies attributed to Caligula, and which culminated in his inevitable assassination. Camus has incorporated many of these features of Caligula's madness in his play: his moon fixation and his fondness for staring at himself in a mirror, for example, are two of the idiosyncrasies which are potentially most suggestive, from a symbolic point of view, in a play about metaphysical *speculation* and illusion and reality. Other legendary deeds or customs of Caligula are built into the plot without any significant modification and serve to motivate the assassination on which the play ends. Caligula reputedly abused women in front of their husbands, forced the rich to bequeath their wealth to the state, tortured a child to death in its father's sight, and obliged poets to lick their slates clean at a competition. Many similar incidents are laid at his door. And yet although Camus kept to the broad outlines of Caligula's career and relied entirely on the incidents described in Suetonius for the plot of the play, he nevertheless stated that in its fundamentals *Caligula* is not a historical play. An examination of its plot, characterization and philosophical theme soon makes it clear why this claim is justified.

Camus opens his play at the heart of a crisis and on the brink of disaster. The whole of the first act takes place at a time when Caligula has been Emperor for about a year. By all accounts he has been a very good one: "tout allait trop bien. Cet empereur était parfait." However, his sister and mistress Drusilla has died, and his immediate reaction has been to flee from his palace into the Roman countryside. For the semicomic chorus of inane patricians this is the natural effect on "un sentimental" of the loss of a lover. Caligula returns after three days, exhausted and dishevelled, and informs his friend, the freed slave Hélicon, that he has been looking for the moon: "Mais je ne suis pas fou et même je n'ai jamais été aussi raisonnable. Simplement je me suis senti tout d'un coup un besoin d'impossible." Contrary to the belief of the patricians, "cette mort n'est rien." Caligula has been affected not by the personal loss of Drusilla but by his discovery of the absurd: "Les hommes meurent et ils ne sont pas heureux." To attempt to possess the moon, to hold it in his hands—a symbol of impossible attainment—is his reaction to the effect which his sudden awareness of the absurd has made on his sensibility. Just as it is impossible for man to evade death so it is impossible for Caligula to hold the moon between his hands. Camus makes Caligula the first man in history to rebel against this certainty. He will not accept the message of the absurd in its most striking manifestation, that the inevitability of death means that man's happiness on this earth must be relative, not absolute. Or rather he accepts the message but follows it through with a "logic" which no man previously has been lucid or powerful enough to pursue.

The men around Caligula are the realists, the relativists, who, like the ordinary human beings who surround Anouilh's rebel heroines, survive more or less happily, usually by means of illusions, sometimes by lies, always by compromise. But Caligula is not one of Anouilh's frail young women. He is the Roman Emperor, and when he cries "tout, autour de moi, est mensonge, et moi, je veux qu'on vive dans la vérité!" he has the power to make the whole world discover the absurd. The remainder of the play is devoted to this education and its consequences. Still obsessed by the moon, Caligula becomes for the mass of mankind, represented by the patricians, a *lunatic* absolutist. It is in his philosophical interpolation that Camus makes the most ingenious use of his legendary theme. His Caligula turns upon society, to which he is superior by virtue of his intelligence and sensitivity and unique sudden vision of truth. There have been many rebels before in French literature, particularly in the Romantic period: outcasts, hypersensitive misfits, *poètes maudits,* challenging society in all its established might with no certainty of achieving anything other than their own destruction. But Caligula operates initially from strength. Thus much of the power of the climax to act 1 stems from a combination of two factors. Camus is using a semi-mythic, semi-historical theme which preconditions an audience in much the same way as do the myths of Troy, Thebes and Argos as used by so many of Camus's contemporaries in the French theatre. We know that Caligula was a tyrant, a monster of depravity, who eventually went too far and was assassinated. It is clear as act 1 draws to a close that Caligula is about to become all that Suetonius said he was. And yet Camus, with a fair degree of credibility and ingenuity, has created a highly pregnant first act interval by making it clear that it is the tyrant who has the ideals. For once the outsider who has taken upon himself the task of transforming society is endowed with immense power. With such credibility in fact that at least two critics have persuaded themselves that Suetonius' characteristic line *hactenus quasi de principe, reliqua ut de monstro narranda sunt* means that Caligula was a perfect emperor until the death of Drusilla but thereafter became irrevocably mad and evil; whereas the Caligula portrayed by Suetonius showed signs of depravity during his adolescence, went mad for physiological reasons (and not overnight), possessed little or no virtue, and was not irrevocably unhinged by the death of Drusilla who was only one of the three sisters (but admittedly the favourite) with whom Caligula allegedly committed incest. Thus it is not only because he grafted the absurd on to a historical situation that Camus rightly disclaimed any intention of creating a historical play: the very factual basis of the history in the first place is unsound.

The enigmatic reshaping of the legendary material is further complicated in act 1 by the fact that Camus has taken care to enlist our sympathy for Caligula right from the start. Every character who appears in the play at any time is presented at the earliest possible moment in act 1, and Caligula comes out of the juxtaposition very well. On the one hand there is the choric group of more or less anonymous patricians. They are fatuous, petty, hypocritical figures, symbolizing the supine conservatism of the establishment and serving the same function as the chemist and the grocer in *Révolte dans les Asturies.* But between them and Caligula is juxtaposed a second group of characters, the four supporting roles, who, in their relationships either with one another or with Caligula, create the philosophical ambiguity—and subtlety—of the play. Each of these characters has some sort of bond with Caligula. With Hélicon it is social. A freed slave who acts as the Emperor's henchman, he is a witty cynic who loathes the establishment as much as Caligula does but for personal reasons. He throws himself enthusiastically into the task of organizing the disruption of society without the philosophical understanding of why, according to Caligula's logic, such action may be considered justified. A somewhat similar figure is Caesonia, "la vieille maîtresse," who has a purely sensual relationship with Caligula. She fills what will be an increasingly familiar slot in Camus's work, that of a sort of composite wife-mother-mistress figure (her prototype was the mature Pilar in *Révolte dans les Asturies*). With an appropriately doglike fidelity both Hélicon and Caesonia will stick by Caligula in his last moments. With the far more important characters of Scipion and Cherea, however, we move to much higher levels of human attachment. Scipion, the young poet whose father has been murdered by Caligula, is allied to him by a spiritual and emotional bond: "quelque chose en moi lui ressemble pourtant. La même flamme nous brûle le coeur." He is Caligula's only successful pupil, the only one who understands the point of Caligula's brutal pedagogy and who becomes aware of and accepts the absurd in all its implications. Irrevocably contaminated, he refuses to join in the conspiracy and leaves Rome, incapable of action either for or against Caligula. Cherea, the last and most important of these four characters, understands and to a certain extent sympathizes with both Caligula and Scipion. He is an intellectual, a lover of books, a retiring, Apollonian figure contrasting with the Dionysian Caligula. He knows what has happened to Caligula, and what is happening to Scipion, through having himself resisted the philosophical implications of the absurd when younger: "j'ai fait taire en moi ce qui pouvait lui ressembler." A moderate and a respecter of peace and compromise, Cherea will assume increasing importance during the course of the play as he is called down from his ivory tower to act in the name of the sanity which is more important to him than idealism. Put simply, in the terms from *Le Mythe de Sisyphe* which I explained [elsewhere], Cherea, like most people whether they are aware of it or not, believes in a qualitative ethic—"je crois qu'il y a des actions qui sont plus belles que d'autres," whereas Caligula does not—"Je crois que toutes sont équivalentes." As Caligula says to Caesonia at the end of act 1, "Tout est sur le même pied: la grandeur de Rome et tes crises d'arthritisme": there is no hierarchy of values. The remaining three acts are devoted to Caligula's systematic destruction of relative values.

Act 2 takes place when Caligula's campaign is three years old. The patricians are outraged by Caligula's atrocities and have met at Cherea's house to plot the Emperor's assassination. Acts 3 and 4, taking place in the days or weeks immediately following, continue the movement towards the inevitable consummation. Much of the material of these three acts consists of the more notorious of Suetonius' incidents dramatized. There is one major set-piece per act: one of Caligula's characteristically nerve-racking banquets in act 2, his Venus-masquerade in act 3 and the poetry competition in act 4. A possible criticism of the play from the structural point of view is that there is too great a lapse of time between act 1 and the remaining three acts. Thus without making any formal use of flashbacks Camus spends a lot of time, for almost three-quarters of the play, presenting atrocities of the sort which motivated the plotting which began as early as the beginning of act 2. One feels that a dramatist with a surer grasp of dramatic form would have either situated act 2 much closer in time to the beginning of Caligula's campaign and kept the start of the resistance movement entirely for act 3, or else made almost the whole of act 3 one long flashback. My own feeling, however, is that the leisurely, chronological (and some would say old-fashioned and typically Camusian) movement of these three acts is not a bad thing, considering the complexity of the philosophical arguments which have assailed an audience throughout act 1. The audience now has time to digest Camus's thesis, especially as it is clarified and developed during the crucial scenes between Caligula, Cherea and Scipion, while at the same time enjoying the black comedy of the patrician scenes. The long confrontation with Cherea in act 3, scene 6, and with Scipion at the end of the poetry competition (act 4) prepare for the anagnorisis, for Caligula's admission to Caesonia: "soyons justes, je n'ai pas seulement la bêtise contre moi, j'ai aussi la loyauté et le courage de ceux qui veulent être heureux."

I discussed in chapter 1 one of the major pitfalls into which interpreters of Camus's theatre commonly fall: the temptation to schematize *grosso modo* into two periods, the "absurd" period (up to 1945) and the period of "revolt" thereafter. The two concepts are in fact indissociable throughout Camus's theatre, although of course the emphasis may vary from play to play. *Caligula* illustrates this better than most, partly for the reason that a large number of manuscripts and variants exist, from the first jottings in Camus's *Carnets* in 1937 and continuing through the published editions of the play in 1945, 1947 and 1958. Take first of all the absurd as a theme of the play. Here it is important to realize just what Camus has made of the Caligula–Drusilla incident in Suetonius, and to understand why he has singled it out from amidst a mass of equally grotesque incidents. The responsibility for making Caligula's transformation an abrupt one and attributing it to the death of Drusilla belongs entirely to Camus. What he sought in his raw material was an incident which he could refashion to illustrate the "meaning of death"; i.e., the mathematical certainty of death makes one aware of "le caractère dérisoire de cette habitude, l'absence de toute raison profonde de vivre, le caractère insensé de cette agitation quotidienne et l'inutilité de la souffrance" (*Le Mythe de Sisyphe*). Camus also wished to show the *manner* in which this meaning is perceived. Far from emerging as a result of a "slow incubation" as one critic has suggested, the absurd bursts upon the consciousness as a result of a *sudden* access of lucidity. *Le Mythe* once again makes the point clear: "Le sentiment de l'absurdité au détour de n'importe quelle rue peut frapper à la face de n'importe quel homme. Tel quel, dans sa lumière sans rayonnement, il est insaisissable. Mais cette difficulté même mérite réflexion." "Reflection"—this is exactly the reaction which contact with death provokes in *Caligula*, according to Scipion: "Il s'est avancé vers le corps de Drusilla. Il l'a touché avec deux doigts. *Puis il a semblé réfléchir,* tournant sur lui-même, et il est sorti d'un pas égal." Thus the death of the beloved is the occasion for the "naissance misérable" and is assimilated to the category of banal discovery from which the absurd draws its "commencement dérisoire." Credit must go to Camus for the ingenuity with which he has adapted this incident in a way which is credible in the context of Caligula's life, and at the same time is perfectly consistent with the author's view of death and other manifestations of the absurd in his work at this time.

Le Mythe de Sisyphe serves perfectly adequately to explain the "absurd" basis of *Caligula,* and Camus's first notes for the play in his *Carnets* make it clear that the whole of the play as it was first conceived would have been explicable in these terms. The scenario which Camus sketched out in January 1937 is built around Caligula and Drusilla and it was not until near the end that he proposed to deal with "Mort de Drusilla. Fuite de Caligula." When Camus rejected this project and drafted his first manuscript he still portrayed a hero obsessed with the horror of his discovery, but the emphasis changed slightly. Partly because of the difficulty of communicating the absurd on the stage without a totally different concept of form and style—a problem which the so-called "absurd playwrights," notably Beckett and Ionesco, attempted to solve in a radical way—but mainly because of his own philosophical development, Camus gave the play a new slant, and one to which *Le Mythe* would not be relevant. For just as Camus stressed that "Ce qui m'intéresse, je veux encore le répéter, ce ne sont pas tant les découvertes absurdes. Ce sont leurs conséquences," so in *Caligula* he revealed an increasing concern for the moral and philosophical consequences of the Emperor's reaction at the expense of a purely dramatic presentation of the discovery which unleashed it. In other words revolt will have just as important a part to play in *Caligula* as the absurd. But the consequences examined in *Le Mythe* of the discovery that "aucune morale, ni aucun effort ne sont *a priori* justifiables devant les sanglantes mathématiques qui ordonnent notre condition" are very different from those examined in the more mature versions of *Caligula* from 1938 onwards. The play is still basically the tragedy of the man who is unable to maintain the tension of the two terms of the "pari déchirant et merveilleux de l'absurde," but his way out of the impasse does not correspond to any of the three possibilities discussed in *Le Mythe*.

In *Le Mythe* Camus rejected the two traditional, but to him unsatisfactory, reactions to the discovery of the absurd, which result from the cancellation of one of the terms. These were (1) physical suicide, i.e., suppressing term A (the self) and maintaining term B (the world—inscrutable, irrational and meaningless), and thus capitulating to the absurd (the unbearable relationship A plus B), and (2) philosophical suicide, the leap of faith, according to which term A, although preserved as a *living* entity, is destroyed as an agent of intellectual inquiry. In other words term A, the self, does not literally commit suicide but simply ceases to think, and in this sense commits *philosophical* suicide. Term B is negated: reasoned scrutiny of the world is rejected and refuge is sought in religion, with the effect of escaping from, rather than capitulating to, the absurd. The third possible reaction, and the one advocated by Camus, requires both terms to be maintained in equilibrium: the absurd is preserved. *Caligula,* much more from the time of its drafting in 1938 than probably at its conception, illustrates a fourth possible reaction, and one not examined in *Le Mythe*. The play is about the danger of disturbing the equilibrium not by the physical or philosophical suicide of A but by an attack upon B. The self both combats the absurd in a sense and also allies with it to universalize an awareness of it in the whole of humanity, which is a component of term B. The result is that the relationship A plus B is broken in a welter of universal homicide and chaos. B is partly destroyed, and A totally, for in the end the self virtually commits suicide: Camus accentuated this point by adding to his 1947 version of the play the scene in act 3 in which the Old Patrician informs Caligula of the plot, to which news the latter remains indifferent. Caligula is unable to live the difficult compromise, to walk the tightrope between *Tout* (the vision of an ideal world, in which the totality of human experience would be logical and at the same time morally acceptable) and on the other hand *Rien* (the evidence of the real world, where nothing is tolerable: Nihilism). Camus originally used as a working title for the play *Caligula ou le Joueur,* and we may see the Emperor as the man who gambles on the absolute, who tries to pierce the "walls of the absurd" by being "logique jusqu'à la fin." Thus, like *Le Mythe de Sisyphe*, *Caligula* illustrates a quantitative ethic. The difference is that now it is not an ethic of creation, aiming at a positive although qualified happiness, but on the contrary an ethic of destruction. The difference between the two consequences is the difference between *L'Etranger* and *Caligula*, as Carina Gadourek has observed:

> Au lieu de se faire le professeur de l'humanité qui pousse le reste des mortels dans la voie de la vérité et de la liberté, un tempérament plus calme pouvait décider d'aller son chemin tout seul et sans discours, sans essayer de rien changer pour les autres. Ainsi considéré, Meursault s'oppose à Caligula comme le Rien au Tout.

As well as being of the greatest importance for a study of the absurd, *Caligula* is thus crucial in the development of the theme of revolt. For not only does the play demonstrate the catastrophic consequences of a quantitative ethic allied to a combative attitude towards the absurd—taking the form of absolute revolt—but it goes a considerable part of the way towards establishing a more valid alternative. From the start Camus had stressed the provisional nature of *Le Mythe*. It was a *point de départ* and could hardly be anything else in view of the highly abstract circumstances in which he placed the four manifestations of the absurd hero. But this is where the importance of Cherea comes in. Camus makes it clear that he has a philosophical understanding of the absurd, although he has doubtless not made contact with it by means of such a traumatic experience as Caligula's. He is nevertheless an individual in a much more concrete situation than the four modern descendants of Sisyphus. He lives in a world of contingency, and is lucid enough to determine the conditions and consequences for others of any choice he is forced to make. His articulate objections to Caligula's form of revolt are a clear indication that even before *Le Mythe* was written (September 1940–March 1941) Camus was finding the highly personal ethic expounded in that work to be an untenable solipsism in the face of current political events.

Although in his earliest form prone to flippancy and cynicism—characteristics which Camus appears to have redistributed to Hélicon whom he created later—Cherea existed in *Caligula* as a fairly well-developed character right from the start. Thus as early as 1938 he understood the nature of Caligula's revolt, his desire for the identification of thought with action, the ideal with the real: "par Caligula et pour la première fois dans l'histoire, la pensée agit et le rêve rejoint l'action. Il fait ce qu'il rêve de faire." The peril of absolutism is equally clear to him: "qu'un seul être soit pur, dans

le mal ou dans le bien, et notre monde est en danger," and in the same
harangue to the patricians in act 2 he envisages the full consequences: "oui,
laissons continuer Caligula. Poussons-le dans cette voie. Organisons cette
folie. Un jour viendra où il sera seul devant un empire plein de morts ou de
parents de morts." However, it is particularly in the crucial confrontation
with Caligula in act 3, scene 6, that Cherea, in his advocacy of moderation
and condemnation of extremism, most explicitly anticipates the concept of
"limited revolt" and the *qualitative* ethic which are to be the most salient
features of Camus's thinking and writing after the war. Cherea assumes his
"devoirs d'homme" and in acknowledging a moral responsibility towards
society, despite being tempted by the same "logical" conclusion as Caligula,
he announces the communal ethic of human solidarity which is to be extolled
in *La Peste* and *L'Homme révolté*.

To situate this antinihilist and positive aspect of *Caligula* more accurately in the context of Camus's developing thought we may refer to a work
which is much more the contemporary of the play than *La Peste* or *L'Homme
révolté*. This is the series of four *Lettres à un ami allemand* of 1943–4. In the
fourth letter Camus, addressing his fictitious German friend, might almost
be paraphrasing Cherea in the scene just described:

> Nous avons longtemps cru ensemble que ce monde n'avait pas de
> raison supérieure et que nous étions frustrés. Je le crois encore
> d'une certaine manière. Mais j'en ai tiré d'autres conclusions que
> celles dont vous me parliez alors et que, depuis tant d'années,
> vous essayez de faire entrer dans l'Histoire.

And in the same letter, even when the butt of Camus's forensic eloquence
is more obviously the brutal realism of Nazi ambition, the analogy with
Caligula's pedagogic method is none the less striking:

> Vous n'avez jamais cru au sens de ce monde et vous en avez
> tiré l'idée que tout était équivalent et que le bien et le mal se
> définissaient selon qu'on le voulait. Vous avez supposé qu'en
> l'absence de toute morale humaine ou divine les seules valeurs
> étaient celles qui régissaient le monde animal, c'est-à-dire la vio-
> lence et la ruse. Vous en avez conclu que l'homme n'était rien
> et qu'on pouvait tuer son âme, que dans la plus insensée des
> histoires la tâche d'un individu ne pouvait être que l'aventure
> de la puissance, et sa morale, le réalisme des conquêtes. Et à la
> vérité, moi qui croyais penser comme vous, je ne voyais guère
> d'argument à vous opposer, sinon un goût violent de la justice

qui, pour finir, me paraissait aussi peu raisonnée que la plus soudaine des passions.

Où était la différence? C'est que vous acceptiez légèrement de désespérer et que je n'y ai jamais consenti.

(Essais)

The similarities between Camus's objections to Nazism and Cherea's opposition to Caligula are so great that one can easily understand how the audiences of 1945 believed that the play was intended as a direct comment on the contemporary Fascist cataclysm. Camus however was firmly opposed to this association and argued in a letter to Jean Paulhan: "although it was conceived and written in 1938, events have given it a meaning which it did not originally have . . . it was as I conceived it a drama of the mind outside all contingencies." But all that Camus is saying here is that he did not set out to write a consciously committed work containing deliberate allusions to German or Italian Fascism. There is a sense in which Fascism can be philosophical and intellectual as much as political, and a tyrant does not have to be as allusively characterized as Sartre's Aegisthus in *Les Mouches* or Camus's own la Peste in *L'Etat de siège* to be considered remotely relevant to the political climate of Europe in the 1930s and 1940s. Of course *Caligula* originated as a "drama of the mind," but in the letters to his imaginary German friend Camus made it clear that as far as he was concerned Nazism stemmed from precisely the same sort of drama of the mind: the sudden perception that there are no absolute standards and no ultimate divine sanction. The way was clear for the "adventurers" and "conquerors" of the twentieth century to misinterpret and exploit to their own advantage two of the most pregnant hypotheses of the nineteenth century: "God is dead" (Nietzsche) and "If God does not exist, anything is permissible" (Dostoevsky).

In its philosophical atmosphere *Caligula* is very much a characteristic play of its age. Take first of all the subject-matter. There is an undoubted affinity between *Caligula* and the numerous plays on classical Greek themes of the 1930s and 1940s. This rather phenomenal revival has by now been well discussed and documented. Some of the lesser playwrights no doubt hoped to cash in on the lucrative vogue established by Giraudoux and Cocteau (for example André Roussin with his *Hélène ou la Joie de vivre*), and other plays, notably *Les Mouches* and *Antigone,* could only have been performed under the nose of the German censor in their classical guise. But the movement is of greater significance when interpreted out of this strict context of theatrical fad or political contingency, and when seen in the light of Jung and Kérényi's research into archetypes and the collective unconscious. The modern French dramatist, to a far greater extent than his contemporaries in other countries, has made use of a framework of crucial situations and relationships involving death, violence, exile and madness in which to set the crisis of the Western moral consciousness in the modern age, especially during its time of sharpest focus: the Second World War and the events immediately leading up to it. It is not satisfactory to suggest that the modern French return to classical mythology is no more than convenient utilization of existing material, a sort of cultural tomb-robbing as George Steiner sees it, in order to indulge in *jeux d'esprit*. Classical tombs may well have been robbed in France between 1925 and 1950, and the genre has undoubtedly been endowed with an aura of frivolity—some might put it as strongly as sacrilege—by some of the work of Cocteau and Giraudoux. Yet on the whole it was not for easy gain that bodies were lifted from Troy, Thebes and Argos and resurrected in Paris. The very limited range of Greek myths used, and the striking obsession with one or two—rarely the ones which made the great tragedies of the seventeenth century, it should be noted—seem to suggest that the theft was a genuine response to needs of the French collective unconscious, a theft carried out in the dark shadow of a handful of archetypes. Well over a dozen leading French authors each wrote an average of almost two "neo-Greek" plays during this period. Yet of the enormous range of themes and characters which were fully exploited in the Renaissance, the number transposed to the modern period is small. Oedipus and Jocasta, Antigone and Creon, Orestes and Electra, these are the characters and relationships which dominate the age, reflecting, perhaps, some of the most significant aspects of the French malaise at this time: increasing sensitivity to the arrogance of power, a growing consciousness in intellectuals of metaphysical alienation, and a general re-examination of personal (particularly sexual?) values. Few writers of the late 1930s were more concerned with these and kindred dilemmas than Camus. And yet he is one of the few members of the generation of French dramatists who came to the fore at this time who did not draw directly on Greek mythology. He was in fact opposed to the movement, and spoke of the weariness of the theatregoing public with contemporary versions of the *Atridae*. In particular he associated this kind of play with the ostentatious intellectualism of Giraudoux ("l'un des écrivains les moins faits pour le théâtre"), with his constant recourse to "la grâce, l'esprit, le conventionnel et le charmant." But Camus could not resist the pull of the classical archetype at this time, for *Caligula*, although Roman and in its factual essentials historical as opposed to Greek and mythological, acts upon our consciousness in much the same way as do the myths adapted by Gide, Sartre, Anouilh and the others.

Suetonius was a scandalmonger and propagandist. A healthy corrective to the *Lives of the Caesars* is Tacitus, but Tacitus' Life of Gaius Caligula is not extant. Thus of the Julio-Claudian Emperors Caligula is the one whose character has been, and always will be, embellished with all the lusts and quirks which are commonly attributed in the popular imagination to the monster-tyrant figures of history. The raw material which Camus has used for the plot and characters of his play is prurient sensationalism and highly suspect history, destined to be for ever doubted but never completely corrected. It is tempting to suggest that it is precisely because it is such material, whether Camus knew it to be such or not, that it has suited his purpose so well. Caligula has attained an almost mythical stature, rivalling in the popular imagination such figures as Herod, Attila the Hun, Genghis Khan, the Borgias, Richard III, Ivan the Terrible—and Adolf Hitler. He is a giant of depravity and tyranny who cannot, for want of a historical corrective, be reduced in size by comparison with the other eminent figures in the field at this time: Nero, Claudius, Tiberius, Galba, Vitellius and Domitian. Of all the *Lives,* that of Caligula, with its atmosphere of terror, suspicion and decadence and its twin themes of death and gratuitousness, is the ideal raw material out of which to forge a myth of the absurd.

No one need be surprised to know that it was Jean Grenier, who played such a crucial role in Camus's political and philosophical evolution at this time, who put Camus on to the Caligula theme. One of the works which made the greatest impact on Camus in his formative years was Grenier's collection of meditative and semibiographical essays, *Les Iles.* In one of the essays, a particularly sensitive one called "L'Ile de Pâques," Grenier treats the theme of isolation and death ("ce fait aveuglant et écrasant de la mort") in a way that could not fail to appeal to Camus at this time. It is significant that this is one of the few essays to which Camus made specific reference in his preface to the 1959 edition of Grenier's book. It is in this essay that Grenier explains the title of the whole collection:

> D'où vient l'impression d'étouffement qu'on éprouve en pensant à des îles? Où a-t-on pourtant mieux que dans une île l'air du large, la mer libre à tous les horizons, où peut-on mieux vivre dans l'exaltation physique? Mais on y est "isolé" (n'est-ce pas l'étymologie). Une île ou un homme *seul.* Des îles ou des hommes *seuls.*

The narrator describes his relationship with an invalid, a simple, uneducated man and very much "un homme seul," being a paranoiac, who esteems his company for his enlightened conversation. The invalid senses that death may be imminent and tries to elicit the narrator's opinion about the possibility of life after death, evidently considering him a likely actuary of such metaphysical hazards ("vous qui avez fait des études"). But the narrator hedges, for this is by no means his province: "Je ne sais si le boucher s'en rendait compte: ce qui rendait possibles nos conversations à nous qui n'avions rien de commun, c'était une épouvante commune et quotidienne de mourir." And in fact just as it has always been his own custom in the past to avoid such speculation by means of a heavy programme of reading, so he now tries to distract his friend: he brings him the *Lives of the Caesars* to read. The butcher is delighted. Having been thus distracted from mortal speculation by this macabre encyclopaedia of death he dies, and the essay ends on this ironic note. What is interesting is that Grenier alludes particularly to Caligula's crimes, and concludes: "je ne goûtais guère que la couleur locale de ces histoires dont quelques-unes sont bien plus belles—*et n'en voyais pas le sens profond*." This enigmatic attribution of significance where none would at first sight exist has subsequently been explained by Grenier: "j'ai dû en parler [de Suétone] plusieurs fois à Albert Camus en en faisant ressortir le sens nietzschéen de vies comme celles de Caligula." In one of his earliest works, an "Essai sur la musique," written shortly after he had come under the influence of Grenier in the *première supérieure* at the Lycée d'Alger, Camus was writing of Greek civilization in precisely Nietzschean terms, those of the *Birth of Tragedy*, which will find a direct echo in *Caligula* a few years later:

> En effet, l'apollonisme et le dionysisme résultent du besoin de fuir une vie trop douloureuse. Les Grecs ont été déchirés par les luttes politiques, par l'ambition, par la jalousie, par toutes sortes de violences. Mais, direz-vous, il en est de même pour d'autres peuples? En effet. Mais par leur sensibilité et par leur émotivité, les Grecs ont été les plus aptes à la souffrance. Ils ont plus cruellement senti l'horreur de leur vie et ont été ainsi fatalement destinés au dionysisme barbare. De là le besoin de remédier à ces horreurs sauvages, en créant des formes ou plutôt des rêves, plus beaux que chez aucun autre peuple.
> Et pour cela ils se sont servis de la danse et de la musique.
>
> (*Essais*)

This immediately suggests a link between *Caligula* and "le sens nietzschéen" which Grenier attached to the original Suetonius account. Camus's Emperor transforms himself into Venus, "Déesse des douleurs et de la danse," and

justifies himself with an argument which appears to be inspired directly by
Der Wille zur Macht:

> Tout ce qu'on peut me reprocher aujourd'hui, c'est d'avoir fait
> encore un petit progrès sur la voie de la puissance et de la lib-
> erté. Pour un homme qui aime le pouvoir, la rivalité des dieux
> a quelque chose d'agaçant. J'ai supprimé cela. J'ai prouvé à ces
> dieux illusoires qu'un homme, s'il en a la volonté, peut exercer,
> sans apprentissage, leur métier ridicule.

It is the failure of Hélicon to bring the moon which elevates Caligula to the
truly Nietzschean plane of anagnorisis at the end of the play: "Je n'ai pas
pris la voie qu'il fallait, je n'aboutis à rien. Ma liberté n'est pas la bonne."
It remains for Caligula to shatter the mirror of delusion and be struck down
by the mediocre, but relatively harmless, representatives of humanity. Some
have interpreted the direction *"Cherea* [le frappe] *en pleine figure"* to indicate
Cherea's loyalty in contrast with the treachery of the Old Patrician, who
stabs Caligula in the back. Yet this is not altogether logical since it would
have been just as loyal, and yet less brutal, for him to stab Caligula from
the front *but in the body* instead of in the face. There is, I think, another
reason for Camus's precise direction. Cherea's earlier remark to Caligula
that "on ne peut pas aimer celui de ses visages qu'on essaie de masquer en
soi" suggests that there is rather a symbolic significance to this precise blow.
Cherea, the true Dionysus-Apollo synthesis, shatters the mask of the false
one, of the unbridled and self-deluding Dionysus which he himself might
have become.

It is from this Nietzschean perspective that it is most appropriate to
end this examination of *Caligula.* At the prompting of Jean Grenier, Camus
has succeeded in turning a late Roman ragbag of prurience and propaganda
into a tragedy which, relative to the transpositions of Cocteau, Giraudoux,
Anouilh and the others, is more metaphysical, more primordial and—why
not?—more Greek. *Caligula* is proof of the development that was made from
the Théâtre du Travail to the succeeding company, and in every way indicates
an appreciable maturing of Camus's art and thought. The massed workers
of Oviedo, Prague and Algiers no longer fight oversimplified political and
economic issues. Now, as we see with Caligula, Cherea and Scipion, there
are no easy solutions. It is clear that in the evolution of Camus's politics and
his theory and practice in the theatre, ethics and aesthetics are closely linked:
"In the 'epic' theatre, therefore, there is no attempt to create fixed, highly
individualized characters. Character emerges from the social function of the

individual and changes with that function"—Esslin's description suggests a
reason for Camus's rejection of both Communism and the "Communist theatre" of Brecht and Piscator. It was no more possible for Camus to subjugate
his individualism at this time than at any other. Ultimately liberty was more
important to him than justice. *A fortiori* the very dubious Communist notion
of justice in Algeria between 1935 and 1937 could make no lasting hold on
his allegiance. Likewise the future creator of some of the most individualistic
characters of French literature in the middle of the century—Caligula, Meursault, Tarrou, Kaliayev, Martha, Clamence—was ill suited, temperamentally,
to both "epic" and "proletarian" theatre.

Just as Camus constantly asserted that *Caligula* had no overt political
significance (although it is clearly a product of its age in a general philosophical sense), so the Equipe at this time, according to the manifesto of October
1937, would be "sans parti-pris politique ni religieux." A far greater flexi-
bility and aesthetic pragmatism was proclaimed—and practised: "la liberté
la plus grande régnera dans la conception des mises en scène et des décors.
Les sentiments de tous et de tout temps dans des formes toujours jeunes,
c'est à la fois le visage de la vie et l'idéal du bon théâtre." A far greater aesthetic and literary preoccupation is discernible. Camus's "dégagement" from
Communism is complete, and there is no obvious political bias in any of
the five plays in the repertory (*La Célestine, Retour de l'enfant prodigue, Le
Paquebot Tenacity, Les Frères Karamazov, Le Baladin du monde occiden-
tal*), or nine if one includes the envisaged productions of *Caligula, Othello,
Les Esprits* and *La Comédie des bagnes d'Alger,* to compare with that of *Le
Temps du mépris* and *Révolte dans les Asturies.* Unlike the two anti-Fascist
experiments, *Caligula,* as we have seen, possesses a totally ambiguous moral
atmosphere, and is a much closer biographical reflection of the circumstances
in which the play germinated. The inklings of ethical and metaphysical doubt
which close examination revealed to be just below the surface of *Révolte
dans les Asturies* now become the core of Camus's dramatic activity: "Le
Théâtre de l'Equipe . . . demandera aux oeuvres la vérité et la simplicité, la
violence dans les sentiments et la cruauté dans l'action. Ainsi se tournera-t-il
vers les époques où l'amour de la vie se mêlait au désespoir de vivre."

It should now be clear why Camus preferred to regard the Théâtre de
l'Équipe—the company for whom he originally wrote *Caligula*—as the real
beginning of his mature theatrical career, rather than the Théâtre du Travail.
By 1937 the first seeds of disillusionment were firmly implanted in Camus's
sensibility. His first marriage had broken up, and he had been prevented by
his serious ill-health from taking the *agrégation* and continuing with the university career for which he was so obviously suited intellectually. In Algeria

the Communist concern for human justice had been revealed as a sham. In metropolitan France Blum's noninterventionist policy confirmed the inability of the Popular Front to assist the Spanish Republicans. Fascism marched onward in Spain, Italy and Germany. The present time was indeed for Camus one of the "époques où l'amour de la vie se mêlait au désespoir de vivre." *Caligula* is a crystallization of this experience.

DONALD LAZERE

The Myth *and* The Rebel:
Diversity and Unity

The Myth of Sisyphus is Camus's most difficult work, particularly in the first, forty-eight-page sequence, "An Absurd Reasoning," which presents stylistic challenges similar to the lyrical essays—dense construction, digressive asides, elliptical jumps between sentences, cryptic aphorisms—and compounds them with a lengthily sustained, involved line of argument in a combination of philosophy and literary essay reminiscent of Kierkegaard or Nietzsche. The book is filled with nearly as many points of ambiguity as *The Stranger*, which would undoubtedly be a defect from a purely philosophical point of view but which makes it all the more engrossing as an aesthetic creation, embodying in its own structure the epistemological pluralism that comprises one aspect of the absurd.

Despite these difficulties, however, *The Myth* makes a strong initial impression, even on casual readers who may simply be struck by the incisiveness of many individual passages. Readers who are mature enough to have experienced a measure of disenchantment with life are also likely to feel the shock of recognition in the author's enumeration of the absurd's various aspects, which are nonspecific enough to prompt everyone to fill in examples from his personal brushes with absurdity. Perhaps you see a man killed (a rare event for well-insulated, middle-class American whites between World War II and the rash of violence initiated in the 1960s with the assassination of President Kennedy, the Vietnam War, ghetto riots, and college campus rebellion) or hear about the sudden death of a youthful friend or relative.

From *The Unique Creation of Albert Camus.* © 1973 by Yale University. Yale University Press, 1973.

A jarring auto accident on the way to a party or sports event wipes out your anticipation of it and exposes the triviality of such diversions. One day you are overwhelmed by the superhuman magnitude of mountains or the sea and by the indifference to human existence of this natural world that you have been accustomed to viewing as a stage set existing for purposes of your recreation. You witness abdominal surgery and see human life reduced to an animal organism, a slab of beef on the butcher's block. You suddenly perceive a sign of aging in yourself, with its chilling premonition of what you will look like at seventy—or when you are dead. You feel the eerie sensation of perceiving yourself as an Other when you see your picture on film or hear your recorded voice. You find yourself deserted in sickness or adversity, realize the indifference of most people to anyone else's suffering but their own, and make the infuriating discovery that the rest of society goes on doing business as usual, oblivious to your personal calamities.

Another factor contributing to the book's emotional power is its dramatic techniques like the buildup of narrative tension and dynamic modulations in tone. Camus displays his flair for drama in the startling opening— "There is but one truly serious philosophical problem, and that is suicide" —and in the way he systematically demolishes all the illusory values that sustain conventional life, then amid this seeming wasteland builds a new scale of values consistent with the absurd in which "everything resumes its place and the absurd world is reborn in all its splendor and diversity." *The Myth* shares with the fiction and lyrical essays Camus's characteristic of rising in climactic paragraphs to a rhapsodic tone and intensely poetic diction, as for example in the descriptions of the absurd man's lucid, polar night on page 48 or Sisyphus's pride in his fate and in his underworld memories of the beauties of this world on page 91, which recall Meursault's scene with the chaplain.

A dramatic shift in tone comes again when, after the relative abstractness and impersonality of "An Absurd Reasoning," Camus brings his themes down to human scale, in the manner of Kierkegaard or Gide, in the character sketches of Don Juan, the actor, the conqueror, and later Sisyphus. His Don Juan, an absurd hero in the guises both of seducer and blasphemer, ranks with his most appealing fictional characters. Camus, obviously a kindred male soul, rescues Don Juan from his associations by the romantic movement with insatiable questing and by modern psychiatry with misogyny: " 'At last,' exclaims one of [his women], 'I have given you love.' " Can we be surprised that Don Juan laughs at this? " 'At last? No,' he says, 'but once more' ['Enfin? non, dit-il, mais une fois de plus' (*Essais*).]" Camus adds to the legend a touching end: the commander's statue fails to keep his dinner date, and Don Juan is damned not to fire and brimstone but to a ripe old age in a senior citizen's home.

The Myth's ambiguities begin with the central term itself, "the absurd," partly because Camus isn't entirely consistent in its usage, partly because he considers it essentially an indefinable, emotional quality, such as beauty: "Solely appearances can be enumerated and the climate make itself felt." Still it is puzzling, when the climate unquestionably does make itself felt, that it is so difficult to define even a common denominator covering this complex of appearances. One might venture to say, in the broadest possible terms, that the various aspects enumerated in "Absurd Walls" are all experienced as an alienation from or breakdown in our habitual patterns or expectations of life. These patterns and expectations, then, are absurd in the sense of being illusory, ephemeral, or parochial. And the absurd man is one who lucidly recognizes that his normal routine is subject to collapse at any moment and is steeled to go on living after that collapse—indeed, to see it become his routine and to thrive in a permanent state of alienation.

The book's expository structure also contributes to several ambiguities, some doubtlessly intentional, some probably not, that tend to mislead unwary readers. The shock opening leads one to expect a discourse on suicide in general, despite Camus's subsequent qualification that he is only dealing with suicide as a response to the absurd. The expectation of a comprehensive discussion of suicide is furthered by the statement in the 1955 preface to the American edition, "Even if one does not believe in God, suicide is not legitimate," which also leads one to expect that the question of God's existence will be more central than it is. In the essay itself the question does not arise until pages 24–25, where Camus sneaks it in by the back door in describing Jaspers's and Chestov's leap to faith as an evasion of the absurd. Considering the importance of God's existence in the subsequent discussions of Kierkegaard and Dostoevsky, in "Absurd Freedom" and the appendix on Kafka, Camus could have placed the problem more effectively in the book's organizational framework by including it among the aspects of the absurd in "Absurd Walls."

There are several more organizational weaknesses that make the line of argument unnecessarily difficult to follow while lacking sufficient literary merit to redeem them: the jumps back and forth between metaphysical and epistemological absurdity in "Philosophical Suicide" and "Absurd Freedom"; Camus's failure to expand the reference to Heidegger in "Absurd Walls" into "Philosophical Suicide" as he does with the other philosophers he refers to there; the digressions on the existential philosophers and Husserl in "Philosophical Suicide," which are too sketchy to do justice to any of them but long enough to distract from the main line of argument; and finally, the circuitous exposition of the argument in favor of preserving the absurd centered in "Philosophical Suicide" and "Absurd Freedom," which is one of the most ambiguous and difficult points in the book even when it is reassembled into a more straightforward order—as I shall now attempt to do.

II

This argument can be interpreted in at least two distinct ways. The first centers on the paradox that the absurd is an evil, but that in order to oppose it we must preserve it: "What seems to me so obvious, even against me, I must support" (*Myth*). The human condition is inextricably tied to the absurd, like Sisyphus and his rock; there is no escaping the absurd without destroying life itself. The paradox can perhaps best be clarified by comparing the absurd to a disease, which can only be treated so long as the patient remains alive. Killing the patient eliminates the disease rather than directly combating it and in fact signals its victory. Suicide, then, is a surrender to the disease of the absurd, eliminating the absurdity of one's particular life instead of keeping it alive so that it can be opposed: "It may be thought that suicide follows revolt—but wrongly. For it does not represent the logical outcome of revolt. It is just the contrary by the consent it presupposes."

If one decides that it is worthwhile to combat the absurd (only a hypothetical proposition at this point in the argument, since the value of revolt has not yet been established), he must, first, do everything he can to stay alive. Second, he must fully acknowledge the truth of life's absurdity rather than evading it through the existential leap to faith in God (Chestov, Kierkegaard, Dostoevsky, Jaspers) or through a total irrationalism that destroys the intellectual faculties necessary to perceive the absurd. Finally, since the absurd is by definition a state of mind, existing only through the mental act of perceiving it, one must not only acknowledge the absurd on principle but must apply this acknowledgment by constantly either thinking explicitly about the absurd or making his every action consistent with its terms, without giving in to the temptation toward mindless distraction, Pascal's le *divertissement*. To stop thinking about the absurd is to kill it, the intellectual equivalent of suicide: "Living is keeping the absurd alive. Keeping it alive is, above all, contemplating it. Unlike Eurydice, the absurd dies only when we turn away from it."

These, then, are the conditions one must meet *if* he judges that the absurd is worth preserving. Its worth still remains to be established at this point, when the question becomes "whether I can live with what I know and with that alone." The answer comes in "Absurd Freedom" with the affirmation of the values of revolt, freedom, and passion summarized in chapter 3 above. This interpretation, then, simply establishes maintaining awareness of the absurd as a precondition for revolting against it, whose value is established elsewhere—in contrast to the alternate interpretation, which follows, according to which maintaining absurd awareness becomes a value, even an ethical necessity, in itself.

A second dimension to the foregoing argument, more complex and ambiguous logically, originates on page 5: "The principle can be established that for a man who does not cheat, what he believes to be true must determine his action. Belief in the absurdity of existence must then dictate his conduct." Camus in effect is making intellectual truthfulness into a moral imperative and another value to be found within the boundaries of the absurd. Since the absurd is not inherent in the objective world but survives only as an attitude within the human mind, adhering to the truth of the absurd entails keeping both the mind and its awareness of the absurd alive:

> And it is by this elementary criterion that I judge the notion of the absurd [which he has distinguished on page 21 from the unarticulated, emotional experience of it] to be essential and consider that it can stand as the first of my truths. . . . If I judge that a thing is true, I must preserve it. If I attempt to solve a problem, at least I must not by that very solution conjure away one of the terms of the problem. For me the sole datum is the absurd. [O'Brien's translation inexplicably leaves out the following sentence here: "The problem is where to proceed from it and if suicide must be deduced from this absurd" (*Essais*).] The first and, after all, the only condition of my inquiry is to preserve the very thing that crushes me, consequently to respect what I consider essential in it. I have just defined it as a confrontation and an unceasing struggle.

He repeats the same argument on page 38, concluding, "And what constitutes the basis of that conflict, of that break between the world and my mind, but the awareness of it? If therefore I want to preserve it, I can through a constant awareness, ever revived, ever alert."

This apparent attempt by Camus to demonstrate the logical necessity of preserving the absurd has provoked refutations by several critics and philosophers, including John Cruickshank and Herbert Hochberg. Hochberg claims that Camus makes an "unfortunate play on the notion of preserving, or alternatively, denying a truth or a fact. Need one do more than point out that it is quite one thing to deny that some one has a wart by stating that it is not so; it is quite another thing to 'deny' that fact by removing the wart. Of course, in Camus's case one removes the disease by removing the patient, but the point is still the same." I do not think that the point *is* still the same or that Camus does in fact fall into this fallacy, even though he at times appears to.

If Camus meant his assertion "If I judge a thing is true, I must preserve it" to be categorical, as Hochberg takes it to be, it would obviously be fallacious: although a wart really exists, nothing obliges one not to remove it. We can infer, however, that Camus's assertion is not universal, but applies only to the unique truth of the absurd. The wart still exists even if one stops thinking about it or denies that it exists, but the absurd continues to exist only through thinking about it. It lies, for example, not in the irrationality of the natural world or fate alone, which would continue to be facts even if I were not aware of them, but in the tension between "my appetite for the absolute and for unity and the impossibility of reducing this world to a rational and reasonable principle"; it does not lie in the imminence of my death alone, which likewise will still be fact even if I stop thinking about it, but in the anxiety created between my recognition of that inevitability and my innate sense of and craving for immortality. All I need to do to end the absurdity of my particular life is to stop thinking about it—intellectual suicide. But doing so is to betray Camus's earlier principle of always acting in accordance with what reasoning consciousness judges to be true, i.e., that the authentic mental state is that of the absurd.

This syllogistic argument, more formally contrived than most of Camus's thought, does have an aura of being sophistic even if it isn't, and its conclusion barely carries enough emotional force to make it worth the mental gymnastics demanded to grasp it. Assuming that the argument is logically sound, all it really ends up saying is that intellectual honesty favors maintaining the absurd consciousness, all other things being equal. Intellectual integrity alone, however, would be a shaky basis for remaining alive if the absurd condition were so painful, or even barren, otherwise that it eclipsed the gratifications of integrity. What really redeems his argument is his subsequent affirmation of the values within the absurd—freedom, revolt, and passion—which provide reasons for not committing suicide that are emotionally far more persuasive.

Logicians may challenge Camus's line of reasoning, or at least my account of it, and I confess that having wrestled with this book about once a year for a dozen years I have changed my interpretation and evaluation of Camus's argument—sometimes agreeing with Hochberg—with every rereading, often several times during one rereading. But all of this only indicates that from a literary viewpoint it is only secondarily important whether we finally judge his logic to be completely valid or not. What is most important is the argument's—and the book's—enigmatic power to engage the reader's mind protractedly over a span of years. Camus has once again constructed an aesthetic labyrinth, a verbal objective correlative for that absurd world which "resembles the data of experience in that it is both infinitely simple and infinitely complicated."

III

After what we have already seen of Camus's practice of balancing metaphysical with sociopolitical themes in different works, it should scarcely be necessary to reiterate that the most common criticism of *The Myth* by left-wing critics, that it deals with existence only on the metaphysical plane to the neglect of social reality, is based on an ill-informed consideration of this work, and sometimes *The Stranger,* in isolation from Camus's total creation. In a footnote near the beginning of the book, Camus makes it clear that he is purposely restricting his present scope: "Let us not miss this opportunity to point out the relative character of this essay. Suicide may indeed be related to much more honorable considerations—for example, the political suicides of protest, as they were called, during the Chinese revolution." Nevertheless, it is necessary to ask whether *The Myth* is consistent with radically critical political thought even while excluding it.

As his aesthetic theory has indicated, Camus's writing generally does not convey a highly developed sense of specific social or historical situation. Although in his reportage he did criticize the inequities of class society, in his fiction, drama, and literary and philosophical essays he purposely strove for universal truths even when he located them in recognizable social settings. The price he paid was a certain loss of fidelity to those specifics of existence that vary enormously between different social strata and historical moments. The gap left by the absence of these specifics can be remarked even in the ostensibly asocial, ahistorical world of *The Myth.* The very awareness of metaphysical absurdity, resulting from a breakdown in habitual routine and expectations, is a bourgeois privilege, even with all its attendant anxieties. Exploited or unemployed workers, colonized or ghettoized peoples, the victims of war cannot even afford the luxury of habits and expectations to be alienated from; absurd alienation is their habitual condition. Thus Norman Mailer, in "The White Negro: Superficial Reflections on the Hipster," describes the Negro as the American existentialist:

Any Negro who wishes to live must live with danger from his
first day, and no experience can ever be casual to him, no Negro
can saunter down a street with any real certainty that violence
will not visit him on his walk. The cameos of security for the
average white: mother and the home, job and the family, are not
even a mockery to millions of Negroes; they are impossible.

On the other hand, there are more implications for social reality in *The
Myth* than granted by critics like the German Marxist Ernst Fischer, who
chastises "writers, ranging from Camus to Beckett, who set out to divorce
man from society, to dissolve his identity and to wrap him in mystery as
the agent of 'eternal being' and 'formless original forces.' Any man is more
than the mere mask of a social character. But the tendency to turn him into
a hieroglyphic in a play of cosmic mysteries, to blot out his social as well
as his individual face in a mystical archaic fog, leads to nothingness." I find
Fischer's characterization wholly appropriate to Beckett but not Camus. As
indicated [elsewhere] *The Myth* and *The Stranger* (which Fischer seems to be
referring to more specifically) already contain implications that, followed to
their logical conclusions, lead directly to the social philosophy of *The Rebel,
The Plague,* and *The Just Assassins.*

The Myth first points out the absurd insignificance of each individual's
subjective consciousness, then asserts its irreplaceable importance. Once we
affirm every individual consciousness as an absolute value, we become bound
to seek a social system that promotes maximal length, intensity, and freedom
for each individual's life. Hence we must oppose war, capital punishment,
and any ideology that subordinates human flesh and blood to abstractions
such as nationalism or bourgeois propriety. On its epistemological level,
The Myth's exhortation for the absurd man constantly to follow the dictates
of truth and to challenge the inscrutability of the universe with his utmost
capacity for lucidity carries over into Camus's later notions of the artist's
and intellectual's responsibility to pit their understanding against the equally
absurd enigmas of contemporary politics and to oppose political lies and
euphemisms that obfuscate carnal truth and separate those whom absurd
solitudes should unite. *The Stranger,* too, tacitly criticizes bourgeois verbal
abstractions and arbitrary restraints on individual life and liberty, notwith-
standing Meursault's utter lack of political consciousness as such. The pri-
macy of fleshly reality in *The Myth* and *The Stranger* constitutes the matrix
for the explicit anticapitalism of "Create Dangerously":

For about a century we have been living in a society that is not
even the society of money (gold can arouse carnal passions) but

that of the abstract symbols of money. The society of merchants can be defined as a society in which things disappear in favor of signs. When a ruling class measures its fortunes, not by the acre of land or the ingot of gold, but by the number of figures corresponding ideally to a certain number of exchange operations, it thereby condemns itself to setting a certain kind of humbug at the center of its experience and its universe. A society founded on signs is, in its essence, an artificial society in which man's carnal truth is handled as something artificial.

(*Resistance, Rebellion, and Death*)

This far in his thinking, Camus is quite at one with Marxist denunciations of bourgeois society for its wage slavery, verbal mystifications, alienating separation of individuals in lonely crowds, reification of human beings and their subordination to commodity fetishism that rationalizes war, capital punishment, and police shooting of petty larcenists. His disagreements with what he considered doctrinaire Marxists and the Communist party come at later stages of his political philosophy, in *The Rebel*. Camus's thought, in sum, is more authentically dialectical than Fischer's in his fragmentary account of Camus, although their general aesthetics are quite similar. The sophisticated Marxist should be able to see in *The Myth*, as well as *The Stranger*, the generation of theses and antitheses that will be resolved in the syntheses of *The Rebel*.

IV

Although *The Rebel* is three times as long as *The Myth* and demands more historical and literary background from the reader, it is easier to follow because Camus holds to a straight line of exposition and strives on principle for clarity rather than ambiguity—a principle that is betrayed by Bower's clumsy, obfuscating translation. Camus does maintain the customary ambiguity of his titles in *L'Homme révolté*, which translates either as "Man in Revolt" or "The Revolted [or 'Disgusted'] Man." The essay's artistic complexity is mainly contained in its monumental structure and a world view synthesizing metaphysics, political and literary history and theory. In lieu of his projected 1500-page "The System," it is the closest approximation to his *summa*, encompassing virtually all aspects of his formal thought and all the stages in the dialectical development of his themes.

Critical appreciation of the book's total scope has been impeded because its appearance in 1951, at the height of the Cold War, resulted in a nearly exclusive focus by Francis Jeanson and Sartre in *Les Temps modernes* and other critics on Camus's attack against Hegelian-Marxian dialectical philosophy and the political history of communism, which takes up only seventy-five of three hundred pages. The Jeanson-Camus-Sartre exchange matched three highly intelligent and farsighted opponents on the central political issues of our time and still retains its urgent importance for Americans today (although unfortunately at this writing only Sartre's reply has been translated here; Camus's letter to *Les Temps modernes* was reprinted as "Révolte et servitude" in *Actuelles II* and *Essais*). The political themes, however, will be considered here only in their due proportion to the complete work as a literary essay.

In some ways *The Rebel*'s ideological weaknesses are literary strengths. Jeanson, in fact, charged that its structure was so elaborate and its style so elegant that the political issues became subordinated to a literary virtuosity calculated to win approval in bourgeois literary circles. Camus in turn objected to the implication that a polished style must be a sign of cultural reactionism. Undoubtedly, Camus's vast syntheses, categories, and polarities indicate intellectual oversimplifications, especially in contrast to the essay style of the more recondite Sartre, who is less inclined to reduce ideas to clear-cut dualities. Sartre's counterstatement to *The Rebel* in political theory, *Critique of Dialectical Reason,* required the projection of two large, densely written volumes; the one volume that has appeared, however, like much of Sartre's writing and that of his associate Beauvoir, is open to the opposite criticism, that it is excessively protracted, with repetitious and obscure stretches. Camus's clarity, conciseness, and judicious editing in almost all his works at least constitute a persuasive case for his belief in the autonomous value of artful literary style.

One recent American critic, Leo Bersani, has gone so far as to say that *The Rebel* "makes no sense at all except as a bizarre and unsuccessful stylistic exercise in the lyricism of abstract antinomies." Even as hyperbole, this is an extremely glib dismissal of a work that can be profitably studied over many years for its unique application in our times of a classical humanistic perspective to the most pressing modern literary and political disorders. (Bersani compares Camus disadvantageously to Samuel Beckett, Alain Robbe-Grillet and other French New Novelists, as well as to recent structuralist critics. These writers may well have superseded Camus in abstruse thought or literary technique—they are often, in fact, far more abstract than Bersani claims Camus is—but they have not invalidated his commonsense fidelity to the immediate, fundamental truths of individual existence.) Whatever the drawbacks of *The Rebel*'s massively symmetrical structure, it effectively underscores the theme of man's perpetual passion for unity, forming an organizational counterpart to the reflection of absurd pluralism in *The Myth*'s fragmented exposition.

The introduction is one of the key passages of his entire works, encapsulating the transition between the phase of the absurd and that of rebellion. Picking up from where *The Myth* leaves off, Camus moves from the problem of suicide to that of murder. Although he does not mention the titles of his earlier works, he implicitly contrasts the nihilistic implications of the absurd, those followed by Meursault and Caligula, with the affirmative implications in *The Myth,* whose line of argument, if followed accurately and to its end, rejects nihilistic suicide and now by extension rejects nihilistic murder as well: "To say that life is absurd, the conscience must be alive. How is it possible, without making remarkable concessions to one's desire for comfort, to preserve exclusively for oneself the benefits of such a process of reasoning? From the moment that life is recognized as good, it becomes good for all men" (*Rebel*).

As a corollary to Camus's thesis of the inconsistency of deducing nihilism from the absurd, he adds the self-contradictions implicit in metaphysical and epistemological absurdity discussed [elsewhere], the point of which in this context is that if absurdist despair neither ends in suicide nor is surpassed it runs the danger of turning into a pleasure-giving pose in which "the absurd, which claims to express man in his solitude, really makes him live in front of a mirror." Two pages later he expresses the necessity of transcending the absurd similarly: "The mirror, with its fixed stare, must be broken." (The mirror imagery, of course, alludes back to *Caligula* and ahead to *The Fall,* although the connotations are slightly different in the various contexts. Caligula's mirror symbolizes his nihilistic moral solipsism and is shattered at his death. In "The Dandies' Rebellion" it represents not only the narcissistic *Schadenfreude* of the romantic agony but also the dependence of the dandyish rebel on an audience: "He can only be sure of his own existence by finding it in the expression of others' faces. Other people are his mirror" (*Rebel*). The latter description also fits Clamence, who uses other people, especially the confidant of his confession, as a mirror for his self-satisfaction before the fall and his self-laceration afterward.)

Absurdist narcissism itself can lead to murder, either actively, through "tragic dilettantism" in which "human lives become counters in a game" (*Rebel*), or passively, through self-absorbed paralysis: "not to act at all, which amounts to at least accepting the murder of others, with perhaps mild reservations about the imperfection of the human race." Furthermore, in the mid-twentieth century nihilism not only is an individual creed but has been institutionalized by governments, which commit murder on a wider scale than ever before in history. If the absurd man is to rebel against death, then his revolt must be not only metaphysical but political, directed against legalized murder by the State. The detailed history of how nihilism evolved and turned from an individual, metaphysical philosophy into a collective, political one and the problem of how to revolt against a murderous history without becoming a murderer oneself will comprise the main substance of *The Rebel*.

V

"Metaphysical Rebellion" (*Rebel*) stands by itself as a significant work of literary criticism, a cogent history of this theme from the Prometheus of Aeschylus through the surrealist movement. Camus's criticisms of individual authors are sometimes biased or superficial, but they are all interesting for the insights they give into his own thought.

"The Sons of Cain" outlines the values of moderation he admired in classical Greece, in contrast to the excesses of modern romanticism. He denies that rebellion in Greek literature was truly metaphysical, since it was directed only against individual gods who were themselves fallible, not against the whole of creation or nature, which was impersonal: "The acme of excess to the Greek mind was to beat the sea with rods—an act of insanity worthy only of barbarians." Furthermore, the tragic hero's outrage against the capriciousness of destiny is ultimately tempered by his enlightened resignation to the world's fatality: "The Greek mind has two aspects and in its meditations almost always re-echoes, as counterpoint to its most tragic melodies, the eternal words of Oedipus, who, blind and desperate, recognizes that all is for the best. Affirmation counterbalances negation." For the romantics, on the other hand, fatalism dictates all-or-nothing total negation. Qualifying his affinities to epicureanism and stoicism in his other works, he remarks that Epicurus, Lucretius, and the Roman stoics, in their ascetic minimizing of life's pleasures, mark a transition toward the modern disbalanced preoccupation with death over life.

He touches only lightly on most of the Christian era, then focuses on the eighteenth to twentieth centuries, the same period he will cover at length in "Historical Rebellion." The Marquis de Sade in "A Man of Letters," the romantic hero in "The Dandies' Rebellion," Ivan Karamazov in "The Rejection of Salvation," and Maldoror in "Lautréamont and Banality" are, like Caligula, "compelled to do evil by [their] nostalgia for an unrealizable good." Revenge against the absurdity of the universe or a murderous God impels them all to become rivals in murder, and while Nietzsche, in "Absolute Affirmation," replaces the very concepts of good and evil with his great yea-saying to all of creation, "to say yes to everything supposes that one says yes to murder." Furthermore, romantic rebellion tends to become a platform for poseurs who, congenitally deficient in normal emotions, can only fulfill themselves in excessive ones: in a love that is perverse, as with Sade, or ill fated, as with "the Byronic hero, incapable of love, or capable only of an impossible love"; in paroxysms of narcissistic despair; in mystical transcendentalism or apocalyptic destruction that purports to transfigure the world but actually leads only to annihilation, as with Lautréamont, Rimbaud, and the more extreme expressions of surrealism. He does acknowledge that some writers recognized the sterility of the romantic pose and turned from narcissism toward political commitment, in a passage that is worth quoting as another example of Bower's loose and confusing translations: "Between the times of the eighteenth-century eccentric and the 'conquerors' of the twentieth century, Byron and Shelley are already fighting, though only ostensibly, for freedom." [More accurately, "Between Rameau's nephew and the 'conquerors' of the twentieth century, Byron and Shelley are already fighting, even though ostentatiously, for freedom."]

The title of "The Dandies' Rebellion" alludes to Baudelaire's 1853 essay "The Dandy," one of the subjects of the engravings of Constantin Guys that he interprets in *The Painter of Modern Life*. Baudelaire's essay coins the term "the cult of oneself" to describe romantic narcissism, as well as perceiving the paradoxical theatricality of dandyism's nonconformity—"It is, above all, a burning need to acquire originality, within the apparent bounds of convention"—and its exaltation of what Camus calls tragic dilettantism— "A dandy can never indulge in anything vulgar. If he committed a crime, he would perhaps not be too upset about it; but if this crime had some trivial cause, his disgrace would be irreparable." While Guys's and Baudelaire's dandy is the vestigial aristocrat in bourgeois society, Camus applies the idea to the romantic movement in general as well as to absurdist nihilism. Since anguish is the strongest emotion that the romantic rebel's peculiar temperament enables him to feel—or is at least a more dramatic one than positive forms of revolt—he develops a vested interest in maintaining it: "Pain, at this stage, is acceptable only if it is incurable." If the spontaneous overflow of powerful feelings can only be inspired by death and despair, so be it, whether one participates in the carnage actively or only vicariously. While the romantics' taste for apocalypse is expressed only in literature, theirs are "desires that a later generation will assuage in extermination camps." Thus, for all

the distortions in the Nazis' preemption of romantic *Geist,* their nihilism
can be seen as a logical though perverse extension of this tendency in the
romantic literary tradition.

Although the unhealthy tendencies that Camus criticizes may only be
deviations rather than the essence of romanticism, this analysis remains one
of his most astute points, appearing as it did in the America of the mid-
1950s when it was applicable to a neoromantic revival in the American
drug cult, beat writing, and Actors Studio theater, and in French New Wave
cinema. His attack follows lines similar to Irving Babbitt's *Rousseau and
Romanticism* (a book that strongly resembles *The Rebel* in its style and classical humanist viewpoint, aside from Babbitt's conservative social philosophy), Denis de Rougemont's *Love in the Western World,* and Leslie Fiedler's
Love and Death in the American Novel. Out of these works emerges a pattern of insights to the romantic psychology: idealized or unattainable love
may conceal an incapacity for real love, replacing palpable objects of desire
with infinite, indeterminate longing. An excess of sexual or other emotions
is likely to stem not from satiation with normal ones but from a defi-
ciency of them, the frustrated passions frequently being channeled perversely
into necrophilic violence. The longing for apocalyptic transformation of the
world can become an indolent evasion of the effort necessary to make intellectual distinctions and value judgments or to revolt directly against clear
and present evils. And the quest for mystical transcendence of the ego may
be a form of intellectual suicide, leading only to annihilation of the ego or
a vegetable mentality as banal as the conformist mentality against which it
rebels.

VI

The parallel between metaphysical and historical rebellion in part three
is an elaboration on a theme from *The Brothers Karamazov,* expressed in a
passage that Camus quotes on page 60: "If Aliosha had come to the conclusion that neither God nor immortality existed, he would immediately have
become an atheist and a socialist. For socialism is not only a question of the
working classes; it is above all, in its contemporary incarnation, a question
of atheism, a question of the tower of Babel, which is constructed without
God's help, not to reach to the heavens, but to bring the heavens down to
earth."

The anti–Church-State revolutions that, since 1789, have been aimed
at establishing earthly justice and freedom have, like nihilistic metaphysical
rebellion, lost sight of their affirmative origins and ended up reestablish-

ing tyranny and murder on an even wider and more institutionalized scale through capital punishment and total war. In the Western European democracies, Camus claims, this has happened for the same reasons he has given in the lyrical essays: the life-denying bureaucracy of industrial capitalism and the hubris of governments that, arrogantly believing themselves capable of attaining total justice, have stifled individual liberty. Under communism he attributes the suppression of freedom to betrayal of the revolution by nihilistic leaders, to Soviet Russia's aping of capitalist technocracy, and most importantly to Marxist-Leninist utopianism that sacrifices present liberties toward the end of a classless society in a future that turns out to be perpetually receding. He regards the Soviet five-year-plan mentality as the direct offshoot of Hegelian and Marxian dialectical theory. Although he largely agrees with Marx's critique of bourgeois society and, as we have seen, has certain affinities to Marxism in the dialectical turn of his mind, he considers dialectical materialism equivocal in claiming to be at once deterministic and messianic, scientific and hortatory, thus lending itself to the expedient, self-contradicting shifts in Communist party line under Stalin.

What emerges from this analysis is in effect a theory of historical absurdity parallel to the metaphysical absurdity of *The Myth,* in which the course of history is unpredictable and capricious and in which aspiration for political progress is virtually doomed to frustration if not to utter betrayal or reversal. What path is left open, then, for the authentic historical rebel that is comparable to the absurd man's life-affirming options for revolt?

Before answering this question, or perhaps on the way to answering it, he makes a detour into "Rebellion and Art," part four. This apparent disruption of the book's expository development becomes justified as art and the vocation of the artist emerge as one model for antinihilistic revolt. "Rebellion and the Novel" and "Rebellion and Style" respond to "Metaphysical Rebellion"; here the writer, rather than simply venting his spite against the disunity and obscurity of the universe, corrects creation through literary form, style, and lucidity. And "Creation and Revolution" is a delineation of the artist as historical rebel that anticipates the "Artist and His Time" interviews and Stockholm speeches. Against bloodshed and bureaucratic dehumanization the creator opposes his love of life and beauty. Camus gives art wider significance by using the figure of the artist, somewhat in the manner of Pater, Wilde, or Gide, to exemplify a creative attitude in all realms of life, in the same way that he equates the artist and lover in "The Enigma." He reiterates the theme common in Marxist literary criticism (although, perhaps with a touch of Cold War squeamishness, failing to acknowledge it) that the integration of form and content in art can provide a model for an organic society reversing the division of labor imposed by industrial capitalism. He again echoes Marx in his ideal of a postindustrial society that will erase capitalism's alienating distinctions between manual and mental labor, work and artistic creation: "Industrial society will open the way to a new civilization only by restoring to the worker the dignity of a creator; in other words, by making him apply his interest and his intelligence as much to the work itself as to what it produces."

From *The Myth, Neither Victims nor Executioners* [all further references to this work will be abbreviated as *NVNE*], and Tarrou's monologue in *The Plague,* one could deduce that Camus's conclusion in part five, "Thought at the Meridian [La Pensée de midi]," would express a philosophy of resistance to historical absurdity, an opposition of absolute nonviolent revolt against murder, whether sanctioned by individual nihilism, the State, or revolution. But what we get is a modification of his earlier pacifism. Whereas in 1946 he avowed, "I could no longer hold to any truth which might oblige me, directly or indirectly, to demand a man's life" (*NVNE*), now he concedes, "In the world today, only a philosophy of eternity could justify nonviolence" (*Rebel*) and "Absolute non-violence is the negative basis of slavery and its acts of violence" (*Rebel*). Complicity in killing in a just revolt or war of self-defense cannot be completely avoided without lapsing into a quietism that acquiesces to killing by the prevailing powers, but limits can be set that establish a reasonable culpability: "Authentic acts of rebellion will only consent to take up arms for institutions that limit violence, not for those that codify it. A revolution is not worth dying for unless it assures the immediate suppression of the death penalty; not worth going to prison for unless it refuses in advance to pass sentence without fixed terms."

One point on which his position does follow directly from *The Myth* is his rejection of communist (as well as Christian) messianism that defers social gratifications until the millennium of the classless society: "Real generosity toward the future lies in giving all to the present." As practical alternatives to present political establishments and revolutionary movements, he suggests the models of the Scandinavian republics, syndicalism, the trade-union movement—broadly, a democratic, decentralized socialism similar to that advocated by other mentors of the New Left in the late 1950s and 1960s such as C. Wright Mills, Erich Fromm, Herbert Marcuse, and Paul Goodman. And as a precondition to any specific program he urges a regenerated political ethic scaled to humane principles rather than expediency, to individuals rather than masses, plus a renaissance of the classical sense of proportion and limits without which both established powers and revolutionaries are fated to continue the cycle of violence and counterviolence until it ends in the apocalypse of nuclear war. Differences between the ideologies of capitalism, communism, and socialism are secondary; no ideology can be valid unless its exponents have the capacity to exercise a measured balance between means and ends, present and future needs, justice and freedom, the individual and the community.

Within a broad, humanistic perspective, Camus's analysis retains several valuable lessons. First, the course of history can be mercurial and inscrutable, which should serve to caution though not completely discourage revolutionary proponents. (This argument can, incidentally, also be applied to established powers and thus turned against Camus's own anticommunism and that of the more rigid Cold Warriors who failed to take adequate account of the possible flux in the communist world after the death of Stalin.) No matter how frustrated revolutionary hopes may be, men will always retain the freedom to resist political tyranny even if they cannot overthrow it. Finally, his call for a revival of classical temperance reasserts precious values that, simple as they may seem, are indeed woefully absent from the prevailing political and cultural mentality of the twentieth century. While his appeal for a sense of restraint in governmental violence may appear on the face of it to be a rather vague or mild prescription, going into the 1970s one had only to look around at Indochina, the Middle East, Czechoslovakia, American police actions in ghettos, prisons, and college campuses, or listen to the theoreticians of nuclear overkill and a perpetually escalating arms race, to recognize that governments on all sides, far from having heeded Camus's program, were still prone to use violence as a first rather than last resort.

The Rebel's overall political perspective, however, in its association of all contemporary revolution with the U.S.S.R., has become somewhat dated since the late fifties with the breakup of communism as a monolithic world power and the shift in the focus of the Cold War to Third World liberation fronts. These changes have lent support to the position of Jeanson, Sartre, and subsequent leftist critics of Camus, which may be briefly summarized as follows. His understanding of Hegelian and Marxian dialectical philosophy is rather shallow. Sartre tells him, "I have at least this in common with Hegel. You have not read either of us." While his account of Stalinist manipulations of dialectical thought is accurate, it is highly disputable whether Stalinism is the logical consequence of Marxism or a perversion of it. Camus closed himself off from the possibility that some aspects of dialectical materialism were still viable. In this, he may have had the bias of the marginal bourgeois and colonial who feels his life to be relatively free from class determination, hence is reluctant to acknowledge an element of dialectical inexorability in the economic necessity for European and American capitalism to expand imperialistically into Africa, Asia, and Latin America—and in the consequent violent revolt of the colonized. Instead, he would prefer to believe that these forces might be reversed by hortatory appeals for liberal humanitarianism.

It is all very well, say Camus's opponents, for intellectuals to exhort those in power to exercise restraint, but the latter are little inclined to be influenced by humanitarian appeals. This being the case, it is even less meaningful to prescribe moderation to the rulers' victims who have no alternative to fighting for their lives or liberation by any means possible. Herbert Marcuse, in his controversial 1965 essay "Repressive Tolerance," approvingly quotes Sartre's preface to Fanon's *The Wretched of the Earth* and adds, "Non-violence is normally not only preached to but exacted from the weak—it is a necessity rather than a virtue, and normally it does not seriously harm the case of the strong. . . . To start applying [ethical standards] at the point where the oppressed rebel against the oppressors, the have-nots against the haves is serving the cause of actual violence by weakening the protest against it." While Camus's prognosis of the vicious cycle of revolutionary violence may be accurate, it, like his aesthetic theory, is formulated outside the flux of historical situation and consequently is largely irrelevant to the actual circumstances of "men who for example would be hungry," as Jeanson says sarcastically, "and who would try, following their very inferior logic, to struggle against those responsible for their hunger."

In the end, Camus's exhortations are only fully applicable to volunteer rebels, especially intellectuals, within the bourgeoisie—one of whom, as Sartre reminded him, Camus himself had become. Camus's political theory in general is most meaningful as a program for middle-class intellectuals and artists involving themselves and their distinctive sensibility in historical struggle. These men, however, are apt to play only a marginal political role at best. Camus recognized this and at times gives the impression in *The Rebel* that he is trying mainly to formulate an ethic of minimal nonviolence for himself while conceding, like Tarrou, that other men must go on murderously making history. In this light, *The Rebel* stops short of proposing a universal political program, which is undoubtedly a grave limitation. On the other hand, perhaps the reader can best do it justice by approaching it with the understanding that its title applies mainly to the intellectual *engagé* and perhaps even more specifically to Camus himself.

RENÉ GIRARD

Camus's Stranger Retried

We have always pictured Meursault as a stranger to the sentiments of other men. Love and hatred, ambition and envy, greed and jealousy are equally foreign to him. He attends the funeral of his mother as impassively as he watches, on the following day, a Fernandel movie. Eventually, Meursault kills a man, but how could we feel that he is a real criminal? How could this man have any motive for murder?

Meursault is the fictional embodiment of the nihilistic individualism expounded in *Le Mythe de Sisyphe* and commonly referred to as *l'absurde*. Meursault is possessed by this *absurde* as others, in a different spiritual context, are possessed by religious grace. But the word *absurde* is not really necessary; the author himself, in his preface to the Brée-Lynes edition of the novel, defines his hero as a man "who does not play the game." Meursault "refuses to lie" and, immediately, "society feels threatened." This hero has a positive significance, therefore; he is not an *épave*, a derelict; "he is a man poor and naked who is in love with the sun."

It is easy to oppose *L'Etranger* to a novel like *Crime and Punishment*. Dostoevsky *approves* the sentence that condemns his hero, whereas Camus *disapproves*. *L'Etranger* must be a work of innocence and generosity, soaring above the morass of a guilt-ridden literature. But the problem is not so simple as it looks. Meursault is not the only character in the novel. If he is innocent, the judges who sentence him are guilty. The presentation of the trial as a parody of justice contains at least an implicit indictment of the judges. Many

From *"To Double Business Bound": Essays on Literature, Mimesis, and Anthropology*. © 1978 by the Johns Hopkins University Press, Baltimore/London.

critics have made this indictment explicit and so has Camus himself in the preface to the American edition of *L'Etranger*. After presenting the death of his hero as the evil fruit of an evil collectivity, the author concludes: "In our society, a man who does not cry at the funeral of his mother is likely to be sentenced to death." This striking sentence is really a quotation from an earlier statement; it is labeled "paradoxical," but it is nevertheless repeated with the obvious intent to clear all possible misunderstanding as to an interpretation of *L'Etranger* that, in a sense, is beyond questioning.

La Chute was published in 1956, one year after the American edition of *L'Etranger*. In it, a fashionable Parisian lawyer named Clamence has made a great reputation defending those criminals whom he could, somehow, picture as victims of the "judges." Clamence has a very high opinion of himself because he has always sided with the "underdog" against the iniquitous "judges." One day, however, he discovers that moral heroism is not so easily achieved in deeds as it is in words, and a process of soul searching begins that leads the "generous lawyer" to abandon his successful career and take refuge in Amsterdam. Clamence realizes that mercy, in his hands, was a secret weapon against the unmerciful, a more complex form of self-righteousness. His real desire was not to save his clients but to prove his moral superiority by discrediting the judges. Clamence, in other words, had been the type of lawyer whom Salinger's hero, in *The Catcher in the Rye,* would hate to become:

> Lawyers are right . . . if they go around saving innocent guys' lives all the time, and like that, but you don't *do* that kind of stuff if you're a lawyer. . . . And besides. Even if you *did* go around saving guys' lives, and all, how would you know if you did it because you really *wanted* to save guys' lives, or because what you *really* wanted to do was be a terrific lawyer, with everybody slapping you on the back and congratulating you in court when the goddam trial was over. . . . How would you know you weren't being a phony? The trouble is, you *wouldn't*.

The "generous lawyer" wants to be *above* everybody else and to sit in judgment over the judges themselves; he is a judge in disguise. Unlike the ordinary judges who judge directly and openly, he judges indirectly and deviously. When anti-Pharisaism is used as a device to crush the Pharisees, it becomes another and more vicious form of Pharisaism. This point is a pertinent one, especially in our time, but it is not new and it would not be so striking if Camus, in order to make it, did not return to the themes and symbols of his earlier works, in particular those of *L'Etranger*.

In *La Chute* as in *L'Etranger,* there are a court, a trial, the accused, and, of course, the inevitable judges. The only new character is the generous lawyer himself, who defends his "good criminals" just as Camus, the novelist, defended Meursault in *L'Etranger.* The good criminals lose their cases, and so did Meursault, but the loss, in either case, is more than regained in the wider court of public opinion. When we read *L'Etranger,* we feel pity for Meursault and anger with his judges, the very sentiments that the "generous lawyer" is supposed to derive from his practice of the law.

The pre-*Chute* Camus is quite different, of course, from his hero Clamence, but the two have a common trait in their contempt for the "judges." Both of them have built an intellectually complex and socially successful life around this one hallowed principle. The contemporary advocate of literary "revolt" is perpetually challenging social institutions and values, but his challenge, like that of the lawyer, has become a part of the institutions themselves; far from entailing any personal risks, his activities bring fame and comfort in their wake.

If Camus had conceived any doubts as to the validity of his ethical attitude and if he had wanted to express these doubts in another work of fiction, he could not have hit upon a more appropriate theme than that of *La Chute.* All the earlier works of the author are based upon the explicit or implicit tenet that a systematic hostility to all "judges" provides the surest foundation for an "authentic" ethical life. *La Chute* openly derides this tenet. It is natural, therefore, to conclude that the work contains an element of self-criticism. It is no less natural to reject a conclusion that threatens all established ideas concerning Camus, the writer and the man.

We live in an age of middle-class "individualism" in which self-consistency is rated as a major virtue. But a thinker is not bound by the same rules as a statesman or a banker. We do not think less of Goethe because he repudiated *Werther.* We do not blush at the thought of Rimbaud repudiating his whole work or of Kafka refusing to have his manuscripts published at the time of his death. Progress in matters of the spirit is often a form of self-destruction; it may entail a violent reaction against the past. If an artist has to keep admiring his own works at all times in order to remain admirable, Monsieur Joseph Prud'homme, the caricatural French bourgeois, is certainly greater than Pascal, Racine, Chateaubriand, or Claudel.

A writer's creative process has become a major, if not *the* major, literary theme of our time. The lawyer of *La Chute,* like the doctor of *La Peste,* is, at least to a certain extent, an allegory of the creator. Can this assertion be denied on the grounds that it involves a "naive confusion" between the author and his fictional work? Fear of the "biographical fallacy" must not be an excuse to evade the truly significant problems raised by literary creation. This fear is itself naive because it conceives of the rapport between an author and his work as an all-or-nothing proposition. When I say that Clamence *is* Albert Camus, I do not mean that the two are identical in the sense that an original document is identical to its carbon copy or that a traveler is identical to the snapshot that figures on the first page of his passport. When a work is really profound, the existential significance of its characters and situations can never be stated in terms of straight biography, but why should it have to be so stated?

I may admit that Camus's past is present in *La Chute* and still evade the most difficult consequences of this discovery. By placing the emphasis upon the political and social allusions, I may interpret the confession of Clamence as an attack against whatever is implied in the word *engagement*. Camus's quarrel with Sartre as well as his restrained public attitude during the last years of his life could provide some additional evidence for this view. If *La Chute* is a reaction against the recent past only, is it not, as such, a return to the earlier past and a vigorous—if enigmatic—restatement of the positions defended in *Sisyphe* and *L'Etranger?* This minimal interpretation is attractive; unfortunately, it rests not on internal evidence but on the implicit assumption that Camus's entire itinerary can and must be defined in terms of that *engagement/dégagement* polarity that reigned supreme a dozen years ago. The trouble with this polarity is that it excludes the one possibility that is actually realized in *La Chute,* that of a change in vision radical enough to transcend both the *engagement* of *La Peste* and the *dégagement* of *L'Etranger.*

Engagement can rarely be distinguished from the other targets of satire in *La Chute* because, from the standpoint of Clamence, it no longer con-stitutes a truly autonomous attitude. The first Camus, as well as the later advocate of *engagement,* can fit the description of the "generous lawyer." The only difference is that the "clients" are characters of fiction in the first case and real human beings in the second. From the cynical perspective of Clamence, this difference is unimportant. To the generous lawyer, the clients are never quite real since they are not an end in themselves, but they are never quite fictional since they are a means to discredit the judges. *Engagement* represents only a variation on the theme of "bad faith," one of the many forms that a secretly self-seeking dedication to the downtrodden can assume. Behind the clients, therefore, we can see the characters created by the early Camus, such as Caligula, the two women murderers in *Le Malentendu,* and, preeminently, Meursault no less than the real but shadowy people whose cause a writer is supposed to embrace when he becomes *engagé.*

The passage in which Clamence describes his kindness to old ladies in distress and other such people is probably the one direct reference to *engagement* in *La Chute*. And we may note that this boy-scoutish behavior is presented as nothing more than an extension of the lawyer's professional attitude. Clamence has become so engrossed in his legal self that he goes on playing the part of the generous lawyer outside of the court; the comedy gradually takes over even the most ordinary circumstances of daily life. Literature and life have become one, not because literature imitates life but because life imitates literature. Unity of experience is achieved at the level of an all-pervasive imposture.

La Chute must be read in the right perspective, which is one of humor. The author, tired of his popularity with all the *bien-pensants* of the intellectual élite, found a witty way to deride his quasiprophetic role without scandalizing the pure at heart among the faithful. Allowance must be made for overstatement, but the work cannot be discounted as a joke or safely extolled as art for art's sake. The confession of Clamence is Camus's own, in a broad literary and spiritual sense. To prove this point, I shall turn first to *L'Etranger* and uncover a structural flaw that, to my knowledge, has not been previously detected. The significance of that structural flaw will provide the evidence needed to confirm the reading of *La Chute* as self-criticism.

From a purely textual standpoint, Meursault's condemnation is almost unrelated to his crime. Every detail of the trial adds up to the conclusion that the judges resent the murderer not for what he did but for what he is. The critic Albert Maquet expressed this truth quite well when he wrote: "The murder of the Arab is only a pretext; behind the person of the accused, the judges want to destroy the truth he embodies."

Let there be no murder and a good pretext to get rid of Meursault will, indeed, have been lost, but a pretext should be easy to replace, precisely because it does not have to be good. If society is as eager to annihilate Meursault as it is pictured by Maquet, the remarkable existence of this hero should provide more "pretexts" than will ever be needed to send an innocent to his doom.

Is this assumption well founded? We ask this question in all awareness that we are abandoning, for the time being, pure textual analysis for common sense realism. If we feel, when we are reading the novel, that Meursault lives dangerously, this impression evaporates under examination. The man goes to work regularly; he swims on the beaches of the Mediterranean and he has dates with the girls in the office. He likes the movies but he is not interested in politics. Which of these activities will take him to a police station, let alone the guillotine?

Meursault has no responsibilities, no family, no personal problems; he feels no sympathy for unpopular causes. Apparently he drinks nothing but café au lait. He really lives the prudent and peaceful life of a little bureaucrat anywhere and of a French petit bourgeois in the bargain. He carries the foresight of his class so far that he waits the medically recommended number of hours after his noonday meal before he plunges into the Mediterranean. His way of life should constitute a good insurance against nervous breakdowns, mental exhaustion, heart failure, and, a fortiori, the guillotine.

Meursault, it is true, does not cry at his mother's funeral, and this is the one action in his life that is likely to be criticized by his neighbors; from such criticism to the scaffold, however, there is a distance that could never be bridged if Meursault did not commit a murder. Even the most ferocious judge could not touch a single hair on his head, had he not killed one of his fellow men.

The murder may be a pretext, but it is the only one available, and upon this unfortunate event, the whole structure of meaning erected by Camus comes to rest. It is very important, therefore, to understand how the murder comes to pass. How can a man commit a murder and not be responsible for it? The obvious answer is that this murder must be an *accident,* and many critics have taken up that answer. Louis Hudon, for instance, says that Meursault is guilty of involuntary manslaughter at worst. How could Meursault premeditate murder, since he cannot premeditate a successful career in Paris or marriage with his mistress? Involuntary manslaughter, as everyone knows, should not send a man to the guillotine. This interpretation seems to clinch Camus's case against the "judges."

There is a difficulty, however. If Meursault must commit a crime, we agree that he must be an involuntary rather than a voluntary criminal, but why should he commit a crime in the first place? Accidents will happen, no doubt, but no general conclusion can be drawn from them, or they cease, quite obviously, to be *accidents.* If the murder is an accident, so is the sentence that condemns Meursault, and *L'Etranger* does not prove that people who do not cry at their mothers' funerals are likely to be sentenced to death. All the novel proves, then, is that these people will be sentenced to death if they also happen to commit involuntary manslaughter, and this *if,* it will be conceded, is a very big one. The accident theory reduces Meursault's case to the proportions of a pathetic but rather insignificant *fait-divers.*

Let a million devotees of *l'absurde* copy Meursault's way of life down to the last dregs of his café au lait, let them bury their entire families without shedding a single tear, and not one of them will ever die on the guillotine, for the simple reason that their *imitatio absurdi* will not and should not include the accidental murder of the Arab; this unfortunate happening, in all probability, will never be duplicated.

The accident theory weakens, if it does not destroy, the tragic opposition between Meursault and society. That is why it does not really account for the experience of the reader. Textually speaking, the relationship between Meursault and his murder cannot be expressed in terms of motivation, as would be the case with an ordinary criminal, but it is nevertheless felt to be essential, rather than accidental. From the very beginning of the novel we sense that something frightful is going to happen and that Meursault can do nothing to protect himself. The hero is innocent, no doubt, and this very innocence will bring about his downfall.

The critics who, like Carl Viggiani, have best captured the atmosphere of the murder reject all rational interpretations and attribute this event to that same *Fatum* that presides over the destinies of epic and tragic heroes in ancient and primitive literatures. They point out that the various incidents and objects connected with this episode can be interpreted as symbols of an implacable Nemesis.

We still invoke fate today when we do not want to ascribe an event to chance, even though we cannot account for it. This "explanation" is not meant seriously, however, when we are talking about real happenings taking place in the real world. We feel that this world is essentially rational and that it should be interpreted rationally.

An artist is entitled to disregard rational laws in his search for esthetic effects. No one denies this. If he makes use of this privilege, however, the world he creates is not only fictional but fantastic. If Meursault is sentenced to death in such a fantastic world, my indignation against the iniquitous judges must be fantastic too, and I cannot say, as Camus did in his preface to the Brée-Lynes edition of *L'Etranger,* that, *in our society,* people who behave like Meursault are likely to be sentenced to death. The conclusions that I infer from the novel are valid for this novel only and not for the real world, since the laws of verisimilitude have been violated. Meursault's drama does not give me the right to look with contempt upon real judges operating in a real court. Such contempt must be justified by a perfectly rational sequence of causes or motivations leading from the funeral of the mother to the death of the hero. If, at the most crucial point in this sequence, *Fatum* is suddenly brandished, or some other deity as vague as it is dark, we must note this sudden disregard for the rational course of human affairs and take a very close look at the antisocial message of the novel.

If supernatural necessity is present in *L'Etranger,* why should Meursault alone come under its power? Why should the various characters in the same novel be judged by different yardsticks? If the murderer is not held responsible for his actions, why should the judges be held responsible for theirs? It is possible, of course, to read part of *L'Etranger* as fantasy and the rest as realistic fiction, but the novel thus fragmented presents no unified world view; even from a purely esthetic point of view it is open to criticism.

The fate theory looks satisfactory as long as the episode of the murder remains detached from the novel, but it cannot be integrated with this novel. Sympathy for Meursault is inseparable from resentment against the judges. We cannot do away with that resentment without mutilating our global esthetic experience. This resentment is really generated by the text, and we must somehow account for it even if it is not logically justified.

The search for the significance of Meursault's murderous gesture leads nowhere. The death of the Arab can be neither an accident nor an event inspired from "above," and yet it must be one of these two things if it is not voluntary. It is as difficult to ascribe an "ontological status" to the murder as it is easy to ascertain its function in the story. Meursault, as I have said, could never have been tried, convicted, and sentenced if he had not killed the Arab. But Camus thought otherwise, and he said so in the preface to *L'Etranger:* "A man who does not cry at the funeral of his mother is likely to be sentenced to death." Is this an a posteriori judgment deduced from the facts of the story, as everybody has always taken for granted, or is it an a priori principle to which the "facts" must somehow be fitted? Everything becomes intelligible if we choose the second solution. Camus needs his "innocent murder" because his a priori principle is blatantly false. The irritating cult of motherhood and the alleged profundities of *l'absurde* must not obscure the main issue. Let us translate the brilliant paradoxes of the author back into the terms of his story, let us remove the halo of intellectual sophistication that surrounds the novel, and no one will take its message seriously. Do we really believe that the French judicial system is ruthlessly dedicated to the extermination of little bureaucrats addicted to café au lait, Fernandel movies, and casual love affairs with the boss's secretary?

One of the reasons we do not question the tragic ending of *L'Etranger* is the lowly status of its hero. Little clerks are, indeed, potential and actual victims of our modern societies. Like the other members of his class, Meursault is vulnerable to a multitude of social ills ranging from war to racial and economic discrimination. But this fact, on close examination, has no bearing on Camus's tragedy. The work is not one of social but of individual protest, even though the author welcomes the ambiguity, or at least does nothing to dispel it. The main point is that Meursault is the incarnation of unique qualities rather than the member of a group. The judges are supposed to resent what is most Meursault-like in Meursault. Unfortunately, the alleged uniqueness of this hero has no concrete consequences in his behavior. For all practical purposes, Meursault is a little bureaucrat devoid of ambition and, as such, he cannot be singled out for persecution. The only real threats to his welfare are those he shares with every other little bureaucrat, or with the human race as a whole.

The idea of the novel is incredible; that is why a direct demonstration is unthinkable. The writer wanted to arouse an indignation that he himself felt, and he had to take into account the demands of elementary realism. In order to become a martyr, Meursault had to commit some truly reprehensible action, but in order to retain the sympathy of the readers, he had to remain innocent. His crime had to be involuntary, therefore, but not so involuntary that the essential Meursault, the man who does not cry at his mother's funeral, would remain untouched by the sentence. All the events leading to the actual scene of the shooting, including that scene itself, with its first involuntary shot followed by four voluntary ones, are so devised that they appear to fulfill these two incompatible exigencies. Meursault will die an innocent, and yet his death sentence will be more significant than a mere judicial error.

This solution is really no solution at all. It can only hide, it cannot resolve, the contradiction between the first and the second Meursault, between the peaceful solipsist and the martyr of society; it *is* that contradiction in a nutshell, as revealed by the two conflicting words, "innocent" and "murder," whose combination sounds unusual and interesting, somewhat like a surrealistic image, precisely because they cannot form a real concept and be fused together any more than a surrealistic image can evoke a real object.

The skillful narrative technique makes it very difficult to perceive the logical flaw in the structure of the novel. When an existence as uneventful as that of Meursault is described in minute detail, without any humor, an atmosphere of tense expectation is automatically created. As I read the novel, my attention is focused upon details that are insignificant in themselves but that come to be regarded as portents of doom just because the writer has seen fit to record them. I sense that Meursault is moving toward a tragedy, and this impression, which has nothing to do with the hero's actions, seems to arise from them. Who can see a woman knitting alone in a dark house at the beginning of a mystery story without being led to believe that knitting is a most dangerous occupation?

In the second half of *L'Etranger*, all the incidents recorded in the first half are recalled and used as evidence against Meursault. The aura of fear that surrounds these incidents appears fully justified. We are aware of these trifles as trifles but we have been conditioned to regard them as potentially dangerous to the hero. It is natural, therefore, to consider the attitude of the judges both unfair and inevitable. In a mystery story, the clues ultimately lead to the murderer; in *L'Etranger,* they all lead to the judges. The murder itself is handled in the same casual and fateful manner as the other actions of Meursault. Thus, the gap between this portentous action and an afternoon swim in the Mediterranean or the absorption of a cup of café au lait is gradually narrowed, and we are gently led to the incredible conclusion that the hero is sentenced to death not for the crime of which he is accused and that he has really committed, but for his innocence, which this crime has not tarnished and which should remain obvious to all people at all times, as if it were the attribute of a divinity.

   L'Etranger was not written for pure art's sake, nor was it written to vindicate the victims of persecution everywhere. Camus set out to prove that the hero according to his heart will necessarily be persecuted by society. He set out to prove, in other words, that "the judges are always in the wrong." The truth deeply buried in *L'Etranger* would have been discovered long before it became explicit in *La Chute* if we had read the tragedy of Meursault with truly critical eyes. A really close reading leads, indeed, to questioning the structure and, beyond it, the "authenticity" of *L'Etranger* in terms identical with those of Clamence's confession. The allegory of the generous lawyer stems from the structural flaw of *L'Etranger,* fully apprehended for the first time and interpreted as the "objective correlative" of the author's "bad faith." Further evidence can be provided by the explication of some obscure passages and apparent contradictions in the text of *La Chute.*

   Here is a first example. At one point in the description of his past professional life Clamence remarks: "Je ne me trouvais pas sur la scène du tribunal mais quelque part, dans les cintres, comme ces dieux que, de temps en temps, on descend, au moyen d'une machine, pour transfigurer l'action et lui donner un sens." Readers acquainted with the terminology of postwar French criticism will remember that Sartre and his school accuse novelists of mistaking themselves for "gods" when they warp the destiny of a character and when, consciously or not, they lead him to some preordained conclusion. If we recognize the figure of the writer behind the mask of the lawyer we shall immediately perceive, in this bizarre statement, an allusion, and a very pertinent one, to the wrong kind of novelist. Can this same statement be made meaningful if *La Chute* is not understood as an allegory of the writer's own literary past?

   The image of the god is originally Sartrian, but the Greek element brings us back to those critics who have rejected all rational interpretation of the murder. They themselves are solely concerned with problems of esthetic symbolism, but their writings may well have helped Camus realize what he now implicitly denounces as the "bad faith" of his own creation. The murder of the Arab, in a novel otherwise rational and realistic, is a *deus ex machina,* or rather a *crimen ex machina* that provides the author not with a happy ending but with a tragic one that is really precluded by the character he himself has given to his hero.

Here is a second example. Clamence tells us that he chose his clients "à la seule condition qu'ils fussent de bons meurtriers comme d'autres de bons sauvages." This sentence is absolutely unintelligible in a nonliterary context. It is a thinly disguised reference to Meursault, who plays, in his fictional world, a role similar to that of the good savage, a well-known pre-Romantic stranger, in the world of eighteenth-century literature. Here again, the image may have been suggested by Sartre, who, in his *Situations* article, defined *L'Etranger* as a twentieth-century *conte philosophique.*

Like the "bon sauvage," Meursault is supposed to act as a catalyst; his sole presence reveals the arbitrariness of the values that bind the "insiders" together. The *bonté* of this abstract figure is an absolute that no amount of *sauvagerie* can diminish. Meursault's excellence has the same quality. He is no less innocent and the judges no less guilty for punishing him, a confessed criminal, than if no crime had been committed. Innocence and guilt are fixed essences; they cannot be affected by the vicissitudes of existence any more than Ormazd and Ahriman can exchange their roles as the principle of good and the principle of evil.

In *La Chute,* the author questions his own motives for writing fiction within the framework of this fiction itself. Meursault, as a "client" of Clamence, has retreated in the background and become anonymous, but he is still a dramatis persona, and the structural incoherence of *L'Etranger* must be expressed primarily in terms of *his* personal motivations. In order to denounce what he now regards as his own moral illusions and creative weakness, Clamence must say, as he does, that *his clients were not so innocent after all.* Their allegedly spontaneous and unmotivated misdeeds were, in fact, premeditated. If Camus is to abide by the rules of the fictional game initiated in the first novel, he must attribute to the hero the "bad faith" that really belongs to his creator, and this is precisely what he does. The "good criminals" killed, not for any of the ordinary reasons, as we are well aware, but because they *wanted* to be tried and sentenced. Clamence tells us that their motives were really the same as his: like so many of our contemporaries, in this anonymous world, they wanted a little publicity.

Meursault, however, is a character of fiction; responsibility for his crime lies, in the last resort, with the creator himself. The present reading would be more convincing if Clamence, instead of placing the blame upon his "clients," had placed it squarely upon himself. But Clamence is already the lawyer; how could he be the instigator of the crime without absurdity? Such transparent allegory would deal the last blow to *La Chute* as art for art's sake and the present exegesis would be pointless. Let me apologize, therefore, for belaboring the obvious since Clamence does, indeed, present himself both as the passionate defender and as the accomplice of his good criminals. He does not hesitate to assume these two incompatible roles. If we reject the obvious implications of this inconsistency, we must dare condemn *La Chute* as an incoherent piece of fiction.

This is a curious lawyer, indeed, who manipulates the court from high above, as he would a puppet show, and who discovers the guilt of his clients *after* they are sentenced, even though he himself had a hand in their crimes. We must observe, on the other hand, that this collusion with the criminals should destroy the image of the generous lawyer as a stuffy, self-righteous, upper-middle-class man if the reader did not realize, subconsciously at least, that these criminals are only paper ones. The account of Clamence's law career is really a collection of metaphors, all pointing to "unauthentic creation," and Camus uses them as he sees fit, tearing as he goes the thin veil of his fiction. Clamence really suggests that the author of *L'Etranger* was not really conscious of his own motivation until he experienced his own *chute*. His purpose, which disguised itself as "generosity," was really identical with egotistical passion. *L'Etranger* must not be read as a *roman à thèse*. The author did not consciously try to deceive his audience, but he succeeded all the better because he managed to deceive himself in the first place. The dichotomy between Meursault and his judges represents the dichotomy between the Self and the Others in a world of intersubjective warfare.

L'Etranger, as the expression of egotistical values and meanings, forms a structure, a relatively stable "world view." Camus "sincerely" believed in his and, consequently, in Meursault's innocence, because he passionately believed in the guilt of the "judges." The incoherence of the plot does not stem from an awkward effort to prove something that was only half believed or not believed at all. On the contrary, the author's conviction that the iniquity of the judges can always be proved was so strong that nothing could shake it. The innocent will inevitably be treated as a criminal. In the process of proving this point, Camus had to turn his innocent into a real criminal, but his faith was such that he did not perceive the tautology. We can understand, now, why the "generous lawyer" is presented to us both as the sincere defender of his clients and as the accomplice of their crimes.

As long as the egotistical Manicheism that produced *L'Etranger* held its sway over him, the author could not perceive the structural flaw of his novel. All illusions are one. They stand together and they fall together as soon as their cause, egotistical passion, is perceived. The confession of Clamence does not lead to a new "interpretation" of *L'Etranger* but to an act of transcendence; the perspective of this first novel is rejected.

The rejection of the world view expressed in *L'Etranger* is not the fruit of an empirical discovery but of an existential conversion, and it is, indeed, such a conversion that is described ironically but unmistakably throughout the novel, in terms of an ego-shattering *chute*. This spiritual metamorphosis is triggered, so to speak, by the incident of the drowning woman but, basically, it has nothing to do with exterior circumstances. Neither can our own reevaluation of *L'Etranger* in the light of *La Chute* rest on external evidence such as scholarly arguments and "explications de textes," however massive the material proof available through these channels. The evidence will not be judged convincing until there is a willingness to go along with the self-critical mood of the creator. I, the reader, must undergo an experience, less profound to be sure, but somewhat analogous to that of this creator. The true critic must not remain superbly and coldly objective; he is the one most profoundly affected and transformed by the work of art; he truly *sympathizes*, suffers with the author. I, too, must fall from my pedestal; as an admirer of *L'Etranger*, I must accept the risk of an exegetical *chute*.

A refusal to probe the confession of Clamence must not be rationalized on the grounds that it makes the literary reputation of Camus more secure. It is the reverse that is true. The fact that *La Chute* transcends the perspective of *L'Etranger* does not mean that, in a comparison with other works of recent fiction, the earlier work ranks lower than had been previously thought; it certainly means, however, that *La Chute* ranks higher.

A gingerly approach to *La Chute* obscures the true greatness of Camus. This work can already be defined as a forgotten masterpiece. Camus is praised to the high heavens by some, while others deride his role as "directeur de conscience" of the middle class, but all this is done with only passing reference, or no reference at all, to *La Chute*. Most people ignore the fact that Albert Camus was the first one to react against his own cult. Here and there, some voices are raised in defense of a truth that no one, it seems, is really eager to hear. Philippe Sénart, for instance, maintained that Camus refused to be the infallible pope of his own new neohumanism:

Il ne voulait être que le *pape des fous* et il écrivait *La Chute* pour se tourner en dérision et il s'accusait en se moquant. Clamence, avocat déchu, qui avait "bien vécu de sa vertu," qui se trouvait, avec coquetterie, "un peu surhomme," était, dans le bouge où il se déguisait en juge pour mieux rire de lui, le Bouffon de l'humanité, d'aucuns disaient le Singe de Dieu, comme Satan. Clamence, l'Homme-qui-rit, c'était l'Anti-Camus.

In one of the speeches pronounced when he received his Nobel Prize, Camus opened still a new line of investigation to the critics of his work:

> Le thème du poète maudit né dans une société marchande (Chatterton en est la plus belle illustration), s'est durci dans un préjugé qui finit par vouloir qu'on ne puisse être un grand artiste que contre la société de son temps, quelle qu'elle soit. Légitime à son origine quand il affirmait qu'un artiste véritable ne pouvait composer avec le monde de l'argent, le principe est devenu faux lorsqu'on en a tiré qu'un artiste ne pouvait s'affirmer qu'en étant contre toute chose en général.

Throughout the *Discours de Suède,* Camus dissociated himself from his own past as much as the occasion permitted. Here, he relates the type of literature he himself had practiced for so long not to an awe-inspiring philosophical tradition, as in *L'Homme révolté,* but to French Romanticism. He chooses as the archetype of *révolte, Chatterton,* the one work of Alfred de Vigny with which contemporary readers are likely to find most fault. He suggests that the tragic conflicts set forth in his own early works are really a *degraded* form of Vigny's Romantic drama.

An earlier Camus would certainly have rejected this rapprochement out of hand in spite or rather because of its extreme relevance. *L'Etranger* is really much closer to *Chatterton* than to the *conte philosophique* because the *conte* has a concrete content and it fights for definite objectives, whereas *Chatterton,* like *L'Etranger,* is primarily an abstract protest of the discontented ego. A work that is against everything in general is really against nothing in particular and no one actually feels disturbed by it. Like Dostoevsky's underground man, Meursault says: "I am alone and *they* are together." The work spells the final democratization of the Romantic myth, the universal symbol of the separated ego in a world where almost everyone feels like an "outsider."

Chatterton, like Meursault, was conceived as a lonely figure, as a man who refuses "to play the game." Both men live in a world of their own that contrasts with the unauthentic world of other men. Both of them suffer and die because society makes it impossible for them to live according to their own lonely, infinitely superior ways.

There is a difference, however. When Chatterton is offered the same type of third-rate job Meursault holds, he refuses haughtily. In his eyes, this menial way of life is incompatible with his mission. We find it rather easy to interpret Chatterton's destiny in terms of Romantic pride. Camus's hero appears very humble by contrast; he does not view himself as a man with a mission; he has no visible pretensions and he is ready to do whatever is necessary to sustain his mediocre existence.

This modest appearance really hides a more extreme form of Romantic pride. Between Chatterton and other men there is still a measure of reciprocity, whereas none is left in the case of Meursault. Chatterton gives his "genius" and the community must give him food and shelter in return. If society does not fulfill its share of the contract, the poet cannot fulfill his role as a great poet; the crowd grows spiritually hungry and the poet grows physically hungry. This general starvation is less tragic, no doubt, than Greek or classical tragedy and it is so because Chatterton is less deeply involved with his fellowmen than earlier tragic heroes. Real tragedy demands genuine involvement. It is somewhat ironic, let us note in passing, that a doctrine with such ethereal pretensions as 1830 Romanticism could produce only alimentary tragedies of the Chatterton type. But this last meager resource is still truly present, whereas it is gone in the case of Camus. The poetic life cherished by Chatterton has become a part of the shameful game that the real individual must refuse to play in order to remain "authentic." L'Etranger should not end in a Chatterton-like tragedy; it should revolve around the closed circle of a perfectly self-sufficient personality. An endless succession of cafés au lait, Fernandel movies, and amorous interludes should provide a scale model of the Nietzschean eternal return.

Romantic pride separates Chatterton from his fellowmen; greater pride cuts Meursault off so completely that no tragic possibilities remain. In order to grasp this point, we may compare Meursault with another Romantic in disguise, Monsieur Teste, the solipsistic hero of Valéry's youth. Monsieur Teste is infinitely brilliant and original but he alone is aware of his own worth. He is satisfied, like Meursault, with a third-rate job; he does not mind looking *quelconque* and remaining unknown. He will never be a *grand homme* because he refuses to sacrifice anything to the spirit of the crowd. Meursault is really a Teste without a Ph.D., a Teste who prefers café au lait to higher mathematics, a super-Teste, in other words, who does not even bother to be intelligent.

The idea of turning Teste into a martyr of society would have sounded ludicrous to Valéry. The only thing a solipsist is entitled to ask of society is indifference, and indifference he will get if he behaves like a Teste or a Meursault. Valéry was perfectly aware that, as individualism becomes more extreme, the possibilities offered to a writer shrink; and he rejected as "impure" all types of dramatic literature.

L'Etranger begins like *Monsieur Teste* and it ends like *Chatterton*. Unlike Valéry, Camus does not perceive or he refuses to assume the consequences of his literary solipsism. He resorts to the device of the "innocent murder" in order to retrieve the structure of the *poète maudit* or, more generally, of the "exceptional man persecuted by society." The *crimen ex machina* saves the author from the limitations of his own attitude.

Contemporary readers sense that there is something contrived in *Chatterton*, and yet Vigny did not have to turn his exceptional man into a murderer in order to present him as a martyr of society. *L'Etranger* should appear even more contrived, but we do not understand the disturbing role that violence plays in it, probably because the novel is the latest successful formulation of the myth of the Romantic self.

Chatterton already prefers to be persecuted rather than ignored, but we cannot prove the point because it is plausible that society will prevent a poet from fulfilling his destiny as a poet. In the case of Meursault, this same preference for egotistical martyrdom can be proven, because it is not plausible that society will prevent a little bureaucrat from fulfilling his destiny as a little bureaucrat. Camus takes his hero out of society with one hand only to put him back with the other. He wants Meursault to be a solipsist, then turns him into the hero of a trial, that quintessence of diseased human relations in our modern society.

Why does Camus crave solitude and society at the same time; why is he both repelled and fascinated by *les autres*? The contradiction is really inherent in the Romantic personality. The Romantic does not want to be alone, but *to be seen alone*. In *Crime and Punishment*, Dostoevsky shows that solitary dreams and the "trial" are the two inseparable facets, the dialectically related "moments" of the Romantic consciousness. But this proud consciousness refuses to acknowledge openly the fascination it feels for the others. In the days of Vigny a discreet return to society was still possible because a few bridges were left between the individualist and his fellowmen. The "mission of the poet" was one, romantic love another. Camus has destroyed these last bridges because the urge to be alone is stronger in him than ever before. But the unacknowledged urge to return to other men is also stronger than ever.

And this second urge can no longer be satisfied within the context created by the first.

The murder is really a secret effort to reestablish contact with humanity. It reveals an ambivalence that is present in all art with solipsistic tendencies but that has probably never been so visibly written into the structure of a work. This contradiction is also present in *Monsieur Teste* because it can never be eliminated completely. Monsieur Teste lives and dies alone, but not so much alone that we, the readers, are left in the dark about his superhuman and invisible qualities. The egotistical *Deus* is never so *absconditus* that it does not have its priests and mediators. The ambiguous narrator plays the part of the "innocent murder" in *L'Etranger*. He is an artificial bridge between the solipsist and ordinary mortals. He is close enough to Teste to understand him and close enough to us to write for us. Such a man, by definition, should not exist and the work should never have been written. Valéry was so aware of it that he remained silent for twenty years after writing *Monsieur Teste*.

Camus, too, should be silent and he is at least partly aware of it since, in *Sisyphe,* he discusses literature and concludes that it is a fitting pastime for the knight-errant of *l'absurde*—provided, of course, it is not oriented to *les autres*. This a posteriori justification must be read primarily as evidence that the problem was a significant and important one for Camus at the time. The pure doctrine of solipsism is not in *Sisyphe* but in *L'Etranger*. Meursault does not read or write; we cannot imagine him submitting a manuscript to a publisher or correcting galley proofs. All such activities have no place in an "authentic" existence.

Both the young Valéry and the young Camus cherished literature; both knew that it offered an avenue of escape from their equally mediocre stations in life. And yet both of them held views that made the practice of their art almost impossible. Romantic individualism becomes so exacerbated with these writers that it verges on a certain type of neurotic behavior.

We all know, outside of literature, that certain people are too proud to acknowledge a situation as painful. These people may even do their utmost to perpetuate or even aggravate this situation in order to prove to them-selves that it is *freely chosen*. The creation of Meursault certainly reflects an attitude of this type. The life of this hero is objectively sad and sordid. The man is, indeed, a derelict; he has no intellectual life, no love, no friend-ship, no interest in anyone or faith in anything. His life is limited to physical sensations and to cheap pleasures of modern mass culture. The uninformed readers—American undergraduates, for instance—often perceive this essential wretchedness; they grasp the *objective* significance of the novel because the *subjective* intention of the creator escapes them. The "informed" reader, on the other hand, rejects the objective significance as naive because he readily perceives the subjective intention, and he feels very sophisticated—until he reads and understands *La Chute*. Clamence alone is aware that there are two layers of significance, subjective and objective, and he picks the latter as the essential one when he states that his "good criminals" were wretched people *at bottom*. The most lucid view justifies the most naive; the truth belongs to the reader who takes *nothing* or *everything* into account, and to no one in between.

The undergraduates quickly learn, of course, that it is not smart to pity Meursault, but they vaguely wonder, for a while, why his living hell should be interpreted as paradise. This hell is the one to which, rightly or wrongly, Camus felt condemned in the years of *L'Etranger*. There are psychological, social, and even metaphysical reasons, as well as literary ones, for *L'Etranger*'s mood of repressed despair. These were troubled times; opportunity was scarce; the health of the young Camus was not good; he was not yet a famous writer and he had no assurance that he would ever become one. He *willed*, therefore, as many did who came before and after him, the solitude and mediocrity from which he did not see any escape. His was an act of intellectual pride and desperation reminiscent of Nietzschean *amor fati*. Valéry's *Monsieur Teste* stems from a comparable experience in a world somewhat less harsh. A young man who feels doomed to anonymity and mediocrity is compelled to repay with indifference the indifference of society. If he is very gifted, he may devise a new and radical variety of Romantic solipsism; he may create a Teste or a Meursault.

Even more relevant here than a purely psychiatric interpretation are the passages of *The Sickness unto Death* dedicated to what Kierkegaard calls "defiance," or "the despair of willing despairingly to be oneself."

> This too is a form of despair: not to be willing to hope that an earthly distress, a temporal cross, might be removed. This is what the despair which wills desperately to be itself is not willing to hope. It has convinced itself that this thorn in the flesh gnaws so profoundly that he cannot abstract it—no matter whether this is actually so or his passion makes it true for him—and so he is willing to accept it as it were eternally. So he is offended by it, or rather from it he takes occasion to be offended at the whole of existence. . . . To hope in the possibility of help, not to speak of help by virtue of the absurd, that for God all things are possible—

no, that he will not do. And as for seeking help from any other—
no, that he will not do for all the world; rather than seek help he
would prefer to be himself—with all the torture of hell, if so must
be. . . . Now it is too late, he once would have given everything to
be rid of this torment but was made to wait, now that's all past,
now he would rather rage against everything, he, the one man in
the whole of existence who is the most unjustly treated, to whom
it is especially important to have his torment at hand, important
that no one should take it from him—for thus he can convince
himself that he is in the right.

The absurd of which Kierkegaard is speaking, needless to say, is not
Camus's *absurde*. It is rather the opposite of it, since it is the final rejection
of nihilism, rejected by Camus himself and dismissed as facile optimism in
Sisyphe. The young Camus thought he could dispose of Kierkegaard in a few
sentences but Kierkegaard on Camus goes much deeper, paradoxically, than
Camus on Kierkegaard: "such self-control, such firmness, such ataraxia, etc.,
border almost on the fabulous. . . . The self wants . . . to have the honor of
this poetical, this masterly plan according to which it has understood itself.
And yet, . . . just at the instant when it seems to be nearest to having the
fabric finished it can arbitrarily resolve the whole thing into nothing."

This highest form of despair, Kierkegaard informs us, is encountered
solely in the works of a few great poets, and we perceive the bond between
the Vigny of *Chatterton*, the Valéry of *Teste*, and the Camus of *L'Etranger*
when the philosopher adds: "one might call it Stoicism—yet without thinking only of this philosophic sect." The genius of Kierkegaard cuts through
the maze of minor differences that help a writer assert his own individual-
ity, thus obscuring the fundamental significance of his literary posture. The
whole spiritual structure is grasped through a single act of intuition. The
essential features are revealed, common, as a rule, to two or more writers.
The following passage enables us, for instance, to account for the similarities
between Teste and Meursault:

One might represent the lower forms of despair by describing or
by saying something about the outward traits of the despairer.
But the more despair becomes spiritual, and the more is the self
alert with demoniac shrewdness to keep despair shut up in close
reserve, and all the more intent therefore to set the outward appearance at the level of indifference, to make it as unrevealing and
indifferent as possible. . . . This hiddenness is precisely something

spiritual and is one of the safety devices for assuring oneself of
having as it were behind reality an enclosure, a world for itself
locking all else out, a world where the despairing self is employed
as tirelessly as Tantalus in willing to be itself.

This last reference might as well be to Sisyphus rather than to Tantalus.
Camus's *Sisyphe,* like *Teste,* is a "rationalization" of Kierkegaardian despair,
whereas *L'Etranger* is the esthetic, or naive and, as such, most revealing
expression of that same despair.

Here again, we must not let the hollow specter of the "biographical
fallacy" interfere with our comprehension of an author's fundamental problems. We do not confuse the creator with his creation. The relationship is
not a simple one. Meursault is the portrait, or even the caricature, of a man
Camus never was but swore to be, at the end of his adolescence, because he
feared he could never be anyone else. The scene with the employer is revela-
tory. Meursault, as we all know, is offered a trip to Paris and the possibility
of a permanent job there. He is not interested. The incident has only one
purpose, which is to demonstrate Meursault's total lack of ambition. And
it does what it is supposed to do; it does it, in a sense, too well; it is just
a little too pointed. Why should *any* little clerk with a penchant for sun
bathing want to move to Paris, with its dreary winter climate? At the lower
echelon, which is Meursault's, sunny Algeria offers the same possibilities
for advancement as the French capital. As Meursault refuses, with studied
indifference, to live in Saint-Germain-des-Prés, we can hear Camus himself
protesting that he has no literary ambitions.

Camus left Algeria for Paris; he wrote and published quite a few books;
he submitted, at least for a few years, to the various indignities that the fab-
rication of a *grand homme* demands. The conclusion is inescapable: Camus,
unlike his hero, was not devoid of ambition, especially literary ambition.
This truth is as obvious as it is innocuous, but it sounds almost blasphemous;
we are still living in the atmosphere of puritanical egotism that fosters such
works as *L'Etranger* and that prevents us from reading them critically.

The urge to escape solitude was stronger than the self-destructive dy-
namism of repressed pride. But this urge had to prevail in an underhanded
fashion. Camus could not contradict himself too openly. The style of the
novel reveals how he managed to deceive himself. Rhetorical ornaments are
systematically avoided; the author uses none of the gestures that serve to
emphasize a good point. We feel that he is not looking at us and that he
hardly unclenches his teeth. He rejects even the affectation of vulgarity and

profanity that the preceding generation had adopted in an earlier attempt to destroy rhetoric—with the sole result, of course, of creating a new one. The famous rejection of the preterite—or of the present—the two tenses of formal narration, for the *passé composé* that is a conversational tense, amounts to an abandonment of all approved techniques of story telling. The author refuses to be a *raconteur* who performs for an audience. His *écriture blanche* gives an effect of greyish monotony that is the next best thing to silence, and silence is the only conduct truly befitting a solipsist, the only one, however, that he cannot bring himself to adopt.

This style bears a striking resemblance to the style of Meursault's actions prior to the murder. We feel that someone, on some fine day, handed Camus a pen and a piece of paper and Camus did the natural and mechanical thing to do, in such circumstances, which is to start writing, just as Meursault did the natural and mechanical thing to do, when you receive a gun, which is to start shooting. The book, like the murder, appears to be the result of fortuitous circumstances. The overall impression is that *L'Etranger* was written in the same bored, absentminded, and apathetic fashion as the Arab was murdered. We have a crime and we have no criminal; we have a book and we have no writer.

Camus and his hero have sworn to forsake all but the most superficial contacts with their fellow men. Overtly, at least, they both kept their oaths. Meursault refused to go to Paris; Camus criticized writers and thinkers naive enough to believe in communication. But the oath was not kept so firmly that Meursault refrained from killing the Arab or Camus from writing *L'Etranger*. A murder and a book are not superficial contacts but, in the case of the murder, the destructive nature of the contact as well as the casual way in which it was obtained make it possible to deny that there is any contact at all. Similarly, the antisocial nature of the book, as well as the furtive nature of its creation, make it possible to deny that the solipsist is really appealing to other men.

Camus betrays solipsism when he writes *L'Etranger* just as Meursault betrays it when he murders the Arab. The close analogy between the murder of the Arab and the style of the novel is not difficult to explain; every aspect of the work bears the imprint of a single creative act that stands in the same relation to its own consequence, the book, as Meursault's behavior to his murder. The "innocent murder" is really the image and the crux of the whole creative process. Clamence is aware of that fact when he insists that he, as a lawyer, had the same hidden motives as his clients. He, too, craved publicity but he did not have to pay as dearly as the actual criminals for the satisfaction of that impure desire. He should have shared in the punishment as he had shared in the crime, but he was acclaimed, instead, as a great moral leader:

> Le crime tient sans trêve le devant de la scène, mais le criminel n'y figure que fugitivement pour être aussitôt remplacé. Ces brefs triomphes enfin se paient trop cher. Défendre nos malheureux aspirants à la réputation revenait, au contraire, à être vraiment reconnu, dans le même temps et aux mêmes places, mais par des moyens plus économiques. Cela m'encourageait aussi à déployer de méritoires efforts pour qu'ils payassent le moins possible; ce qu'ils payaient, ils le payaient un peu à ma place.

Camus does not want us to believe that his motives, as a writer, were those of a literary opportunist writing cheap best sellers. From the higher standpoint of *La Chute,* he realizes that his own involvement in the tragic conflicts represented in his work was rooted in his own ambitions and in that stubborn need for self-justification to which we all succumb. *L'Etranger* is a real work of art since it can be apprehended as a single structure; its stylistic features are reflected in its plot and vice versa. We must not speak of the novel's *unity,* however, but of its consistent duality and of its radical ambiguity. How could the novel be one when its creative process is truly "divided against itself"? Every page of the work reflects the contradiction and the division inherent in the murder; every denial of communication is really an effort to communicate; every gesture of indifference or hostility is an appeal in disguise. The critical perspective suggested by *La Chute* illuminates even those structural elements that the esthetic approach makes its essential concern but that it ultimately leaves out of account because it isolates them from the content of the work and its many-sided significance.

Can we really understand the murder of the Arab, the structure of the novel, its style, and the "inspiration" of the novelist as a single process? We can if we compare this process to certain types of immature behavior. Let us imagine a child who, having been denied something he wanted very much, turns away from his parents; no blandishments will make him come out of his retreat. Like Meursault, like the first Camus, this child manages to convince himself that his sole desire is to be left alone.

If the child is left alone, his solitude quickly becomes unbearable but pride prevents him from returning meekly to the family circle. What can he do, then, to reestablish contact with the outside world? He must commit an action that will force the attention of the adults but that will not be interpreted as abject surrender, a *punishable* action, of course. But an overt challenge would still be too transparent; the punishable action must be committed covertly and deviously. The child must affect toward the instruments of his future misdeed the same casual attitude as Meursault toward his crime or as Camus toward literature.

Look at Meursault: he starts mingling with underworld characters inadvertently and casually, just as he would associate with anyone else; the matter is of no real consequence since other people do not really exist for him. Meursault, gradually, becomes involved in the shady dealings of his associates but he is hardly aware of this involvement. Why should he care, since one action is as good as another? The child's behavior is exactly the same; he picks up, for instance, a box of matches; he plays with it for a while, absent-mindedly; he does not mean any harm, of course, but all of a sudden, a match is aflame, and the curtains too if they happen to be nearby. Is it an *accident* or is it *fate?* It is "bad faith" and the child feels, like Meursault, that he is not responsible. Objects, to him, are mere fragments of substance lost in a chaotic universe. The *absurde*, in the sense popularized by *Sisyphe*, has become incarnate in this child.

L'Etranger was written and is usually read from the warped perspective that has just been defined. The secretly provocative nature of the murder is never acknowledged and the reprisals of society are presented as unprovoked aggression. The relationship between the individual and society is thereby turned upside down; a lonely individual, Meursault, is presented as completely indifferent to the collectivity, whereas the collectivity is supposed to be intensely concerned with his daily routine. This picture is false, and we all know it. Indifference really belongs to the collectivity; intense concern should be the lot of the lonely and miserable hero. The real picture is found in the few truly great works of fiction of Cervantes, Balzac, Dickens, Dostoevsky, and, we might add, the Camus of *La Chute*.

The truth denied in *L'Etranger* is really so overwhelming that it comes out almost openly at the end of the novel, in Meursault's passionate outburst of resentment. Many readers have rightly felt that this conclusion rings more true than the rest of the novel. The resentment was there all along but pride silenced it, at least until the death sentence, which gave Meursault a pretext to express his despair without losing face in his own estimation. The child, too, wants to be punished, in order to express his grief without confessing its real cause, even to himself. In the last sentence, Meursault practically acknowledges that the sole and only guillotine threatening him is the indifference of *les autres*. "Pour que tout soit consommé, pour que je me sente moins seul, il me restait à souhaiter qu'il y ait beaucoup de spectateurs le jour de mon exécution et qu'ils m'accueillent avec des cris de haine."

The structural flaw in *L'Etranger* becomes intelligible when the novel is assimilated to a type of behavior that has become very common, even among adults, in our contemporary world. Meursault's empty life, his sullen mood, his upside-down world, no less than his half-hearted and secretly provocative crime, are typical of what we call "juvenile delinquency." This social aspect can easily be reconciled with the ultra-Romantic conception of the self that underlies the novel. Observers have pointed out the element of latter-day Romanticism in juvenile delinquency. In recent years, some novels and films dealing openly with this social phenomenon have borrowed features from *L'Etranger,* a work that, outwardly at least, has nothing to do with it. The hero of the film *A bout de souffle,* for instance, half voluntarily kills a policeman, thus becoming a "good criminal" after Meursault's fashion. The *theme* of juvenile delinquency is absent from *L'Etranger* because the novel is the literary equivalent of the action, its perfect *analogon.*

L'Etranger is certainly no accurate portrayal of the society in which it was created. Should we say, therefore, as the formalists do, that it is a "world of its own," that it is wholly independent from this society? The novel *reverses* the laws of our society but this reversal is not an absence of relationship. It is a more complex relationship that involves negative as well as positive factors and that cannot be expressed in the mechanical terms of the old realism or positivism. It is an indirect relationship that must be apprehended if we want to apprehend the esthetic structure itself. We have just seen that the only way to illuminate the esthetic structure of *L'Etranger* as an integrated structure is to resort to the social phenomenon called "juvenile delinquency." *L'Etranger* is not independent from the social reality it overturns, since this overturning is a social attitude among others and a very typical one. The autonomy of the structure may appear absolute to the writer at the time of his writing, and to the uncritical reader, but it is only relative. *L'Etranger* reflects the world view of the juvenile delinquent with unmatched perfection precisely because it is not aware of reflecting anything, except, of course, the innocence of its hero and the injustice of his judges.

Camus wrote *L'Etranger* against the "judges" or, in other words, against the middle class who are his sole potential readers. Instead of rejecting the book as the author had half hoped, half feared, these bourgeois readers showered it with praise. The "judges," obviously, did not recognize their portrait when they saw it. They, too, cursed the iniquitous judges and howled for clemency. They, too, identified with the innocent victim and they acclaimed Meursault as a Galahad of sunworshiping "authenticity." The public turned out, in short, to be made not of judges, as the author had mistakenly believed, but of generous lawyers like the author himself.

Since all the admirers of the early Camus share, to some extent, in the guilt of the "generous lawyer," they too should be present in *La Chute*. And they are, in the person of Clamence's silent listener. The man has nothing to say because Clamence answers *his* questions and objections almost before they are formulated in *our* minds. At the end of the book, this man confesses his identity; he, too, is a generous lawyer.

Thus, Clamence is addressing each one of us personally, leaning toward *me* across a narrow café table and looking straight in *my* eyes. His monologue is dotted with exclamations, interjections, and apostrophes; every three lines we have an "allons," "tiens," "quoi!," "eh bien!," "ne trouvez-vous pas," "mon cher compatriote," etc. The style of *La Chute* is the exact antithesis of the impersonal and antirhetorical *écriture blanche*. Gone is the false detachment of Meursault. We have shifted from the "restrained indignation" of the generous lawyer, as Clamence aptly defines it, to the open theatricality of a self-confessed and yet insurmountable bad faith. The studiously cheap and cacophonic symbolism of *La Chute* is a parody of the serious symbolic works of the past.

As he questions the authenticity of *L'Etranger* and similar works, Camus questions the question itself. *La Chute,* no less than *L'Etranger,* is directed against all potential readers because it is directed against the lawyers in a world where only lawyers are left. The technique of spiritual aggression has become more subtle but its aim has not changed.

Why does Clamence point out to us that his new posture is still one of bad faith? He undermines his own position in order to prevent others from undermining it. After deriding the generous lawyer, he mockingly describes himself as a penitent-judge. Slyly anticipating his readers, whom he knows to be adept at gleaning moral comfort from the most sinister parables, he gives a new twist to the now familiar serpent, hoping to keep one step ahead of everybody else in a game of self-justification that has turned into a game of self-accusation.

Let the judge repudiate judgment and he becomes a judge in disguise, a lawyer; let the lawyer repudiate the disguise and he becomes a penitent-judge; let the penitent-judge. . . . We are spiraling down the circles of a particularly nasty hell, but this more and more precipitous *chute* is perhaps not so fatal as it seems. The penitent-judge does not believe in his role half as much as the generous lawyer did. The conclusion of *La Chute* is a final pirouette as well, perhaps, as the image of what may happen to a world entirely given over to the lawyers and the penitent-judges.

The universal need for self-justification haunts all modern trial literature. But there are different levels of awareness. The so-called "myth" of the trial can be approached from several mutually exclusive perspectives. In *L'Etranger,* the real question is that of the innocence and guilt of the pro-tagonists. The criminal is innocent and the judges are guilty. In the more conventional ego-nourishing fiction, the criminal is usually guilty and the judges innocent. But this difference is really secondary. In both cases, "good" and "bad" are rigid concepts; the verdict of the judges is challenged but not their vision.

La Chute goes higher and deeper. Clamence is still busy proving that he is "good" and that other people are "bad," but his systems of classification keep breaking down. The real question is no longer "who is innocent, who is guilty?," but "why do we, all of us, have to keep judging and being judged?" It is a more interesting question, the very question of Dostoevsky. In *La Chute,* Camus lifts trial literature back to the level of this great predecessor.

The first Camus did not realize how far-reaching, how pervasive the evil of judgment is. He felt that he was outside judgment because he con-demned those who condemn. Using Gabriel Marcel's terminology, we may say that Meursault viewed evil as something outside himself, a *problem* that concerned the judges alone, whereas Clamence knows that he himself is involved. Evil is the *mystery* of a pride that, as it condemns others, un-wittingly condemns itself. It is the pride of Oedipus, another hero of trial literature, always uttering the curses that result in his own undoing. Reci-procity between the I and the Thou asserts itself in the very efforts I make to deny it: "The sentence which you pass against your fellow men," says Clamence, "is always flung back into your face where it effects quite a bit of damage."

The outsider is really inside, but he is not aware of it. This lack of aware-ness determines the esthetic as well as the spiritual limitations of *L'Etranger.* A man who feels the urge to write a trial novel is not really "in love with the sun." He does not belong to the sunny Mediterranean but to the fogs of Amsterdam.

The world in which we live is one of perpetual judgment. It must be our Judeo-Christian heritage, still active within us. We are not healthy pagans. We are not Jews, either, since we have no Law. But we are not real Christians, since we keep judging. Who are we? A Christian cannot help feeling that the answer is close at hand: "thou art inexcusable, o man, whosoever thou art that judgest; for wherein thou judgest another, thou condemnest thyself; for thou that judgest dost the same things." Did Camus realize that all the themes of *La Chute* are in Paul's *Epistles?* If he had, would he have drawn from the analogy, and from the answers of Paul, the conclusions that a Christian would draw? Nobody can answer these questions.

Meursault was guilty of judgment but he never found out; Clamence alone found out. The two heroes may be viewed as a single one whose career describes a single itinerary somewhat analogous to the itinerary of the great Dostoevskian heroes. Like Raskolnikov, like Dmitri Karamazov, Meursault-Clamence first pictured himself as the victim of a judicial error, but he finally realized that the sentence was just, even if the judges were personally unjust, because the Self can provide only a grotesque parody of Justice.

The universal dimension of *La Chute* can be reached only through its most personal, almost intimate dimension. The two are really one; the structure of the work is one and its significance is one. Openly, at least, this significance is entirely negative. But the positive aspects are summed up in one sentence of the Nobel Prize acceptance speech. Camus opposes, in their order, his two fundamental attitudes, as a creator and as a man, leaving no doubt as to the personal significance of Clamence's confession:

> L'art . . . oblige . . . l'artiste à ne pas s'isoler; il le soumet à la vérité la plus humble et la plus universelle. Et celui qui, souvent, a choisi son destin d'artiste parce qu'il se sentait différent, apprend bien vite qu'il ne nourrira son art, et sa différence, qu'en avouant sa ressemblance avec tous.

PATRICK McCARTHY

The Plague

La Peste seems such a traditional novel. A plague strikes the North African
town of Oran. First the rats come above ground to die and then the people
fall ill and cannot be cured. The authorities are helpless and the population
despairs. A group of men band together to combat the plague: Rieux, the
doctor who can limit the plague's ravages but can no longer heal, the mysterious Tarrou, who has crusaded against the death penalty, the journalist
Rambert, who at first tries to escape but then realizes he must stay, Paneloux,
the Jesuit for whom the plague is a trial of his faith, and Grand, the minor
civil servant who spends his evenings writing the first sentence of a novel.
The group sets up special hospitals and vaccinates people until the plague
disappears as suddenly as it has come. Paneloux and Tarrou have died while
Rieux is left to tell the story.

Camus stressed that *La Peste* was to be a more positive book than
L'Etranger. Rieux and his friends demonstrate the moral values of courage
and fraternity which do not defeat the plague but which bear witness against
it. *La Peste* was read as a parable about the Occupation and Rieux's band
was perceived as a group of resistants who are fighting against the overwhelming power of the Nazis. Yet one doubts whether these more positive
values represent Camus's main achievement. The outstanding feature of *La
Peste* is the way this seemingly simple tale is told and the way in which the
narrative technique breaks with traditional novel-writing.

A quotation from Daniel Defoe stands at the head of the book but
Defoe's narrators are omniscient; they tell their tales like men who are sure

From *Camus*. © 1982 by Patrick McCarthy. Random House, 1982.

they dominate the world. *La Peste,* however, is recounted by a narrator who flaunts the limits of his understanding. Camus is continuing down the path he had traced in *L'Etranger.* Meursault had tried to understand his life and to communicate its meaning to us. He did not succeed but at least there was an "I" in the novel. In *La Peste* the story-teller remains anonymous. Not until the end does he identify himself as Rieux; for most of the novel he is a disembodied voice. He too tries to interpret what is happening but the plague defies his attempt to understand and hence dominate it. The opening lines set the tone: "The strange events which make up the subject of this chronicle, took place in 194–, in Oran. They were untoward and somewhat out of the ordinary, at least in most people's opinion. At first sight Oran is in point of fact an ordinary town, nothing more than a French prefecture on the Algerian coast."

The precision of time and place is banished by phrases like "in most people's opinion." These simple facts are not necessarily true; they depend for their veracity on other unnamed narrators. Nothing is real, Camus is telling us, unless it can be stated by a human intelligence; yet the narrator's intelligence enables him only to speculate without affirming. As if trained in Cartesian logic he draws general conclusions from the specific traits of Oran. But his "therefores" are soon entangled with "buts," while his long paragraphs are composed of statements, developments and contradictions.

Whereas Meursault had relied on his own impressions, this narrator is a dutiful historian who parades his documents and witnesses. But this is a subterfuge because he does not trust them: "he proposes to use them as he thinks fit and to cite them whenever he pleases. He also proposes." The only real witness is a narrator who does not finish his sentences and about whom the reader knows nothing.

The inadequacy of the narration cannot be stated until it has been resolved. Then Camus writes of the bond between Rieux and his mother: "a love is never strong enough to find its own expression so he and his mother would always love each other in silence." Writing should be a confession; instead it circles around its subject. Free indirect speech—the hallmark of *L'Etranger*—recurs in *La Peste* because it weakens the emotional veracity of the confession. In important moments such as Rambert's decision to stay in Oran, Camus allows his characters to speak directly. Rambert states that he will join with the others to fight against the plague; this is an affirmation of human courage. But such moments are rare because the narration must remain remote.

The theme of storytelling lies at the heart of *La Peste* which abounds in discussions of language and in narrators. First come the official storytellers like the town government and the newspapers. The government hides reality behind bureaucratic jargon while newspapers console; they keep forecasting that the plague will soon end. Men in authority make bold, ridiculous pronouncements: "There are no rats in the building," says the janitor while the rats die all around him. By contrast the theatre offers what Camus might have called "upside-down" insights. A play is put on and the actor who takes the part of Orpheus is stricken by plague as he descends into hell.

Each of the main characters—Rambert, Paneloux, Grand and Tarrou as well as Rieux—acts as a storyteller and each is a part of the greater anonymous narration. Rambert poses an intriguing problem. A professional journalist, he is the man who should write about the plague. Yet he does not because Camus feels that journalism is a particularly inadequate form of language.

Paneloux, who is an expert on Saint Augustine, delivers two sermons. The first affirms that the plague is a punishment sent by God and that the people of Oran must repent and do penance. This is a traditional piece of rhetoric and Camus uses another storyteller to mock it: Tarrou says that he is waiting for silence to replace bombast. The second sermon affirms that the plague is not sent by God; it is part of an evil which is present in the universe and which the Christian must confront. This sermon is filtered through the scepticism of Rieux who is sitting in the church. He notes that it is heretical but that its very doubts contain some truth. Paneloux's language is more restrained than in his first sermon, while Rieux's language is even more tentative. The second sermon contains some truth because it depicts evil as a painful riddle.

The difficulty which these storytellers encounter when they start to tell their tales is personified in the figure of Grand. His one-line novel is both an expression of Camus's fear that he will be unable to write and an illustration of the uncertainty of language. Grand puzzles over such words as "promise" and "right"; they have a life of their own and they do not convey what he thinks they should. Grand is a frustrated Cartesian who would like to make general statements, but when he makes them, they come out as platitudes. "Never put off until tomorrow," says Grand. Even then he has to qualify his remark by adding "as people say where I come from."

Grand has another aim which is to express fully what he feels. He has been married to a woman called Jeanne whom he still loves. So he wants to write her a love-letter that will make her realize what she means to him. Once more writing should be a confession but Grand cannot find the words to express his love so he sets about his novel instead. One might see in this a parable about absurd art. Language cannot seize human experience directly or totally; it must offer partial insights by "saying less." Grand's inability to go beyond the first sentence is a parody of the anonymous narrator's inability to explain the plague.

Tarrou's diary is the best example of "saying less" and it contains some of the finest writing in *La Peste*. "Tarrou's chronicle seems to stem," says the anonymous narrator, "from a quest for insignificance . . . he sets out to be the historian of things which have no history." Camus had thought of composing an anthology of insignificance but Tarrou's journal is a substitute for it. Convinced that the world does not make sense, Tarrou describes objects and conversations detached from their context and indicating only the absence of coherence. This seems like Meursault but it is not. Meursault hoped to understand Algiers, whereas Tarrou knows there is nothing to understand in Oran. He asks questions to which he does not expect answers and he spends a page describing the bronze lions on the main square. Irony and brevity are the keys to his art which must surely have appealed to Francis Ponge.

Yet there is a trap in Tarrou's lucidity. Since he knows everything he could become an omniscient narrator, which would contradict everything he knows. In order to preserve the incomplete nature of Tarrou's art Camus presents it via his anonymous narrator who does not understand Tarrou's aim and puzzles over his sentences. He wonders why Tarrou describes the bronze lions; they have no historical or allegorical quality and are just ridiculous objects. Such incomprehension prevents Tarrou's cult of insignificance from becoming an explanation of the world.

As *La Peste* goes on, a tension arises within the narration. In yet another discussion about language the medical authorities shrink from using the term "plague." "It doesn't matter whether you call it plague or growth fever," argues Rieux, "what matters is that you prevent it from killing half of Oran." Language cannot be used propositionally but it can be a weapon. It can combat the plague even if it cannot explain it. So the anonymous narrator turns out, unsurprisingly, to be the plague's chief enemy, Dr. Rieux. If stated at the outset this would have robbed the novel of its remote character; Rieux had to remain anonymous in order to depict the plague as an entity outside man's understanding. But he now states that he has "deliberately sided with the victims" and that he is "speaking for everyone."

The gradual change in the point of view is accompanied by a change in the themes. Camus spells out the values which enable men to battle against their condition. The key theme is indifference which is Rieux's special trait. In order to make his rounds and to isolate the people who are infected he has to repress the pity and sympathy which he feels for them. The doctor–patient relationship turns into inadequacy and hatred; the patients hate Rieux because he cannot cure them. But he must ignore this hatred and get on with his work. He feels that he is growing less and less human and that he is as "abstract" as the plague.

Camus is, characteristically, showing how a destructive force may be creative. The indifference which Rieux feels is a kind of courage which is shared by the men around him. The common bond of courage creates the second value of fraternity. Camus's moral thinking has never been more austere and heroic. Rieux, Tarrou and the others are an aristocracy who sacrifice their personal happiness in order to fight the plague.

The flaw in this moral thinking was pointed out by Sartre and by Roland Barthes. Camus had asserted the need to act but he had not treated the more difficult problems of which action one chooses, how one is changed by it and what influence it will have. Although the plague was nonhuman, it was supposed to be an image of the Occupation. But the Occupation was far from nonhuman and it involved agonizing choices. Tarrou illustrates this weakness when he links his stand against the plague with his rejection of violence. Sharing Camus's views on the death penalty and on left-wing tyranny, Tarrou affirms that he will not kill. So he can combat the plague but he could have combatted the Germans only if one assumes, as Camus did in '43, that the Resistance had its hands clean. Even if one sets aside the problem of the parallels with the Occupation the flaw in *La Peste* remains. Any political or social action would sully the purity in which Tarrou—like Camus—believes.

So the aristocrats of *La Peste* are frozen in their heroic posture. They defy the plague rather as Sisyphus defied his rock and their values are religious rather than practical. This is less a union of men who have very different characters and backgrounds than a communion of indifferent saints whose asceticism has dissolved all character. Tarrou, who broods ironically on sanctity, is writing yet another chapter in Camus's dialogue with his own religious temperament.

Yet these men are not saints, as Camus's Dominican friend, Bruckberger, pointed out. Examining Paneloux's death Bruckberger writes that the Jesuit confronts an absent God in static silence; he does not rail against Him, love Him or live with Him. Grace, love and prayer are all absent from *La Peste*. Bruckberger's criticism complements Barthes's: neither the religious notion of grace nor the human virtue of practicality is present in Camus's moral thinking.

The present-day reader may take yet a different view and he may feel that Rieux and Tarrou are exaggeratedly heroic. Indeed Camus's moral thinking is at its best when it depicts the inadequacy of heroism. The dying

Tarrou is not content with courage so he turns to Rieux's mother in an appeal for love. Rieux himself is desperately lonely when he walks through liberated Oran at the end of the novel. He and Tarrou are the most masculine of men— tough, ascetic and proud. Yet *La Peste* echoes with the absence of what have traditionally been the values of women: tenderness and warmth. This is far more convincing than the philosophically dubious, uselessly saintly heroism.

The need to present these moral values brings about the gradual change in the narration. At the outset Rieux is a character like Tarrou or Grand and he knows no more than they. Then he begins to show a greater understanding of his friends and of himself. He traces the growth of his indifference and he watches Rambert's hesitations. Meanwhile the anonymous narrator strikes a lyrical note in this description of Oran:

> The streets were deserted and the wind sighed out its ceaseless, lonely lament. A smell of seaweed and salt mounted from the raging, invisible sea. The deserted city, white with dust, saturated with briny odours, re-echoes with the cries of the wind and moans like an island of misfortune.

This is a visionary's insight and it reminds us of the moments of oneness in *L'Envers et l'endroit*.

As the novel goes on the two tendencies—Rieux's awareness and the anonymous narrator's lyricism—increase until they fuse into the discovery that Rieux is the narrator. This makes the novel more conventional because Rieux almost becomes a traditional, omniscient storyteller. Camus tries to prevent this by reverting to the earlier, fragmentary manner but even Tarrou's diary has changed. From being whimsical and insignificant it has become a treatise about insignificance. Camus is grappling with a real problem: there is a thin line between depicting men who show courage in the face of the unknowable and affirming that the world is unknowable so men must show courage. Once one tilts towards the second position then omniscient narrators and traditional novels reenter by the back door. Camus's language grows more rhetorical and his antitheses—"man's poor and awesome love"—grow heavier.

Yet the incomplete quality of the narration persists to the end. The last entries in Tarrou's journal are puzzling reflections on Rieux's mother and they open a new and mysterious theme of Tarrou's mother. The closing pages of the novel are written in the same remote style as the opening pages. There are celebrations, reunions and dancing; they take place according to some new order which is as undefinable as the old.

Despite the presence within the narration of a moralist, *La Peste* does not really make the world more human or more penetrable than *L'Etranger* did. Anonymity and amputation remain the watchwords of Camus's art. He tried to offer a viewpoint which would be positive because collective but the pages where it dominates are conventional, whereas the remote narrator who puzzles over Grand and Tarrou is a superb and thoroughly modern achievement. However, most of Camus's contemporaries did not interpret *La Peste* in this way. Camus, the tragic writer who depicted an alien universe, gave way to Camus, the apostle of brotherhood. This view of his writing, which he himself fostered, helped to shape his life over the next years.

DAVID R. ELLISON

The Rhetoric of Dizziness:
La Chute

On vivait avec ou contre sa pensée, telle que nous la révélait ses livres—*La Chute,* surtout, le plus beau peut-être et le moins compris—mais toujours à travers elle. C'était une aventure singulière de notre culture, un mouvement dont on essayait de deviner les phases et le terme final.

Il représentait en ce siècle, et contre l'Histoire, l'héritier actuel de cette longue lignée de moralistes dont les oeuvres constituent peut-être ce qu'il y a de plus original dans les lettres françaises. Son humanisme têtu, étroit et pur, austère et sensuel, livrait un combat douteux contre les événements massifs et difformes de ce temps. Mais, inversement, par l'opiniâtreté de ses refus, il réaffirmait, au coeur de notre époque, contre les machiavéliens, contre le veau d'or du réalisme, l'existence du fait moral.

(We lived with or against his thought, such as his books revealed it to us—*La Chute* [*The Fall*] especially, the most beautiful perhaps and the least well understood of his works—but always through it [i.e., his thought]. His literary enterprise was a singular adventure of our culture, a movement whose phases and end-point we tried to guess and imagine.

He represented in this century, and against History, the current inheritor of that long line of moralists whose works constitute perhaps that which is most original in French letters. His obstinate humanism, narrow and pure, austere and sensual, had to wage a questionable battle against the massive and grotesque

From *Contemporary Literature* 24, no. 3 (Fall 1983). © 1983 by the Board of Regents of the University of Wisconsin System.

events of our time. But, on the other hand, by the obstinacy of his refusals, he reaffirmed, at the very heart of our epoch, the existence of the moral fact. [This and all translations that follow are my own.])
                    —JEAN-PAUL SARTRE, "Albert Camus" in *Situations IV*

Since the end of the war, French literature has been dominated by a succession of quickly alternating intellectual fashions that have kept alive the illusion of a fecund and productive modernity. First came the vogue of Sartre, Camus, and the humanistic existentialism that followed immediately in the wake of the war, soon to be succeeded by the experimentalism of the new theater, bypassed in turn by the advent of the *nouveau roman* and its epigones. These movements are, to a large extent, superficial and ephemeral; the traces they will leave on the history of French literature are bound to be slighter than it appears within the necessarily limited perspective of our own contemporaneity. . . . When we are able to observe the period with more detachment, the main proponents of contemporary French literature may well turn out to be figures that now seem shadowy in comparison with the celebrities of the hour. And none is more likely to achieve future prominence than the little-publicized and difficult writer, Maurice Blanchot.
                    —PAUL DE MAN, *Blindness and Insight*

Is *La Chute* readable? Can its resistance to analytical probing be overcome? Is it possible to arrive at a consensus on the main vectors of its significant multiplicity? To those familiar with Camus criticism such questions might sound both naive and overstated: after all, it can be countered that although *La Chute* is an enigmatic *récit* (narration), the most allusive, textually complex, *and* personally (autobiographically) revealing of Camus's late works, twenty-five years of commentary have uncovered many of its secrets and progressively illuminated its dark recesses. To say that a text is difficult or obscure is not necessarily to brand it as unreadable or condemn it to oblivion: on the contrary, such a text invites a diversity of analyses precisely because of the indeterminate nature of its meanings.

    La Chute is a tantalizing and tempting work in that it *needs* its reader to come into textual existence yet denies the reader the pleasures of interpretive mastery and control. This fact has not stopped critics from accomplishing their task, but it has rendered that task more formidable and less comfortable. Despite the help of secondary material, the reader of today is disconcerted by *La Chute* to the point of dizziness: he falls into the narrator's verbal maze and becomes entangled/enmeshed in the blanket of guilt that the *récit* weaves around the crimes of twentieth-century humanity. The question "Is *La Chute* readable?" can be understood not only on the level of textual complexity—allusiveness, intertextuality, *mise en abyme* (literary mirroring or reflexiveness)—as a problem of interpretation, but also on the level of moral power: are we as readers strong enough to "stomach" the discomforting negative truths uttered by the loquacious protagonist? Can we "digest" a text which causes so much trauma and pain? Are we able to contemplate the mirror image of ourselves held up by a mad lawyer who purports to tell *our* story?

Jean-Paul Sartre eulogized Camus as a *moraliste* (see the first epigraph to this essay). According to Sartre, the reason Camus's thought had to be confronted and respected—even if one disagreed with its lack of historical determination, as did Sartre himself—was that it expressed the necessity of examining the excesses and monstrosities of the times *sub specie aeternitatis,* within a grand perspective whose bounds were set by universally recognizable human values. In his writings, Camus addresses himself to the essential humanity of the reader, and he communicates his message with clarity. As Edouard Morot-Sir has observed in a recent assessment of Camus as philosopher-essayist, Camus's style is that of the classical French moralist in that it subordinates form and expression to thought: "L'artiste camusien discipline . . . les élans poétiques: son texte exprime un *lyrisme contenu;* l'image est mise au service de la logique [Camus the artist suppresses poetic flights of fancy: his text expresses a sober lyricism; the image serves to buttress a logical framework]." This general statement fits not only *Le Mythe de Sisyphe* (*The Myth of Sisyphus*) and *L'Homme révolté* (*The Rebel*) but also *L'Etranger* (*The Stranger*) and *La Peste* (*The Plague*): yet how can we apply it to *La Chute,* a work whose rhetoric of *démesure* (excess) stands in diametrical opposition to the "lyrisme contenu" of the moralist? One wonders if Sartre did not secretly admire *La Chute* precisely because it did not fit the category of *moralisme* as such, because it added considerable obscurity to the perhaps excessively clear schematic ideas of Camus the philosopher.

But for what purposes does Camus relinquish the disciplined stylistic control he exercised in the essays and *récits* preceding *La Chute?* Why does he assume, with Clamence, the mask of a strategic duplicity? There is a self-reflexive dimension in *La Chute* that is not merely autobiographical, but textual. *La Chute* is, among other things, a *mise en abyme* of the act of reading, a meditation on the potential and limitations of the written word. In

this sense, Camus is much closer to the modern experimentation of *écriture*
than he is to "humanistic existentialism" (see the second epigraph)—a term
by which Paul de Man implies the subservience of form to content and a certain lack of deep literary self-consciousness in the avowed literary-humanistic
enterprise of both Sartre and Camus. The possibility exists that *La Chute* is
not merely a text we have difficulty reading, but a text that *stages* the difficulty, or even the impossibility of a controlled and masterful reading, and
that it represents a turn away from the rigorous aesthetic sobriety of *moralisme*. This is the hypothesis that will subtend our progressive encounter with
the vertiginous playfulness of Clamence's ironical lamentations.

In the following pages I propose to enter the abyss of *La Chute* with
Maurice Blanchot as guide. My purpose will not be to uncover specific clues
that would unlock and explain the secrets of a difficult work, for this task
has been assumed and to a large degree accomplished by a number of critics.
Rather, I shall proceed in an indirect and consciously circuitous manner in
order to determine, not what *La Chute* says or declares under the cloak of
a discernible symbolism, but what its potential is for the elaboration of a
theory of literary interpretation, how it functions within a network of barely
audible intertextual echoes, and how its confessional mode relates to its
narrative form. My point of departure will be the elucidation of Blanchot's
suggestive but metaphorically elusive critical vocabulary.

BLANCHOT AND THE METAPHOR OF DIZZINESS

In the volume of collected essays entitled *L'Amitié* (*Friendship*) are two
provocative studies of Camus's work which first appeared in *La Nouvelle
Revue Française:* "Le Détour vers la simplicité" and "*La Chute:* La Fuite." In
the first of these articles is Blanchot's effort to locate the creative source from
which Camus derived his power as writer. Some of the critic's observations
correspond closely with generally received assessments of the author, but
there is a certain opaqueness in his descriptive terminology which introduces
an enigmatic aura into an otherwise crystalline discourse. Toward the beginning of his argument, Blanchot asks a question that he answers in a highly
personal and apparently impressionistic way: "Et pourtant, que veut Camus,
écrivant? Retrouver cette simplicité qui lui appartient, cette communication
immédiate avec le bonheur et le malheur, peut-être toutefois quelque chose
de plus (ou de moins), une autre simplicité, une autre présence [And yet,
what does Camus want, in the act of writing? To find again the simplicity
that belongs to him, the immediate communication with happiness and un-
happiness, yet perhaps something more (or less), another kind of simplicity,

another presence]." Not only are the words "*other* simplicity" and "*other* presence" not definable in this initial context, but the remainder of the essay does nothing to develop explicitly their significance. Rather, Blanchot leads his reader through a labyrinth of commentary destined to illuminate the dangers of misreading Camus. It is only in retrospect, after the meanderings of a complex logic attain some degree of immediate coherence, that one can link the idea of an "other" simplicity to the general problematics of textual interpretation.

Throughout Blanchot's analysis, the reader recognizes a constantly recurring structural principle, that of "centrality." We are told that the unique quality of Camus's itinerary as writer resides in a dogged determination to remain faithful to an original or central discovery. His career is not a progression of changing literary experiments, but an attempt to say the same thing in differing forms. Thus, it can be said that the theme of "indifference" (i.e., the silent force that brings together human beings in a communion beyond existential conflict) and the philosophical idea of *l'absurde,* which are the nodal points of the early works *L'Etranger* and *Le Mythe de Sisyphe,* never cease to inform the author's thoughts, never disappear from the horizon of his subsequent work. Yet the drama and the pathos that characterize the later years of Camus's artistic activity derive, ironically, from the writer's misreading of his own deeper motivations that parallels the early misinterpretations of critics. Thus, when Camus becomes involved in political journalism during the fifties, he is forced to reexamine his earlier writings as if they were a sum of declarations that could be reduced to a series of clear statements. But this form of *engagement,* however necessary or admirable in the political arena, is in fact a vast simplification. In wishing to disengage himself from his philosophy of the absurd, Camus must treat the term *l'absurde* as a fixed concept: this is precisely the mistake made by readers of Camus who have not understood the fragility of the undefinable center that is the secret locus of his inspiration. Blanchot makes an important distinction: "l'absurde n'est pas l'absurdité; entre les deux mots, il y a une grande distance; l'absurdité est de caractère conceptuel, indiquant le sens de ce qui n'en a pas, alors que l'absurde est neutre, il n'est ni sujet ni objet, il n'appartient ni à l'un ni à l'autre, il est *Cela* qui se dérobe à la saisie du sens, comme le divin [the absurd is not absurdity; between the two words there is a great distance. Absurdity is a concept: it defines the meaning of that which has no meaning. The absurd, however, is neutral: it is neither subject nor object; it belongs neither to the subjective nor the objective; it is that thing (*Cela*) which eludes (*se dérobe à*) significance, like the Divine]." If the originality of Camus is to be understood as the uncovering and development of a central obsession with *l'absurde,* then his success as creator of fictions can be measured by the degree to which he respects the neutrality and nonapprehensiveness of the center itself, by the manner in which he forges a "silent" language appropriate to the *dérobade* (elusiveness) of meaning.

According to the interpretive framework of Blanchot, then, it would seem that what fascinates Camus, what compels him to continue writing the same thing under varying guises, is the desire to be within proximity of a properly inexpressible source—not to attain simplicity and the absoluteness of *présence,* but to hover around their periphery, to make the detour of an artistically productive avoidance. This desire is thematized clearly in many of Camus's works, but it appears most poignantly in *L'Etranger,* where the ideal of presence or simplicity is incorporated in the figure of the Mother on whose death the events of the *récit* focus. In Blanchot's terms, the condemnation by society of Meursault's apparently unfeeling reactions at the time of the funeral can be understood best as a fundamental misinterpretation of the essential emptiness that characterizes the mother–son relationship.

> C'est que Meursault porte la vérité de la mère. Comme elle, il est presque sans parole, sans pensée, pensant au plus près de ce manque initial qui est plus riche que toute pensée effective, parlant à la mesure des choses, de leur mutisme, des plaisirs qu'elles donnent, des certitudes qu'elles réservent. Du commencement à la fin, son destin est lié à celui de la mère. Le procès qu'on lui fera consiste à *transformer en faute le pur manque* qui leur est commun et, en même temps, à *retourner en crime la probité de leurs rapports,* cette insensibilité où, sans preuves et sans signes, ils ont vécu loin l'un de l'autre, proches l'un de l'autre, indifférents, mais par ce désintéressement qui est la manière d'accéder à l'unique vrai souci.

> (Meursault carries within him the truth of his mother. Like her, he is almost speechless, thoughtless, thinking as close as possible to that initial void/lack [*manque*] which is richer than any thought, speaking on the level of things, their muteness, of the pleasures they give, of the certainties they reserve. From the beginning to the end, his destiny is linked to that of his mother. The trial he will endure consists of *transforming into a crime the pure lack/void* [*manque*] that brought them together and, at the same time, of turning into a crime the integrity of their relationship, that insensitivity thanks to which, without oral communication,

they lived far from one another yet near to one another, in indifference, but with that form of disinterest which is the way of
access to the only true solicitude.) (My emphasis.)

L'Etranger as text is thus an interiorized fable that presents both the "other"
(mute) simplicity and the dramatic process by which the brute strangeness
of simplicity is *transformed* and *reversed* into crime—that is, it narrates
the violence of misreading whereby a *pur manque* (pure lack, pure void) is
clothed in the pathos of explicit (mis)representation.

Blanchot's reading of *L'Etranger* goes against the grain of traditional
critical approaches in that it does not adhere to the surface of related events
and their moral or existential significance, but demonstrates how fiction as
such originates from an unnamable primal source. It is not the message
of the *récit* that matters so much as the way in which a message can be
attached to a central void, or expressivity derived from the inexpressible.
This raises a question whose technical importance is obvious, and whose
theoretical potential will be the focus of a later development in this essay.
If there were no misreading, no *reversal* of probity into crime, would there
still be anything resembling a text? Is it not true that *L'Etranger* is read and
appreciated because of the dramatic possibilities inherent in such a violation
of simplicity? In *Le Mythe de Sisyphe*, Camus had defined the authentic
"oeuvre absurde" as a work that "furnishes no answers." What needs to be
examined is whether any text can exist without drawing false conclusions
from the unanswerable questions it asks of itself. Is it possible, in other
words, to conceive of a literary form that would not turn the neutrality
of *l'absurde* into the conceptual rigidity of "absurdity"? To encounter this
problem in its complexity, we must turn to *La Chute*.

As is often the case with Blanchot, the essay "*La Chute:* La Fuite"
is written on such a high level of reflective abstraction as to seem completely distant from the object of its scrutiny. The critic makes no attempt
to deal with the significance of Biblical and literary allusions that make of
Clamence's confession a disconcertingly complicated intertextual web; he is
ostensibly unconcerned with the *récit*'s formal identity; he has little to say
about the exacerbated eroticism that is at the core of the protagonist's strat-
egy of self-evasion. In other words, the themes and problems that lend themselves to explanatory analysis and that have produced an impressive sum
of criticism concerning the "hidden meanings" of *La Chute* lie untouched
by Blanchot. But it would be a mistake to assume hastily that this refusal
to enter into the detail of textual structures implies that Blanchot is really
writing his own personal obsessions rather than reading Camus. There can

be no doubt that "*La Chute:* La Fuite" is the fragmentary expression of an implicit theory that runs through *L'Amitié* like the Goethian "red thread"; but one would falsify the precise nature of Blanchot's insight into Clamence's provocations were one to disregard what his essay says, *sotto voce,* about how *not* to interpret *La Chute.*

It is by now well established in the critical literature that *La Chute* is on one level an autobiographical/confessional text, Camus's poignant discovery of his own human fallibility. Blanchot is sensitive to the thinly veiled personal element present in *La Chute;* he finds, for example, in the phrase: "N'était-ce pas cela, en effet, l'Eden, cher Monsieur, la vie en prise directe? Ce fut la mienne [Was that not, in fact, Eden, my dear Sir, life of unmediated contentment? That was my life]" a statement more appropriate to Camus the man than to the ever-devious Clamence (*L'Amitié*). He refuses, however, to interpret the *récit* in a uniquely psychological vein—that is, according to the stance adopted by the vast majority of critics. Prophetically aware of how *La Chute* will be read in succeeding years, Blanchot evokes the temptation of reducing Clamence's discourse to a drama of consciousness: "L'on cherchera sans doute dans ce récit l'âpre mouvement d'un homme satisfait qui, à force de se prêter à un moi vertueux et content, se livre enfin à cette puissance de mécontentement et de destruction qu'il y a aussi dans le moi [People will no doubt find in this narration/story (*récit*) the rigid movement of a self-satisfied man who, by dint of indulging his virtuous and contented ego, gives himself over in the end to the force of dissatisfaction and destruction that also resides in the ego]." This is a concise summary of the book's plot—the process by which a self-satisfied lawyer, defender of widows and orphans, ends up as *juge-pénitent* (judge-penitent) in an Amsterdam bar, with the avowed purpose of coercing all of humanity to share his own guilt. But Blanchot does not see in Clamence the illustrator of La Rochefoucauld's psychology, and does not believe that *La Chute* is essentially a didactic text whose goal is to "enseigner le mécontentement, la vérité inconfortable et l'inquiétude nécessaire [teach dissatisfaction, the uncomfortable truth and necessary anxiety]." Instead, he sees in the *récit* "la grâce de l'ironie . . . [qui] ne nous donne que ce qu'elle nous enlève [the grace of irony—that gives us only what it takes away from us]." This irony can also be called *attirance* (magnetic attraction) or *fuite* (escape)—words that convey both the capacity of the text to draw the reader into its rhetorical spins and turns, and its potential to escape the imprisonment of semantic identification. What the protagonist relates is thus mere ornamentation—however brilliant and seductive—that hides the general "escaping" movement of his discourse.

As in his interpretation of *L'Etranger,* Blanchot inverts the traditional priority of content over form and demonstrates the insubstantiality of content itself: in so doing, he questions the usual reading that defines *La Chute* as a text "about" guilt. What, in fact, is the nature of Clamence's need to confess? "Sa confession n'est qu'un calcul. Son récit d'homme coupable est fait de l'espérance de se croire coupable, car une vraie faute serait une certitude sur laquelle il pourrait ancrer sa vie, repère solide qui lui permettrait de délimiter sa course [His confession is but a calculation. His guilty man's story is made of the hope of believing himself to be guilty, because a true crime would be a certainty in which he could anchor his life, a solid point of reference that would allow him to limit his course]." Just as the representatives of social order had transformed the *pur manque* of the bond between Meursault and his mother into a crime, in the same way, Blanchot would have us believe that Clamence misreads the *fuite* in which he is caught and tries to turn it into a *certitude* or *repère solide* (solid reference point). This misreading inscribed in the text mirrors the analyses of critics who miss the mark if they take the confessed material "seriously" (literally) rather than inquire about the origin of confession as such. Once again, Blanchot's remarks suggest the structural scheme of a central void around which false interpretations can be formulated without limit, but in the case of *La Chute* the center itself is not defined as an enigmatically nonpresent presence, but as a fleeing motion which lends itself to an allegorical correspondence with the temporal process of reading.

In the final paragraph of his essay, Blanchot touches upon the theoretical implications of the *récit*'s dialogic form. Although the goal of the protagonist is quite obviously to implicate the reader in his own personal degradation, to draw him into the tightly constricted space of an individual discourse, the textual process of *fuite* is precisely the opposite: it forces Clamence into a strange realm of transindividual generality that surpasses his egocentric limits; it thrusts him into dizziness [*vertige*]:

> Nous tombons. Nous nous consolons de tomber en déterminant imaginairement le point où nous aurions commencé de tomber. Nous préférons être coupables plutôt que tourmentés sans faute. . . . Tout doit tomber, et tout ce qui tombe doit entraîner dans la chute, par une croissance indéfinie, tout ce qui prétend demeurer. A certains moments, nous nous apercevons que la chute dépasse de beaucoup notre mesure et que nous avons en quelque sorte plus à tomber que nous n'en sommes capables. *Alors peut commencer le vertige par lequel nous nous dédoublons*, devenant, pour nous-mêmes, compagnons de notre chute.

(We fall. We console ourselves for this fall by determining, in our imagination, the point at which we presume to have begun falling. We prefer to be guilty rather than to be tormented for no crime. . . . Everything must fall, and everything that falls must drag along with it in its fall, in an indefinite movement of growth, all that tries to remain. From time to time, we perceive that the fall far exceeds our measure and that we must, in a sense, fall more than we are capable of falling. *Here begins the dizziness through which we divide ourselves,* becoming, for ourselves, companions in our fall.) (My emphasis.)

Dizziness is an apt metaphor to describe the situation of all readers when confronted with the semantic proliferation of texts; and dizziness is the condition of literary dialogue, which originates when the indescribable otherness of the text is recognized and respected. To read himself, Clamence was obliged to create or locate his double—the silent interlocutor who, it turns out, is also a lawyer and perhaps the imaginary projection of the protagonist. This doubling is also the crucial process by which the *récit* presents itself as an object to be understood, yet it renders comprehension in the sense of mastery impossible since it is born of *vertige.* Clamence's wish to control the order and meaning of his speech takes on a pathetic quality. His attempt to violate the laws of dialogue, his desire to *be* the crying voice of a monologue present only unto itself mimic the hubris underlying the literary critic's "natural" tendency to neutralize ambivalences and make definitive the interpretation of literary works.

THE GAME/PLAY: HERMENEUTIC THEORY AND TEXTUAL PRACTICE

From the preceding review of Blanchot's critical essays arise two major questions. First, is it legitimate to read into the critic's reflections on falling and dizziness a genuine theory of literary interpretation, and if so, can that theory be expressed in a more objective, less metaphorical formulation without losing its pertinence and meaningfulness? Second, to what extent does *La Chute* actually perform the textual dizziness of which Blanchot writes; and is it possible to localize with any degree of precision the moments at which the *récit* succumbs to the *démesure* of the fall? In asking these questions and in attempting to find their answers, I assume that what Blanchot has to say about Camus constitutes an abstract design whose textual objective correlative is the narrative called *La Chute*—that is, I assume that there is a demonstrable correspondence between the remarks of the critic and the text he analyzes. It must be admitted, however, that this may not be true. In characterizing Blanchot's method, Paul de Man has contended that the insights of the interpreter, however rich in general significance, do not necessarily make for a change in our view of the author being studied:

> When we read him [Blanchot] on one of the poets or novelists he happens to choose for a theme, we readily forget all we assumed to know up till then about this writer. This does not happen because Blanchot's insight necessarily compels us to modify our own perspective; this is by no means always the case. Returning afterwards to the author in question, we will find ourselves back at the same point, our understanding barely enriched by the comments of the critic. Blanchot, in fact, never intended to perform a task of exegesis that would combine earlier acquired knowledge with new elucidation. The clarity of his critical writings is not due to exegetic power; they seem clear, not because they penetrate further into a dark and inaccessible domain but because they suspend the very act of comprehension. The light they cast on texts is of a different nature. Nothing, in fact, could be more obscure than the nature of this light.
>
> ("Impersonality in Blanchot")

Although it is certainly true that Blanchot's task in writing about other literary creators is not principally one of exegesis in the traditional sense of the term, I would argue that the "suspension" of comprehension seen by de Man as the ultimate effect of the critic's style is in fact an invitation to descend farther into the textual *abyme* (abyss), where fiction and analytical essay mirror each other and elucidate each other's darkness. Keeping this in mind, I will now examine the origin and meaning of dizziness in *La Chute*. As a first stage of clarification I propose to identify the vertiginous process of transsubjective generality according to its theoretical potential and in the detail of its contextual functioning.

If Blanchot's metaphorical scheme of dizziness were translated into a philosophically coherent, discursively elaborated hermeneutic theory, it would resemble and even repeat the model of Hans-Georg Gadamer that relates artistic creativity to a game or play [*Spiel*]. In the second part of *Wahrheit und Methode,* Gadamer distinguishes between the classical use of the term by Kant and Schiller—both of whom anchored the game analogy in the state of mind of a freely creating subject—and his own post-Heideggerian view according to which the game is nothing less than "die Seinsweise des Kunstwerkes selbst [the mode of being of the work of art itself]." For

Gadamer, it is not the subject who controls the game, but the reverse. In fact—to play with words—the subject of the game is not the subject (or subjectivity), but the game comes to be represented *through* the activity of subjects or players. The game as such fulfills itself much as a musical composition does—through performance or "realization"—and affects its performers in a similar fashion, by transforming them, by actively modifying their being:

> Nur dann erfüllt ja Spielen den Zweck, den es hat, *wenn der Spielende im Spielen aufgeht*. Nicht der aus dem Spiel herausweisende Bezug auf dem Ernst, sondern nur der Ernst beim Spiel läßt das Spiel ganz Spiel sein. Wer das Spiel nicht ernst nimmt, ist ein Spielverderber. Die Seinsweise des Spieles läßt nicht zu, daß der Spielende zu dem Spiel wie zu einem Gegenstande verhält. Der Spielende weiß wohl, was Spiel ist, und daß, was er tut "nur ein Spiel ist," aber er weiß nicht, was er da "weiß."

> (The playing of games fulfills its purpose only *when the player becomes caught up [wrapped up] in the playing*. Not the game's relationship to seriousness, but only seriousness in the act of playing allows the game to be itself entirely. He who does not take the game seriously is a spoil-sport. The mode of being of the game does not permit that the player relate to the game as to an object. The player certainly knows what the game is and that what he is doing is "only a game," but he does not know what he thereby "knows" [i.e., he does not know what this "knowledge" has taught him].) (My emphasis.)

A complete reading of the section on games would show that Gadamer's presentation is parallel to Blanchot's less explicit reflections in that the perceiving or interpreting consciousness relates to the game he plays (or book he reads) as an individual subject relates to a generality whose rules determine his mode of existence. In the cited passage, Gadamer insists that the player is bound or wrapped up in the game [*der Spielende geht im Spiele auf*], and since the game surpasses his limited powers, it is therefore a sign of bad faith to treat the game as if it were a mere object. Most importantly, the model according to Gadamer, like Blanchot's metaphorics of dizziness, indicates both the inevitability of the subject's cognitive relationship to the game he plays and also the limits of this relationship. To paraphrase Gadamer and his predecessors in the field of hermeneutics, one might say that the player has a "foreknowledge" of the meaning of the game, or, more precisely, of the boundaries that determine the game's potential significance; but at the moment of his dramatic *Aufgehen im Spiel,* he loses the capacity to know what he knows, and in a strangely literal sense, loses "himself" in the playing. The truth of the game takes on the form of an ironical reversal in which the manipulator of figures is himself manipulated. In Gadamer's succinct terms, the fascination of game-playing results from the fact that the game becomes *master* of the player ("daß das Spiel über den Spielenden *Herr* wird").

The central conflict of *La Chute*—Clamence's immoderate desire to dominate his fellow humans by assuming the mask of a strategic immersion in guilt—is related in psychological terms, but its implications for a theory of reading are apparent once it becomes clear that Camus is speaking Gadamer's language. The third chapter of *La Chute* is a long discourse on *mastery* as such, but it reverses the ideal form of Gadamer's model in that it shows Clamence's refusal to be controlled by the game and his exasperated attempts to invent the rules himself. This defensive narcissism is especially evident in the passages dealing with love or sexuality. In his repeated scenes of seduction, the protagonist admits: "je satisfaisais encore autre chose que ma sensualité: mon amour du *jeu.* J'aimais dans les femmes les partenaires d'un certain *jeu* [I satisfied even more than my sensuality: my love of *games* (of playing, acting). I loved in women the partners of a certain *game/play*]" (my emphasis). As long as Clamence is in charge of the game, eroticism has all the comforts of ritual habit. In this respect his conception of love repeats that of the Proustian narrator-hero, for whom pleasure is equivalent to the absence of pain—which in turn presupposes the anesthesia of habit and ignorance of the beloved's true activity. As in Proust, because the attachment of self to other is nothing more than the projection of self-love, the most adequate metaphor to express the loving relationship is that of imprisonment: "je finis par m'attacher à elle comme j'imagine que le geôlier se lie à son prisonnier [in the end I became attached to her in much the same way as I imagine a jailer relates to his prisoner]." Furthermore, since the subject both needs the confirmation of outside approval and also denies the very right to existence of the outside as such, the women with whom Clamence shares spare moments must be "vacant" and "deprived of an independent life." On the psychological level, therefore, a subject incapable of relating to the *other* as existential reality creates a game in which it is possible to refuse the *other*'s identity by fictionalizing it or otherwise rendering it harmless. This happens not only in the realm of eroticism, where a jailer tries to control the potentially unknowable secretive essence of a prisoner, but also in the political-historical arena, as Camus demonstrates in a short parable on man's need for figures of authority. Readers of *La Chute* will remember the starkly illuminated episode in which Clamence tells how he came to be "pope" in a prison camp. Having accepted, in jest [*par plaisanterie*], to play the role of a holy man who will share the miseries and assume the collective destiny of a group, Clamence eventually uses his power in his own selfish interests and acts out of a personal survival instinct. As he tells it, with a significant metaphor: "Disons que j'ai bouclé la boucle le jour où j'ai bu l'eau d'un camarade agonisant [Let us say that I came full circle the day I drank the water of a dying comrade]."

The anecdotal material chosen by Camus to illustrate the problem of imprisonment—whether literally, as in the war context, or figuratively, as in the sensuality of love-games—is so interesting in itself, so full of allusions to the crises of our modern age and to the private life of the author, that the temptation is to overlook the possible implications of imprisonment as metaphor—that is, how the term expresses *authorial* desires and functions in the literary sense. I am not suggesting that the matter of Clamence's confessions is of itself indifferent. It is only too clear that social decadence and political crimes need to be examined in themselves, and Camus's *récit* elaborates on these themes in a provocative way. But I would contend that what concerns Camus at the level where the act of writing reflects upon itself is also "imprisonment"—defined as the manipulative control exercised by an author over his own work. If this is true, then there is a special meaningfulness in Clamence's admission that he came full circle when he drank his comrade's life-giving water. Read as an allegory of reading, this statement translates into the inauthentic appropriation by the author of that which is not his by rights, but which, when removed from its proper place, produces the life of his text. In other words, Clamence represents the writer who refuses to engage himself into the hermeneutic circle but pretends to close off the infinite regress of the turning circle itself.

THE BAUDELAIRIAN INTERTEXT:
VERTIGINOUS LAUGHTER AND LITERARY LANGUAGE

To what extent can it be demonstrated that Clamence's actions emblematize the predicament of all writers in their efforts to achieve mastery over reality through form? Can it be shown, through concrete textual analysis, that *La Chute* stages the drama of authorial appropriation, thereby performing the conflict between self and transsubjective dispossessing generality which is at the heart of Blanchot's dizziness metaphor and the game model of Gadamer? If these questions are to be answered, we need to identify that which Camus is obliged to "steal" in order to enliven his text, that which, in becoming part of his *récit,* risks expropriating it in a dizzying circle of uncontrolled relations. The most immediate response, if we view *La Chute* now as the story of its own constitution, is that the force against which the author struggles is that of the *other* texts he has woven into the fabric of his own discourse. As has been noted, critics of Camus have long recognized the intertextual effects of Clamence's story and have explained the numerous Biblical and literary allusions in exegetical articles. But their studies necessarily assume the inviolable uniqueness and aesthetic unity of *La Chute,* so that whatever new information is uncovered by their analyses generally serves to consolidate the thematic coherence they had already presupposed to exist before beginning to write. Of course, it is possible to condemn Camus for an "excessive" borrowing, but this negative judgment only serves to confirm the prejudice that a work of art need stand on its own, detached and indifferent to the subversive potential of the texts it cites. In the following section of this essay, I will propose that the intertextual ramifications of *La Chute* be reexamined in their expropriative power: that is, I will suggest that Camus's text is not so much a self-originating creation as a reading of other texts whose central theme is the bizarre movement of *vertige. La Chute* is vertiginous precisely insofar as it repeats or falls into dizziness.

The initial discovery made by Clamence that precipitates his decision to abandon Paris and a successful professional activity is that his own apparent altruism was in truth the mask of a deeper self-love and will to dominate. When he becomes *juge-pénitent* in the shadowy *demi-monde* of Amsterdam, he simply allows the mask to stick and assumes a permanent stance of duplicity: he recognizes his guilt, but does penance while implicating others in his crimes, so that in the end he can judge all of humanity. One does not rid oneself easily of other people, however, and at times Clamence's relations with the outside world become exaggerated and frustrated to the point of violence. In the latter stages of his confessions, by an ironic reversal, the protagonist attempts to convince his readers that the human solidarity whose precariousness he had formerly experienced is in fact possible, as long as it is clothed in the form of cruelty. This reversal is indeed interesting and produces some rather startling textual effects, but it is by no means original with Camus. The wording used by Clamence in the following passages indicates that he is quoting from one of Baudelaire's most disconcerting and disorienting prose poems, "Assommons les pauvres!": "Avec une courtoisie, avec une solidarité pleine d'émotion, je crachais tous les jours à la figure de tous les aveugles [With courtesy, and with a truly emotional sense of solidarity, I used to spit every day on the faces of all blind men]"; and later, in the same vein, "je projetais de crever les pneumatiques des petites voitures d'infirmes, d'aller hurler 'sale pauvre' sous les échafaudages où travaillaient les ouvriers, de gifler les nourrissons dans le métro [I planned to puncture the tires of wheelchairs, to go cry out 'Dirty Pauper' under the scaffolding where working-class men were occupied, to slap babies in the subway]."

If we turn now to Baudelaire's poem for enlightenment on the problem of cruelty as such and for illumination of its role in *La Chute,* we find more (and less) than we had bargained for. It is true that the argumentation adopted by the "je" who relates "Assommons" resembles closely that of Clamence, in that he begins in a state of disillusionment about the possibility of social and spiritual equality among men. Having read numerous tracts "où il est traité de l'art de rendre les peuples heureux [where one (i.e., an author) elaborates on the art of making people happy]," the poet has his own idea, which consists of attaining solidarity through mutual violence: by standing Christian morality on its head, he decides that the reciprocity of bludgeoning is the only authentic method of achieving the respectful exchange generally called "brotherly love." The tone of the poem is decidedly ironic, and the scene in which the poet and the beggar exchange blows is told with relish, with a joyful accumulation of bloody detail whose immediate effect is to shock the reader and involve him deeply in the representational expressivity of a subject's will to power. Yet the very triumphant voice of the poet, coupled with the fact that he has presented his case as a rigorously demonstrated logical theorem make one question the truth-value of such an inflated ego's apotheosis in rhetoric. (As the beggar turns round to strike him, the poet exclaims: "ô miracle, ô jouissance du philosophe qui vérifie l'excellence de sa théorie [O miracle, O delight of the philosopher who verifies the excellence of his theory].") Most importantly, one is led to wonder about the motivations behind the "idée supérieure" which drove the poet from the solitude of his room to the encounter with the beggar.

The origin of the poet's feeling of superiority is not original: that is, it cannot be located in some primal psychological discovery; it is not the essence of a pure drama of solipsism. Superiority is born of reading; it is the defensive reaction of a subject to the books against whose ideas he wishes to construct his own philosophy. In the first paragraph of "Assommons" the poet criticizes "toutes les élucubrations de tous ces entrepreneurs de bonheurs public—de ceux qui conseillent à tous les pauvres de se faire esclaves, et de ceux qui leur persuadent qu'ils sont tous des rois détrônés [all the lucubrations of all these entrepreneurs of public happiness—of those who counsel poor people to become slaves, and of those who persuade them that they are all dethroned kings]." Like the English psychologists whom Nietzsche ridicules in the opening pages of *The Genealogy of Morals,* the "entrepreneurs de bonheurs public" make an easy target for a writer whose ostensible theme is the inversion of traditional Christian values, the radical questioning of morality in its usual guise of self-effacement and self-annihilation. But the condition of possibility of this inversion is the neutralization and elimination of the "mauvaises lectures [bad readings, bad texts]" to which the poet has subjected himself: hence the metaphors of digestion and swallowing that are used to express the act of reading itself ("J'avais donc digéré—avalé, veux-je dire,—toutes les élucubrations [I had thus digested—swallowed, I mean—all the lucubrations]"). Here, to swallow a "bad" text is to render it impotent by assimilation. But one senses that the poet is only partially successful in his efforts, in that he is caught up in "un état avoisinant *le vertige* ou la stupidité [a state resembling *dizziness* or stupidity]" (my emphasis), so that he must leave his room for the fresh air of the outside and the episode of solidarity-proving. It then becomes possible to read the poem as a whole on a deeper level of irony than its thematic content immediately exhibits. In fact, the self's parading and basking in the feeling of his power are implicitly undercut by the first paragraph. The poem constructs itself in a movement of forgetfulness of its own origin, in the refusal to read the *vertige* from which it emerges and simultaneously wishes to escape. The poet's error was to leave his room in the first place and to conceive of his own superiority, when in fact his situation *as* poet is to be engaged in the movement of dizziness, wrapped up in the corpus of texts that traverses and negates the closed limits of his body and mind.

The Baudelairian intertext is not so much a convenient framework of themes and images that Camus uses to buttress his fictional argument as it is the allusive/elusive movement through which *La Chute* falls into the metaphorically expressed story of its own constitution as text. Quotations from Baudelaire's work are not the signs of an intellectual heritage that Camus can interiorize and call his own, but they stand in the *récit* as trap-doors opening into the *abyme* of the poet's most daring literary provocations. Perhaps the most consequential but least obvious allusion to Baudelaire occurs in a deceptively trivial and seemingly realistic anecdote, when Clamence explains how suddenly he has lost control of his usually rapt audience in the law courts, to the point of becoming the object of a general laughter: "Mes semblables cessaient d'être à mes yeux l'auditoire respectueux dont j'avais l'habitude. Le cercle dont j'étais le centre se brisait, et ils se plaçaient sur une seule rangée, comme au tribunal. . . . Oui, ils étaient là, comme avant, mais ils riaient. . . . J'eus même l'impression, à cette époque, qu'on me faisait des crocs-en-jambe. Deux ou trois fois, en effet, je butai, sans raison, en entrant dans des endroits publics. Une fois même, je m'étalai [My fellow men were no longer, in my eyes, the respectful audience to which I had become accustomed. The circle of which I was the center was breaking, and they were placed in one line, as at a trial. . . . Yes, they were there, like before, but they were laughing. . . . I even thought, at that time, that people were trying to trip me. Two or three times, in fact, I stumbled, for no reason, in entering public places. Once I even fell flat on my face]." The hidden source of this passage is "De l'Essence du rire," Baudelaire's philosophical and moral meditation on laughter. In this essay, the aesthetician of *L'Art romantique* grounds laughter in the ego's sense of superiority. If I laugh at someone who falls on the pavement, it is because I am assured of my own ability to avoid obstacles: "C'est là le point de départ: *moi,* je ne tombe pas; *moi,* je marche droit; *moi,* mon pied est ferme et assuré. Ce n'est pas *moi* qui commettrais la sottise de ne pas voir un trottoir interrompu ou un pavé qui barre le chemin [There is the point of departure: *I* do not fall; *I* walk in a straight line; *my* footing is strong and assured. *I* would not commit the foolish error of not seeing a broken-up sidewalk or a paving-stone that blocks my path]" (Baudelaire's emphasis). But what is the origin of superiority as such? The answer is drawn from Christianity: one feels oneself above others because one has lost the original innocence of Eden. Laughter is therefore satanic in essence. In stating that "le rire humain est lié à l'accident d'une *chute* ancienne, d'une dégradation physique et morale [human laughter is linked to the accident of an ancient *fall,* of a physical and moral degradation]" (my emphasis), Baudelaire provides Camus with the title of his book as well as the theological vocabulary which critics most often examine independently of its contextual relationship to the theme of laughter.

At stake in "De l'Essence du rire" is the same dramatic opposition between egocentric domination and the fall into transsubjective generality that generated the ironies of "Assommons les pauvres!," Gadamer's hermeneutic game-theory, and Blanchot's metaphorics of dizziness. In fact, at a crucial stage in the development of his essay, Baudelaire enters into the problematics of *vertige.* In comparing what he calls the "comique significatif" (whose mode of functioning is *double,* based on the contrasts between mask and reality that constitute social comedy) to the "comique absolu" or *grotesque* (whose appearance is that of a closed unity "[qui] veut être saisi[e] par intuition [that must be seized by intuition]"), Baudelaire finds himself at a logical impasse. Since the "comique significatif" involves the duplicity of theatrical hypocrisy, it can be analyzed into its component parts and understood; but the *grotesque,* on the other hand, can be verified only by laughter itself, not by a discourse on laughter. To describe the comical at the absolute of its power, the writer necessarily resorts to metaphor, but not just any metaphor. In his lively and impressionistic recreation of an English pantomime, the theoretician is reduced to a radical impotence with regard to the overwhelming energy of the *grotesque,* so that his prose becomes a series of punctuated exclamations hovering in dizziness:

> Et toutes choses s'exprimaient ainsi dans cette singulière pièce, avec emportement; c'était *le vertige de l'hyperbole.*

> (And everything was expressed, in this singular play, with fury; it was the *dizziness of hyperbole.*) (My emphasis.)

> Aussitôt le vertige est entré, le vertige circule dans l'air; on respire le vertige; c'est le vertige qui remplit les poumons et renouvelle le sang dans le ventricule.
>
> Qu'est-ce que ce vertige? C'est le comique absolu; *il s'est emparé de chaque être.*

> (Immediately dizziness entered the scene; dizziness circulates in the air; we breathe the dizziness; it is dizziness that fills the lungs and replenishes the blood of the heart.
>
> What is this dizziness? It is the absolute comical; *it has seized (dispossessed) us all.*) (My emphasis.)

The most striking example of the excessive or "hyperbolic" manner in which the individual actor-player is appropriated by the absolute comical is provided by the figure of Pierrot, who is guillotined on the stage with a complete lack of deference for the classical French *bienséances* [proprieties]. Undaunted by the loss of his head, he picks it up and pockets it, consumed by the monomania of his compulsion to steal. The violent laughter that moves through the audience proves that the effect of the absolute has been intuited, while on the level of theatrical staging, the scene as such represents the image of human intelligence at work overtime, attempting to recuperate the irrecuperable. Pierrot is the appropriately absurd symbol of the philosopher or aesthetician who believes he can overcome existential loss by the willed mastery of a possession beyond the limits of the knowable, while the laughter that in truth possesses him [*s'empare de lui*] designates the flimsy foundation of his project.

The word *vertige* enters Baudelaire's critical vocabulary when the inexpressible absolute must be expressed. Its repeated use in the essay on laughter indicates the impossibility of the literary theoretician's desire to imprison conceptually the object of his study: there will always be a dizziness in the original text that the analytical treatise can only repeat. According to Baudelaire, the theoretician is not a detached, objective observer in control of his material, but a body agitated, dispossessed: hence the network of digestion and elimination metaphors already noted in "Assommons les pauvres!" At

the beginning of the essay, Baudelaire states that his purpose is simply to
"faire part au lecteur de quelques réflexions qui me sont venues souvent. . . .
Ces réflexions étaient devenues pour moi une espèce d'obsession; j'ai voulu
me soulager [communicate to the reader certain thoughts that have come
to me often. . . . These thoughts had become for me a kind of obsession;
I wanted to *relieve myself*]" (my emphasis). Later on, he uses the words
"digestion," "se débarrasser [to rid oneself]"; and in his characterization of
Maturin's *Melmoth the Wanderer,* "ce rire glace et tord les entrailles [this
laughter freezes and twists the entrails]." The situation of the critic vis-à-vis
the text(s) he reads is that of an individual who is traversed by the food that
descends and departs his body. To swallow the "élucubrations" of writers is
not to interiorize them permanently, but to allow them access to our own
inner sanctum, where they are free to operate upon us with abandon. The
act of reading is that process by which a body opens itself to the outside and
submits to the rule of the *other.*

The proximity of laughter in its physiological function to literature as
such is one of Blanchot's major insights in *L'Amitié.* In fact, his definition
of laughter as that which requires "l'abandon des limites personnelles, parce
qu'il [le rire] vient de loin et, nous traversant, nous *disperse au loin* [the
abandonment of personal limits, because it (laughter) comes from afar and,
passing through us, disperses us to the winds]" is a shorthand version of
what he has to say about "the truth of literary language" in his article on
Louis René des Forêts's *Le Bavard (The Gossip),* a book which may have
influenced *La Chute.* What Blanchot writes concerning the fascinating power
of des Forêts's curious monologue applies also to Clamence's excesses of
bavardage:

> *Le Bavard* nous fascine, il nous inquiète. Mais ce n'est pas parce
> qu'il représenterait, à titre de figure symbolique, la nullité bavarde
> propre à notre monde, c'est parce qu'il fait pressentir qu'une fois
> engagé dans ce mouvement, la décision d'en sortir, la prétension
> d'en être sorti lui appartient déjà et que cette immense érosion
> préalable, ce vide intérieur, cette contamination des mots par le
> mutisme et du silence par les mots, désignent peut-être la vérité
> de toute langue, et particulièrement du langage littéraire, celle
> que nous rencontrerions si nous avions la force d'aller jusqu'au
> bout, avec la résolution de nous abandonner, rigoureusement,
> méthodiquement, lâchement, au vertige.

> (*Le Bavard* fascinates and upsets us. But this is not because it
> represents, symbolically, the inane gossip one finds in our world,

but because it makes us realize that, once engaged in the movement of gossip, the decision to get out, the pretension to be free
from it belongs to it [gossip] already and that this immense pre-
liminary erosion, this inner void, this contamination of words by
muteness and of silence by words, designate perhaps the truth of
all language, and particularly of literary language, that truth we
would encounter if we had the strength to go to the end, and the
resolution to abandon ourselves, rigorously, methodically, in all
cowardice, to dizziness.)

If laughter and the truth of literary language coincide, it is because
they both designate or "mean" the movement of decentralization by which
a body or text loses mastery over its functions. According to Blanchot, it
is easy to underestimate the importance of this strange process since the
work of art also seems to "represent": it is tempting to see in *Le Bavard*
or *La Chute* the symbolic expression of our modern age's "nullité bavarde
[inane gossip]", and more difficult, more disconcerting, to follow the text's
fall into self-representation, into the domain where fiction turns into itself,
generating itself in the dizziness of its noncoincidence with the apparent
"repère solide" from which its representational reading is derived. In the
case of *La Chute*, it is especially difficult to arrive at that endpoint where
there is a giving-up to *vertige*, because Camus himself seemed unwilling to
abandon authorial control. In the epigraph from Lermontov's *A Hero of
Our Time* which was chosen for the American edition of *The Fall*, Camus
calls his work "a portrait, but not of an individual; it is the aggregate of
the vices of our whole generation in their fullest expression." This would
indicate that we as readers should interpret *La Chute* as the indirectly stated
discourse of a *Zeitgeist*, that Clamence's confessions originate in a definable
guilt that is in fact our guilt. But such a reading presupposes the absolute
solidity of a central point around which the *récit* constitutes itself through an
internally verifiable logical coherence. Is guilt a given, the base upon which
Clamence's story is well anchored, or is there a story of the origin of guilt
which, in telling how *La Chute* unravels itself from the center, thrusts the
narrator into the *démesure* of dizziness? To encounter this question directly
is to read the dramatic episode in which Clamence stands by passively while
a woman apparently drowns.

THE MISREADING OF "GUILT": THE ORIGIN OF NARRATION

Like Dante's Hell, the narrative of *La Chute* is constructed concentri-
cally around a point that supports the entire verbal edifice. However, whereas

the movement of the pilgrim and his guide in the *Inferno* is that of a down-
ward spiral toward the figure of Satan, and therefore toward a direct physical
confrontation with the embodiment of Evil, *La Chute* is best described as
a series of circles receding outward from an origin which is subsequently
lost from view, much like the immediately disappearing pattern made by a
pebble thrown into water. The pebble itself, or cause, is quickly forgotten
in favor of its effect—the rippling waves it produces. Similarly, critical readings of *La Chute* have focused on the way Clamence defers his account of
guilt-causation and on the self-revelations that result from the later strategic
use of confessional discourse. The passage that produces guilt is either para-
phrased transparently or repressed, in an interesting mimicry of Clamence's
own repressions. To *read* what happened on the November night of the protagonist's "cowardice," however, is to analyze the rhetorical disruption that
inhabits the exact center of *La Chute:*

> Cette nuit-là, en novembre, deux ou trois ans avant le soir où je
> crus entendre rire dans mon dos, je regagnais la rive gauche, et
> mon domicile, par le pont Royal. . . . Sur le pont, je passai derrière
> une forme penchée sur le parapet, et qui semblait regarder le
> fleuve. De plus près, je distinguai une mince jeune femme, ha-
> billée de noir. Entre les cheveux sombres et le col du manteau, on
> voyait seulement une nuque, fraîche et mouillée, à laquelle je fus
> sensible. . . . J'avais déjà parcouru une cinquantaine de mètres à
> peu près, lorsque *j'entendis le bruit,* qui malgré la distance, me
> parut formidable dans le silence nocturne, *d'un corps qui s'abat
> sur l'eau.* Je m'arrêtai net, mais sans me retourner. Presque aus-
> sitôt *j'entendis un cri, plusieurs fois répété, qui descendait lui
> aussi le fleuve,* puis s'éteignit brusquement. Le silence qui suivit,
> dans la nuit soudain figée, me parut interminable. Je voulus courir
> et je ne bougeai pas. Je tremblais, je crois, de froid et de saisisse-
> ment. Je me disais qu'il fallait faire vite et je sentais une faiblesse
> irrésistible envahir mon corps. J'ai oublié ce que j'ai pensé alors.
> "Trop tard, trop loin . . ." ou quelque chose de ce genre.

> (On that night, in November, two or three years before the even-
> ing I thought I heard laughter coming from behind me, I was
> crossing the Pont Royal to the Left Bank, to return to my apart-
> ment. . . . On the bridge, I passed behind a human form, bent
> over the parapet, that seemed to be looking at the river. From a
> closer remove, I could discern a slender young woman, dressed in

black. Between her dark hair and the collar of her coat, one could only see the back of her neck, fresh and moist, to which I was not insensitive. . . . I had already moved away by some fifty meters, when *I heard the noise,* which, despite the distance, seemed to me extraordinarily loud in the nocturnal silence, *of a body falling into water.* I stopped in my tracks, but without turning around. Almost immediately, *I heard a cry, repeated several times, which also seemed to follow the river's course,* then suddenly was extinguished. The silence that followed, in the now frozen night, seemed to me interminable. I wanted to run yet could not move. I was trembling, I think, from the cold and the shock. I said to myself that I had to act quickly and I felt an irresistible weakness overcome my body. I forgot what I thought then. "Too late, too far . . ." or something in that vein.)

(*La Chute*, my emphasis)

The most apparent effect of the episode is to inculpate Clamence, to condemn him for lack of action. He has seen a woman, heard a suspiciously revealing noise, and has not shown the slightest sign of altruistic behavior. He has allowed a suicide to occur, the critics tell us. But what is the textual origin of this "death"? A literal reading of the passage that respects the evidence of Camus's wording reveals only a series of juxtaposed perceptions: the protagonist sees a woman who appeals to him sensually, hears the sound of a body falling, followed by a cry. The rhetoric of Clamence and the logic of representation cause us to combine these elements in a coherent picture: we conclude quickly that it is the woman seen on the bridge who falls, and that her death is Clamence's crime of passivity. The text is persuasive enough to render all this believable and pathetic. On the purely literal level of the discourse's immediate significance, however, the dramatic center is nothing more than the enigma of an *invisible absence* which, through a subject's erroneous interpretation, becomes clothed in the language of guilt.

By reading *La Chute* from the center outward, by respecting the unbridgeable gap between falsely perceived cause and invented effect, we necessarily reverse the priorities implicit in the usual interpretation of the *récit* as illustration or clarification of the main character's obsessions. The initial moment of the woman's fall is not in itself a given, a proven exemplary event that supports and justifies the meanderings of the protagonist's talk; it is, rather, the act of separation of the center from all conceivable analytical explanations which, paradoxically, "grounds" the text and allows it to function without limit. Clamence loses the substantiality of the knowing subject, since his own origin is not in self-knowledge or even self-debasement—which comes only later, after he has forged a language of guilt to cover the nothingness of the center—but in the *cry* of his Latin name ("clamans"), in the recognition of the inevitable lateness of his words: "Trop tard, trop loin [Too late, too far]." His exclamation, which adds to the pathos of represented events—the woman is gone, perhaps already drowned—is simultaneously an expression of his language's freedom to create, quite literally, from nothing.

The psychological coherence of Clamence's discourse, the clarity of his confessional voice, arise from a misreading of the dizziness that is the textual movement of *La Chute*. It has been the purpose of this essay to show that Camus's enigmatic *récit*, although it may have been consciously (authorially) conceived as a text about our modern imprisonment in guilt, became, in the actual writing, the *dérobade* by which narration reveals its ironic relationship to the subject-matter or message it conveys. *La Chute* hides its significance in the *abyme* of intertextuality, so that its repetition of the dizziness process performed by the texts it "reads" remains enclosed in darkness; and when it illustrates the logical contradiction on which its central drama is based, it does so with such blinding clarity as to go unseen. My study is a bringing-to-the-light of what Blanchot had said with a certain secretiveness. In rendering explicit his interpretation of Camus, I have been obliged to name and rename that generality in which the writer is swallowed up, and which can be called "dizziness," "game/play," "laughter," and "the truth of literary language." No doubt this naming is the result of a fundamental tendency in language to say what is beyond words, to create a coherent metaphorics where there is nothing but a void demanding interpretation. But the naming is inevitable and productive of meanings. If Clamence had not identified his crime and assumed the cloak of guilt, there could have been no representable actions or matter for confession, but only the hovering around an absent center whose proper expression is silence.

ENGLISH SHOWALTER, JR.

"The Growing Stone":
Reconciliation and Conclusion

"The Artist at Work" broke the pattern of the first four stories [of *Exile and the Kingdom*] in several ways; it used a new narrative perspective, it covered an entire life rather than a single day, it was set in Paris rather than North Africa. The final story also departs from the original pattern in some of the same ways. In its simplest outline, "The Growing Stone" relates the arrival of an engineer in an isolated town and his acceptance by the townspeople. The engineer, D'Arrast, is French; the town, Iguape, is in Brazil. The story opens with an extended account of the trip to Iguape, in a car driven by a native of the region, named Socrates; the most remarkable incident is crossing a river on a primitive ferry. In the town, D'Arrast meets the notables, the Mayor, the Judge, the Harbor Captain, and the Chief of Police, who makes trouble over D'Arrast's passport. He then visits the poor area near the river, where he is to design a flood control dike. There he meets a Cook, who becomes a key figure. Iguape has a shrine, centered around a miraculous stone that grows; and the church has a statue of Jesus, which arrived by "swimming" upstream. The Cook has made a vow to carry a large stone to the church in a procession, but he succumbs to his love of dancing the night before and is too weak to fulfill his promise. D'Arrast picks up the stone and carries it past the church to the Cook's hut, where he places it in the center of the room. The Cook's family invite him to sit down with them.

This summary, despite its brevity, gives some idea of the comparatively cluttered action. Peripheral characters abound; numerous incidents remain

From *Exiles and Strangers: A Reading of Camus's* Exile and the Kingdom. © 1984 by Ohio State University Press.

unresolved, although the action is spread over a span of several days. The unifying thread is, of course, D'Arrast; but it is not his desire or will that propels the plot. He has come on a mission, yet the story ends before he has really begun his work. He asserts himself in various ways: he asks to visit the poor section, he insists that the Police Chief not be punished, and he seizes the Cook's stone. Yet in a sense, he is almost pure consciousness, for he seems to have no memories, no feelings, no expectations. In the face of such disturbances as the drunken Police Chief's threats, or the hostility of the old Negro whose hut he is shown, or his exclusion from the dance, D'Arrast's cool tranquillity reminds one of the legendary heroes of the Hollywood western.

The Brazilian setting, itself an anomaly, puts these events in a context radically different from the North African stories. Where they were arid and lonely, Iguape is humid and teeming with life of all kinds, including people. Even Jonas does not encounter as diverse a group, and the crowds in his apartment remain anonymous ciphers, whereas the Iguapeans assume vivid and individual lives in "The Growing Stone." In part, this results from D'Arrast's insistence on visiting the humblest part of town and from his ability to talk to people like his chauffeur or a cook. Even before D'Arrast articulates his comprehensive interest in humanity, however, the reader can sense a new kind of fraternal feeling, in the evocation of the ferryboat men or the Japanese living in the jungle. There is an extraordinary babble of voices and languages around D'Arrast, and a mixture of nationalities, races, and classes.

D'Arrast moves into this world with almost perfect freedom. Although he recalls a recent crisis, in terms that link him to other characters, he remains unencumbered by it. Neither guilt nor frustration surfaces in his thoughts. Moreover, he shows as little concern for the future as for the past. He has come to build a dike, but expresses no impatience to get started. He manifests no desire to return home to France, either. This description makes him sound completely passive, but that is inaccurate; he possesses a great deal of energy and, in certain key situations, takes initiatives. Understanding the story depends largely on identifying the peculiar qualities of those situations. D'Arrast is free, like the heroes of eighteenth-century philosophical tales. Camus has left him undetermined so that he may act freely and, in that freedom, confront the moral issues that the other characters found thrust upon them.

In the foreground of the story are the relations between D'Arrast and the people of Iguape. D'Arrast never suffers the kind of isolation that becomes the lot of the Renegade or Daru, and the end of the story shows him being invited to join a group, as the beginning had shown him on comradely terms with Socrates. This easy sociability does not mean that his contacts with others arise automatically, however, or that they encounter no obstacles. Even the genial Socrates has an annoying, though involuntary, trait: he keeps D'Arrast from sleeping with his "cataclysmic" sneezing.

D'Arrast's friendship with the Cook grows under still more trying circumstances. At their first meeting, when the Cook tells about his vow, "D'Arrast felt slightly annoyed," but he agrees to participate in the ceremony anyway. By evening, when they go to the dancing together, they seem to be on close terms, but the Cook jeopardizes that closeness by sending D'Arrast away. He addresses him "coldly, as if speaking to a stranger," and tells him "they don't want you to stay now." Furthermore, the Cook reneges on his resolution not to dance and rebuffs D'Arrast, who had been invited partly to help him keep the promise. D'Arrast sustains and even imposes the fraternal solidarity between them by ignoring these slights and committing his own energies to what he takes to be the most genuine of the Cook's desires.

The Cook serves in part to represent a special community, the Negroes who live in the huts by the river and who are the most impoverished citizens of Iguape. At first, D'Arrast's efforts to make contacts among them are met with hostility. Only because the Harbor Captain speaks to the Negroes "in a tone of command" is D'Arrast able to gratify his desire to visit one of the huts. When no volunteers come forward, the man to whom the order is delivered obeys it with a hostile look. And it is in the name of the whole community that the Cook requests D'Arrast to leave the dance.

To outward appearances, the Police Chief raises a more daunting challenge. He wears the uniform of authority, and his demand that D'Arrast show his passport would ordinarily presage continual harassment. In fact, he is made to back down almost instantly by the Judge; but for D'Arrast a new problem arises immediately in place of the first: the Judge insists that D'Arrast decide on a punishment for the Police Chief. D'Arrast temporizes, and tries to evade the responsibility; the Judge reminds him several times, however, and requires that he pronounce a sentence. Ultimately, D'Arrast finds the solution in a graceful speech appealing for leniency as a special favor so that his stay in Iguape "could begin in a climate of peace and friendship."

The incident has no further repercussions. Its arbitrary inclusion calls attention to its importance for Camus as a final statement on the theme of justice. We never learn why the policeman behaved so boorishly, except that he was drunk; but if that is the whole explanation, we never learn why the citizens so urgently demand that he be punished. It is a virtually pure exercise in judicial reasoning, thrust upon D'Arrast by the circumstances. D'Arrast, unlike Daru, rises to the occasion. He finds the formula that will both accomplish his wish, that the offender be pardoned, and satisfy the legitimate need of the community to affirm its laws. He finds within the ethical code of the Iguapeans themselves the pretext for the pardon, and at the same time assumes full responsibility for the judgment. It was precisely this gesture that Daru failed to make, either for Balducci or for the Arab.

Once that hurdle has been cleared, however, D'Arrast finds no barriers to communication with the wealthy and powerful citizens. All of them except the Police Chief had welcomed him enthusiastically from the start, and once the Judge has pronounced his verdict acceptable, D'Arrast enjoys the full favor of the community. Instead of settling comfortably into it, D'Arrast moves on to the sterner challenge of the poor people in the huts. When, from his vantage on the balcony, he sees that the Cook has faltered, D'Arrast leaves the company of the notables and rejoins the common people in the crowd. He takes the Cook's burden on his own shoulders, but he does not exactly fulfill the Cook's vow. He passes by the church and instead carries the stone to the Cook's hut. There he awaits the decision of the Cook's family and friends whether his action has earned him acceptance or not. The verdict is again favorable; he is invited to sit down among them. Once more, D'Arrast has succeeded in meeting the standards of the society around him without betraying his own convictions. He has not pretended to have a faith he lacks, and has graphically shown that his own faith is in people. At the same time, he has taken seriously the beliefs of the others, and shared their sense of responsibility if not the faith behind it. Consequently, he achieves the fraternal union that he sought, by reconciling his values and theirs.

The bonds that D'Arrast forms between himself and other individuals represent possibilities of fraternal links across many kinds of social barrier. In virtually every story, the main characters are isolated by the most ordinary differences. They belong to different races or civilizations or economic classes from the people around them. D'Arrast shares all these signs of difference. He comes to Iguape as an exemplar of European civilization, with all that implies of knowledge and power. His sole reason for being there is to put his superior skill as an engineer at the service of a less-advanced society. Of course, both Daru and the Renegade intended to carry out similar missions. The risks of misunderstanding are great, as the industrial nations have learned to their dismay in the real world. The benefits of technology and material gains seem worthless if they must be purchased through self-abasement.

D'Arrast must, then, offer his superior skills without making the beneficiaries feel inferior. Perhaps it is for this reason that Camus so completely neglects the actual construction project for which D'Arrast has come. The engineer begins by trying to learn about, and from, the people of Iguape. The significance of the name Socrates also becomes clear in this context. Despite the initial impression of comic irony, the name should be taken seriously as designating a wise man. The traditional wisdom of the Greek Socrates was to pretend ignorance and question others. The Brazilian Socrates embodies a genuine wisdom in his relative ignorance, and D'Arrast becomes his disciple, a seeker, not a dispenser, of the truth.

It is in very similar fashion that D'Arrast resolves the judicial problem, as we have just seen. For the European, D'Arrast's leniency expresses the highest ideals of liberal justice, whereas the local citizens' demand for punishment seems vindictive and harsh. So it may be, but we may not assume the moral superiority of "ours" over "theirs," of civilization over primitive society. In the end, they prove to be quite capable of encompassing a pardon within their own code, and this resolution of the question of justice is simultaneously a reconciliation of the two civilizations.

Of all the difficulties that D'Arrast must confront, none poses more profound challenges than religion. Class, language, race, or wealth might seem in the real world to be the chief obstacles to human solidarity. From the perspective of the Camusian hero, however, these problems are illusory; it suffices for the person with the apparent advantage to put aside prejudice, in order for the real equality of all people to become manifest. The European's superior technical knowledge was actually a graver difficulty; the engineering skill of D'Arrast is no illusion. In this case, however, the barrier can still be overcome because the technician and the ordinary people share the same sense of purpose. It seems less plausible that they should find a shared sense of faith. Camus's anxious pursuit of the truth about humanity's place in the universe led to a passionate skepticism that seems incompatible with sophisticated liberal religions, much less with the Cook's superstitious faith.

Yet even here, D'Arrast achieves a reconciliation, in part because he listens respectfully to the Cook's ideas about God, but also because the Cook's faith strangely resembles Camus's skepticism. The Cook's religion provides no dogmatic answers to the questions that haunt Camus. The universe retains all of its capricious indifference to human needs, and the good Jesus answers prayers according to his own inscrutable judgments. With so honest a recognition of the truth, the Cook's superstitions about miracles and vows appear no more than a naive formulation of the very problems that concern D'Arrast, and Camus—how human beings fit into the world around them, and how they can act responsibly. The local priest is conspicuously absent from the group of dignitaries who welcome D'Arrast, and with whom D'Arrast establishes the first cordial relations. The reconciliation with religion is not achieved with the likes of the Renegade, or Father Paneloux or the prison chaplain from Camus's earlier works. It is only with a simple man, as direct and honest in his faith as D'Arrast in his unbelief, that this last division between people can be closed.

The severest trial occurs at the Negroes' dance, which is actually a religious ritual reminiscent of the Taghâsans' fetish worship. The dancers' hut shelters an altar with "a magnificent colored print in which Saint George, with alluring grace, was getting the better of a bewhiskered dragon." Even in this apparently Christian image, violence predominates. Beneath the altar, however, stands a little statue "representing a horned god . . . with a fierce look . . . brandishing an oversized knife made of silver paper." Obviously the faith of the Iguapeans spans the whole range from savage ancient deities to modern Christianity. As the ceremony progresses, these hints of bloodshed are realized when the dark girl appears, as a central figure in the dance, holding "a green-and-yellow bow with an arrow on the tip of which was spitted a multicolored bird."

Many elements of the ceremony resemble scenes from the hut of the fetish in Taghâsa, beginning with the rhythmic dance. In Iguape as in the city of salt, the people are transformed into animals, uttering inarticulate sounds, shrieks, howls, and "a strange bird cry." One woman, "rolling her animal face from side to side, kept barking." The participants enter into a collective frenzy, they are "possessed of the spirit," they fall to the floor in exhaustion. Some are masked, and all, even the Cook, are transfigured into distorted forms. In their own view, they become "the god's field of battle," and the double axhead of the fetish reappears as the short saber wielded by the Negro dancers.

D'Arrast's place in this ceremony is problematic. He is, to be sure, an outsider. Almost as soon as he arrives, he is singled out by the leader as an impediment: "Unfold your arms . . . you are hugging yourself and keeping the saint's spirit from descending," the Cook explains to him. D'Arrast complies, and perhaps there is a grain of truth in the implicit criticism of his egotism and withdrawal. Immediately afterward, D'Arrast begins to resemble a "bestial god" himself, albeit a kindly one. He remains pressed against the wall, like the Renegade, drawn unconsciously into the communal experience at moments, but excluded from real participation. The heat and smoke nauseate him, as the bitter drink had sickened the Renegade. Finally he is rejected by his guide and ordered to leave.

We must not, of course, push the parallel between D'Arrast and the

Renegade too far. D'Arrast is never beaten or mutilated or physically mistreated in any way. The similarities permit us to make some connections, but not to equate the two. D'Arrast is, in fact, a false victim, almost a decoy. He could have made his plight worse by stubborn resistance or by self-pity, but as we have seen, he characteristically accepts rebuffs and frustrations with equanimity. And indeed, the real victim of the ceremony is not D'Arrast but the Cook.

The Cook has already once been designated as the symbolic scapegoat, when he was drowning. He was rescued then, he believes, by the good Jesus, to whom he made a vow. At the dance, he gives in to his love of dancing, to the cigars, to the eroticism; and the next day he cannot fulfill his vow. The ritual has been a trap for him, and in his own mind it has caused him to be cast back into the sea. In the procession, we recognize him as the victim again, for he is dying of the effort to carry the stone, and resembles Christ carrying the cross. This time, only when D'Arrast intervenes is the fatal sacrifice thwarted.

D'Arrast survives the ritual because of his respect for others. Unlike the Renegade, he had not come to convert these people. Whatever he may think of the cult of Saint George or the horned god, he feels no need to impose his beliefs on the celebrants. When told to unfold his arms, he offers no resistance; when ordered to leave, he goes willingly. He accepts as much participation as the people will allow him and demands no more.

The next day, at the procession, however, he seizes a role. By relieving the Cook, he assumes for himself the function of the scapegoat. At the same time, he asserts a new doctrine; for when he bypasses the church, he changes the nature of his gesture. Instead of laying the stone, and his exhausted body, as a sacrifice before the sacred altar, he returns the stone to the midst of the people and actually makes a new altar of it. Symbolically, a new order has been founded, no longer dependent on the violent casting out of evil, but devoted to an affirmation of human wholeness and solidarity.

"The Growing Stone" carries the process to an even greater length, however. The profound solitude of the earlier characters meant not only their sense of separation from each other but also their feeling of alienation from the material world. Their moments of illumination involve an ephemeral intuition of oneness with the desert, with the cracking stones and with the wheeling stars. As we noted before, the setting of this last story is no longer an arid landscape, but rather a teeming jungle. As the title suggests, in this climate the very stones may come alive and start to grow. Suddenly there is a joining of the animate and inanimate. The movement that was imperceptible in the Saharan desert can be seen all around in the Brazilian rain forest.

In several of the other stories, water and the sea have appeared fleet-
ingly as images of harmony between the human and the material universe.
In Iguape, the flow is universal. D'Arrast first appears crossing a river, he
awakens into a rain, and he has come to control the flow of yet another river.
The sea too is close by, and the Cook worked on a ship. The plunge into the
water, a motif we have seen in *The Fall* and "The Artist at Work," is most
fully realized in the Cook; but the statue of Jesus too swam in the sea, and
D'Arrast plunges into a symbolic sea, the human tide of the procession. In
the final moment, the river has become part of D'Arrast; he feels his joy as a
flow within him. Thus "The Growing Stone" concludes the collection on a
vision of almost total reconciliation. Not merely all people but all things and
all people are somehow joined in a common feeling and a common purpose.

These happy images do not, however, supply answers to the philosophical questions at the base of Camus's thought. What takes place in Iguape
is no permanent solution, even for D'Arrast and for his newfound friends.
Eventually, they must part; the Frenchman will have to return to France, and
the Iguapeans will go about their lives as before, although presumably without the regular floods. This, as we noted before, is a philosophical tale, which
particularizes abstract ideas while it simplifies reality. Iguape is Camus's El
Dorado, the home of an ideal community.

Candide returned from El Dorado of his own free will. The timeless uni-
formity of Voltaire's utopia was in fact boring, and Candide came to regret
the very evil that had caused his expulsion from the paradise of Thunder-
ten-tronckh, the differences of status among people. Candide wanted to go
home and be richer than anyone else.

Camus's utopia has far more plausibility, and its fatal flaw is not in its
structure but simply in the nature of things: it cannot last. It is a fortunate
combination of circumstances and people ready to appreciate them. Such
moments of shared joy are as much miracles as the stone or the statue of
Iguape. It is as if they too wash up occasionally from the sea, along with
the wreckage, the drownings, the floods. The lesson we should take from
the story is to be prepared to seize the moment when it comes. D'Arrast
contributes his part in creating the miracle of reconciliation, partly through
the very practical actions that we have seen. The central gesture, however,
defies rationality. In seizing the Cook's stone, D'Arrast perfectly illustrates
the need to take the burden one finds at hand. Neither the vow he fulfills nor
the load he bears is what he might have chosen, but our choices are never
entirely free. The hope that Camus offers us is that by making the choices
that do come our way, we may indeed overcome that solitude and despair by
affirming our human solidarity.

As we remarked in the beginning of the chapter, "The Growing Stone" seems anomalous in *Exile and the Kingdom* because of its loose structure, its profusion of characters, and its exotic setting. Furthermore, the ending seems strikingly more hopeful than in any of the first five stories. As the final story, it occupies a position of unusual importance in the collection, for it will largely determine the overall impression. To the degree that readers perceive unity and order, they must depend heavily on "The Growing Stone" to provide the sense of an ending, to make the diverse characters, events, and themes cohere. On closer examination, we will see that the apparent strangeness of this concluding story conceals many strong links to all the other stories—so many, in fact, that the optimism of the ending may require a retrospective rereading of the whole work.

To a remarkable extent, the main characters of all six stories are alike, and begin in like situations. All are middle-aged and feel themselves at a point of crisis. Their dreams have gone unfulfilled, their energies are waning, their hopes are gone. With Janine and Yvars, the detailed realization of their aging occupies much of the story. Of all the characters, the Renegade has most flatly failed; and he tries to murder his own past when he kills the new missionary, who might have succeeded where he had failed. With these three, recollections of their disappointments obsess them. Even Daru, who had apparently found his place in his little desert schoolhouse, is led by the arrival of the prisoner to recall his first days there and his early frustrations. Daru, however, has come to need the colorlessness, the solitude, the silence, just as Janine needs Marcel, Yvars his trade, and the Renegade his masters.

Since Jonas's whole career is told, he presents a slightly different case; the critical moment does not begin until quite late in the story, when his inspiration deserts him. No incident occurs, but a progressive paralysis of the will and a growing indifference to his work. A few key phrases bring out the analogy to the others, however: "for the first time, he was bothered by the people he kept bumping into everywhere" and "the cold pierced him to the marrow." Jonas's progressive breakdown leads, not to a single dramatic revelation, but to idleness, drink, and womanizing, until his wife's sorrow leads him to make one last effort; and his final painting is comparable to the visions of the other characters.

D'Arrast thinks less about his past than the others, and we learn relatively little about it. Outwardly, he seems happy and successful, but there are signs that he too has reached a point of crisis. In response to the Cook's questions, he reveals that he once made a promise, "in a shipwreck?—If you wish," and he goes on to say, "Someone was about to die through my fault. It seems to me that I called out.—Did you promise?—No. I should have liked to promise.—Long ago?—Not long before coming here." And finally: "I used to be proud; now I'm alone." Whatever one infers from this discreet confession, which makes D'Arrast sound a little like Jonas, Clamence, or Tarrou, it plainly implies a recent personal failure of some sort. Moreover, like Janine and the others, D'Arrast feels a vague longing, of which he grows most aware after seeing the stone of the title: "He too was waiting in front of the grotto under the same film of water, and he didn't know for what. He had been waiting constantly, to tell the truth, for a month since he had arrived in this country." D'Arrast's prestige and success as an engineer overlay a dissatisfaction comparable to all the others, expressed in terms that are in fact identical to Janine's.

The six central figures, differing widely in profession and class and intellect, nonetheless all share the trait of physical solidity. D'Arrast is called a colossus; Janine suffers from her large body; Jonas is tall and rugged. Yvars has dry, hard muscles like a vinestock, Daru is broad and powerful enough to break the Arab in half, and the Renegade has a hard, mulish head. To all of them, their bodies seem encumbrances. Janine and Yvars especially feel themselves stiffening and weakening. The Renegade has been tortured and mutilated. Jonas collapses from fatigue at the end of the story, after feeling increasingly cramped in his crowded apartment. Even Daru is bothered by the Arab's presence, and feels vulnerable. D'Arrast feels nauseated, suffers from a migraine, and almost collapses, despite his strength. The importance of their solid bodies is emphasized by the regular contrasts to the other characters. D'Arrast dominates everyone else, especially the short, fat Cook and the small, thin Socrates.

Camus shows no concern for a psychological or sociological analysis of these characters. He makes no effort to sentimentalize their plights, and even less to generalize about the social conditions. Daru and D'Arrast have virtually no past. The factors that have affected the other characters' lives—the war that ruined Marcel's business, the Renegade's peasant origins, Jonas's broken home—are not perceived by the characters themselves as determinant. In every case, the central event concerns a person who must confront his or her own limitations, whether personal, physical, or professional. They have slightly different substance in each story, but in each there is a moment of failure and loss, which gains plausibility from the fact that it corresponds to a well-documented moment of crisis in the average person's life; but Camus always stresses the moral and philosophical implications, never the social or historical causes. The limits encountered by all the characters are, in the final analysis, those of human mortality and human existence in the absurd universe. Janine is most explicit about the underlying source of her anxiety: "She too was afraid of death." As the first story of the collection, "The Adulterous Woman" serves as a kind of preface and suggests that the nameless anxiety that comes to all the central figures springs from a similar origin. The bodies, originally strong and healthy, bring the first warnings of the impending crisis. These characters' vigor, at an earlier date, was a delusion of possibilities, an appearance of superiority to the common fate that allowed them to be indifferent to their place. Their European origins, in the context of Algerian and Brazilian settings, reinforce this notion. Although in various ways they all admit to having held this illusion of infinite capacity or eternal youth, Jonas most concretely expresses the idea in his "star," as if the universe were watching over him. Ultimately, though, reality demands the same price from him as from everyone else, whether he recognizes it or not. He too has to agonize; he too has to sacrifice; he too has to drive his body to the limits of endurance, as D'Arrast most dramatically does in the final pages of the book, carrying the stone.

While the body provides one form of warning, the settings of the stories consistently provide another. At the start of each one, the central character is isolated, spiritually if not physically. For Jonas and D'Arrast, the realization of their solitude comes to them well into the story. But D'Arrast's triumph over isolation is all the more impressive because he is so strikingly alone and out of place. Along with the sense of loneliness, Camus creates an atmosphere of disorientation. The long introductory section of "The Growing Stone," where D'Arrast travels through night and mist, drifting in and out of sleep, waking into dreamlike scenes such as the Japanese settlement, serves in part to recapitulate similar scenes in the other stories—Janine riding through the sandstorm, Yvars and the Renegade in the blinding light, Daru looking at a landscape made featureless by snow, and Jonas sitting long hours in the dark.

Camus constructs his stories so as to emphasize the strangeness of the familiar. As the characters look about them, their habitual settings seem altered and well-known objects unrecognizable. The discomfort they feel in their bodies extends to all the material world. For D'Arrast, as for Janine, a journey into foreign territory provides the initial shock; but with all the characters, the sense of growing separation from the physical world is meant to translate for us the awareness of a radical alienation, the awakening of a rational mind in a meaningless universe of things.

Having set each of the stories in motion with a similar structure, Camus proceeds by means of a number of repeated motifs and themes. By motif, I mean simply a specific object or situation that recurs; by theme, an idea that is explicitly mentioned. Many of these are familiar, not only in these stories, but also in Camus's other works. Many critics have looked for the works' coherence in the themes of exile and the kingdom, for example, or of solidarity and fraternity, or the motifs of the natural environment, sun, sea, desert, and so on.

For Camus, stone is the fundamental image of the concrete universe, and appears in many forms. The mystical stones of the final story, "The Growing Stone," point to the positive symbolism; the stone is humanity's burden of responsibility, akin to Sisyphus's stone. The growing stone of the grotto, consecrated by superstition, nonetheless represents the fruitful cooperation of people and their environment. D'Arrast, one of those (like Dr. Rieux) who fight against creation as they found it by building roads and dikes, may at the same time learn from the humble acceptance he observes among these poor Brazilians. The struggle to dominate nature can never be won; even the stones may grow again. The other stone, which D'Arrast carries to fulfill the Cook's vow, shows human solidarity at its finest, in the struggle with the world. D'Arrast bears it to the Cook's hut rather than to the church, for his faith is in people, not gods. Inside the hut, it occupies the central place, in the middle of the human circle, like a kind of altar to humanity.

As we have seen, stone was important in all the other stories except "The Artist at Work"; but once again, it is the first story, "The Adulterous Woman," to which the concluding story seems most fitting as a response. For Janine, stone represented not only the harsh real world around her but also something spiritual, linked to the Mosaic law. In her climactic swoon, she discovers a oneness with the universe, stars and stones alike. D'Arrast actually becomes part of this universe. Like the miraculous statue, he "bucks the human tide" to come to the Cook's aid; like the miraculous stone, he grows "taller and more massive each time he came back to life" in the beginning, then "straightening up until he was suddenly enormous" at the end. The waters of the river, whose sound fills him with "a tumultuous happiness," also flow within him as a "surge of obscure and panting joy," just as the water of the night had filled Janine.

Most of the characters have not understood their place in the material universe at the start, if they ever do. They learn from a new experience of pain, but also by reaching a point from which to take a broader view. At the same time, this perspective may suggest a feeling of superiority to the world and to others, which must be overcome or surrendered before peace can be felt. All the characters grow aware of their feelings on elevations—Janine on her parapet, Daru on his hill, Jonas in his loft, and D'Arrast on the balcony.

If revelation occurs on the heights, however, the hero must come back down to profit from the experience. Again, D'Arrast illustrates the most positive instance of this descent; on the balcony with the town notables, he awaits the procession, but leaves instantly when the Cook does not appear with the others. Down among the people, he first tries to revive the Cook, then takes up the stone himself. The analogies both of action and of language between Janine and D'Arrast are unmistakable; retrospectively, Janine's return to her husband may be regarded as a necessary resumption of her human responsibilities. Daru and Yvars remain on their elevations at the end of their stories, not necessarily punished, but still unable to integrate their own happiness and the conditions of their lives. The Renegade and Jonas are brought down, the one by force, the other by exhaustion, and therefore with quite opposite expectations. Both were wrong, however—the Renegade to suppose that he could serve a god, Jonas to suppose that a god (his star) existed to serve him. The Renegade must learn the truth in the most brutal fashion, getting a mouthful of salt when he was aching with thirst. Jonas, on the other hand, in painting the ambiguous solidary/solitary canvas, seems to be on the road to a productive compromise, especially since he has reaffirmed his love of his family and the beauty of the noises of humanity without abandoning his art. Still, like his Old Testament namesake, he had to learn love as well as courage.

One of the most common episodes in Camus's stories, as we saw in "The Silent Men," is a meal or a drink. Part of a long heritage of symbolism, the act of consuming links people with the material world on the one hand, and with the divinity, through Communion, on the other. Shared meals have a complex ritual, itself full of meanings to those who understand it. D'Arrast illustrates the full possibilities of the communal meal. Significantly, his friend among the Brazilians is a ship's cook, whose work is to prepare the nourishment of others. D'Arrast shares several drinks of hospitality, and several official dinners; but the most important is the dinner of black beans the Cook makes specially for D'Arrast. At the end of the story, when D'Arrast has borne the stone to the Cook's hut, the circle re-forms around the hearth, and D'Arrast is welcomed to his place. The collection thus ends on a note of harmony and brotherhood.

"The Growing Stone" contains a great deal of dialog compared with the earlier stories of the book. In fact, the first three stories treat silence and the inability to communicate as a major theme. In "The Guest," although Daru can speak Arabic, yet his conversation with his guest goes continually awry. In the end, Daru's refusal to listen may have cost him his kingdom.

Both Jonas and D'Arrast, creative and professional men of the upper class and of Western Europe, escape the kind of muteness that afflicted the earlier characters. Jonas comes to suffer an artist's block, equivalent to a silence; as an artist, though, he takes on the responsibility for breaking through it. D'Arrast never seems troubled by lack of words; he responds forthrightly to the Cook's questions about his own background, about social conditions in France, and about his promise. Several times, Camus notes a hesitation on his part and on the Cook's part; but always the speaker goes ahead. D'Arrast is fortunate that his hosts, although Portuguese is their native language, chatter willingly in bad French or Spanish; but D'Arrast also speaks more than one language. D'Arrast's greatest linguistic accomplishment is to have found the words with which to judge the Police Chief; the rhetoric does no more than make acceptable to the others what D'Arrast had been saying all along. In reality, he avoids judging and punishing the Police Chief. Yet it is precisely the mark of D'Arrast's heroism that he accepts the challenge of communication at all levels. It was not sufficient for him to be morally right; he had to be so within a social context. His flattering speech is the sort of formula that Daru could not find for Balducci.

Language is, then, a key factor in Camus's moral vision. The early stories show that silence is not necessarily a "sin" or even a sign of dullness; many of the characters understand the truth of the human condition without being able to act upon it. The action alone may be a great achievement—the greater if the inarticulate hero goes unsung. Those who would fully realize Camus's ideal must assume a further burden, however, that of the writer himself, to convey something of that knowledge to others. Only by sharing experiences and the fruits of experience can human beings achieve solidarity among themselves. This is what D'Arrast achieves in many different areas, most of them already familiar to us from the other stories.

The six stories have in common not only themes and motif but also a general plot structure. Near the beginning, a character expresses or remembers hopes and expectations that have been disappointed. Then a change of some sort takes place, so that the disappointed character finds a new perspective on the events. By the end, a subtle reversal has occurred, and the original position is transformed into its opposite. The change may not be for the better, at least at the practical level; Daru rediscovers solitude, and the Renegade dies. Moreover, the change usually has little emotional impact on the reader, and frequently leaves us wondering what has actually happened. There are no melodramatic reunions, no heart-rending separations, no poetic justice, and no tragic mistakes.

With D'Arrast, the change is complex, but it produces hope. D'Arrast comes to Iguape as a prestigious outsider, to whom even the highest local officials defer; yet in the final scene, he waits to be invited to sit among the poorest folk of the town. A religious skeptic, he has fulfilled a pious, even superstitious, vow. He has calmly tolerated abuse from the Chief of Police and exclusion from the Negroes' dancing. But the rewards for these reversals are similar, more positive changes: the foreigner has found a kind of home, the lonely man has found friends, the exile has found a kingdom. When D'Arrast arrived, he brought not only his authority as an engineer and plans for construction but also a nameless longing and a recent personal failure. For once, the revelation comes to a person ready to accept it, the opportunity is seized; and if our final view of D'Arrast is a strange one, it is nonetheless hard to see how it can be anything but hopeful. But what has happened to D'Arrast is enough like what happened to Janine, to Yvars, to Daru, to Jonas, and even to the Renegade, that his small victory must imply theirs, too.

The reason for the lack of high drama in the plots is that the changes happen within. Even where a striking event occurs, such as the Renegade's murder or Lassalle's daughter's seizure, the external conditions are not altered so much as the central figure's awareness and understanding of them. The stories show people confronting the realization that things are not what they seem. The underlying purpose, of course, is to force the reader into the same situation; and so each story also induces an expectation on the reader's part that proves false. There is a transaction between author and reader that parallels the one described in the text.

In several cases, the very title sets up a false expectation or prepares an ironic misunderstanding. The Adulterous Woman commits no adultery; The Artist at Work ceases to work; the Silent Men include finally the boss as well as the men; The Guest—l'hôte—may be host or guest, Daru or the Arab, either in either role. Often the apparent action turns out to be secondary as well; Janine has no affair with the jackal-soldier; the workmen do not confront the boss; the prisoner never challenges Daru; even the Renegade's murder of the new missionary matters less than his sudden reconversion to a religion of mercy.

"The Growing Stone" is yet another misleading title, for the miraculous growing stone is not the most important stone, the one carried by the Cook and D'Arrast. In some sense, however, the title informs the whole story; metaphorically, the two stones are the same, and represent the material world successfully invested with human meanings. The stone they carry grows in a metaphorical sense too, as its weight becomes more and more painful and harder to bear. In the context of Exile and the Kingdom, the stone D'Arrast seizes and carries is a reply to the stone Daru flings away; the stone that

grows is a contrast to the stones Janine hears cracking into dust. Because the
story does not fulfill the immediate implications of its title, we must look for
broader symbolic meanings.

In the haphazard development of the plot, "The Growing Stone" resembles some of the other stories as well. The relationship between D'Arrast
and Socrates, so important at the beginning, turns out to be incidental, like
Janine's with the jackal-soldier. D'Arrast's hostile encounter with the Police
Chief has no repercussions, like Daru's conflict with Balducci. The construction of the dike raises no dramatic issues, just as the strikers' return to
work leads to no confrontation in "The Silent Men." "The Growing Stone"
brings together an exceptionally large number of these false leads, potential
actions that never take place; but it is merely echoing a technique Camus
uses throughout. It is, in fact, only our readers' awareness of literary con-
ventions that leads us to see possible plots in every detail or incident. Our
belief in literary meaning resembles the faith of the Iguapeans in the Growing Stone: phenomena cannot be accidental when they appear so clearly to
signify something.

D'Arrast, however, remains uncommitted in his beliefs; Camus gives us
only his actions as clues to his mind. It is significant that in his climactic
gesture, even D'Arrast is portrayed as unaware of his motives: he leaves the
balcony "quick as lightning, without excusing himself," pushes through the
crowd in an "impetuous way," finds himself beside the Cook "without knowing how," takes the stone "suddenly," and changes course, bypassing the
church and heading for the hut, "without knowing why." D'Arrast possesses
from the start a strong sense of brotherhood with people and of unity with
the universe, which Janine glimpses momentarily in her dash to the parapet,
a gesture very much like D'Arrast's. Even D'Arrast, however, must allow
his instinctive fraternal love to direct his actions. His spontaneity, his tolerance, his freedom are partly learned from the people of Iguape, especially
the Cook.

The only strong desire D'Arrast expresses during the story is to visit
the poor section of the town. The traditional form of plot, where the hero's
will encounters obstacles until it imposes itself or is defeated, is present only
in this area. D'Arrast seems to want to be accepted among these people.
More than he wants to build the dike, more than he wants to conciliate
the notables, he wants to know the lives of Socrates, the Cook, the old
man, the dark girl, the pilgrims, the faithful. Besides the conventional virtues
of the poor—openness, directness, simplicity, and so on—the Cook gives
D'Arrast an important insight into his faith and his sense of place within
the universe. To D'Arrast's skeptical question, "Has the good Jesus always

answered you?" the Cook replies, "Always. . . . no, Captain!" D'Arrast triumphs: "Well, then?" But the Cook only laughs and responds, "Well, he's free, isn't he?" The Cook's relationship to reality is a fraternal one, built on an affectionate respect for the Other's freedom—in this case, the freedom of the entire external universe personified as Jesus. It is immediately after this conversation that D'Arrast finds the solution to the problem of the Police Chief, a solution that respects not only D'Arrast's principles and the Chief's freedom, but also the faith of the Judge and other notables in their system of order.

SUSAN TARROW

Exile from the Kingdom

> Si loin que je vive main-
> tenant de la terre où [je
> suis né], elle est restée
> ma vraie patrie et sa
> lumière me nourrit jusque
> dans la ville d'ombres, où
> le sort me retient.
> —"L'Enigme"

In the aftermath of the famous quarrel, Camus withdrew from Parisian social and intellectual circles: nor could he return to his roots, as Algeria resembled less and less the possible kingdom. All the stories in *Exile and the Kingdom,* published in 1957, deal with people who do not belong in the world in which they find themselves. In 1947 Camus had declared Algeria "my true homeland." But by 1950 he would write in his notebook: "Yes, I have a native land: the French language." There was no longer a land to which he belonged, but merely a form of expression; he became increasingly aware of his francophone core, an "Algerian Frenchman," while his sympathy for France and its values declined. And his recurrent episodes of artistic sterility were exacerbated by the fact that the French language was his medium; his inability to use it fruitfully underlined his feelings of exile.

Algeria was a paramount factor in political debate in France during the 1950s. The tug-of-war between East and West in Europe seemed to have ended in a stalemate, at least for the time being, and events in France's colonies were giving cause for alarm. The conflict in Indochina was decided

From *Exile from the Kingdom: A Political Rereading of Albert Camus.* © 1985 by the University of Alabama Press.

in 1954 with the fall of Dien Bien Phu to the Vietminh. Once Mendès-France had negotiated a settlement in 1955, he had to turn his attention to North Africa. Tunisia and Morocco were already suffering terrorist attacks by rebels and European right-wing extremists; the situation in Algeria had not yet deteriorated to the same degree, but the likelihood of violence was imminent, particularly since the problems of poverty and overpopulation were even more acute there than in the two neighboring countries. Decolonization dominated French political life in the fifties and sharply divided the country.

Camus returned briefly to journalism in 1955; he contributed articles to *L'Express* to support Mendès-France's candidacy for the premiership and to express his views on the Algerian situation. After an unsuccessful appeal for a civilian truce in Algiers in 1956, he withdrew from regular journalism, and limited his activities to behind-the-scenes interventions on behalf of imprisoned activists. The publication in 1958 of *Actuelles III: Chroniques algériennes* elicited scant reaction at a moment when violence was at its height, and de Gaulle had once more been called in to save France. Camus's call for a confederation seemed irrelevant, when the ultimate choice now lay between massive repression and the granting of independence.

The short stories of *Exile and the Kingdom* return to Camus's early themes of estrangement and misunderstanding. Many of the characters are misfits in their environment, even when they feel they belong there. Colonialism constitutes a major motif in the collection. Only one story, that of the artist at work, takes place in Paris, and the artist's name, significantly, is Jonas, the Douay name for the man who refused to prophesy against the city. Three of the stories—"The Adulterous Woman," "The Guest," and "The Silent Men"—are set in Algeria. "The Silent Men" presents an ironic portrayal of the myth of colonial conquest, a reversal of the prevailing view in France of the wealthy, oppressive *pied-noir*. In this story, the conflict is not racial but social: the workers, both European and Algerian, are united in defiance of the owner of the small cooper's shop where they are employed. The other two stories reveal an awareness of the changes in the political situation in Algeria that had occurred since Camus lived there, but they seem to deliberately evade an understanding of the polarization which both sides in the conflict underwent during the 1950s. Camus's characters fail to comprehend or even recognize their misunderstanding of the world.

In his preface to the first edition of "The Adulterous Woman," published by Schumann in Algeria in November 1954, Camus acknowledged the autobiographical element in the story: "In Laghouat I met the characters of this story. I am not certain, of course, that their day ended as I have told it.

Doubtless they did not go forth to the desert. But *I* went, some hours after that, and during all that time their image pursued me and challenged what I saw." This impression of opposition, of conflict, is apparent in the portrayal of Janine and her husband Marcel as they travel in unknown territory in the Algerian interior. On the most obvious level, Janine finds the desert the opposite of what she had expected: instead of warm sand and palm trees, there is a bitterly cold wind blowing over a landscape of stone. Physical discomfort is a dominant feature of the couple's experience.

Marcel is a stereotype of the petty-bourgeois *pied-noir* whom Camus ridiculed in his notebooks, who believes that Arabs are uncivilized and whose aim is a house full of furniture from the Galeries Barbès. Marcel's attitude is that of the fault-finding tourist, who complains of anything that is different. Even in the final version of the story, Marcel's comments are full of racial slurs; it is significant that in earlier versions his comments are even stronger. The typical racist epithets—lazy, dishonest, incompetent— are applied to various Arabs. Marcel expresses a commonly held attitude towards emancipation: "They're supposed to be making progress, said Marcel. To make progress, you have to work. And for them, work is like pork, forbidden."

Camus may, in Quilliot's view, have diluted Marcel's racism because of the worsening situation in Algeria between 1952, when the story was first drafted, and 1954, when it was published in Algiers. It seems more likely, however, that Camus wanted to make his character more sympathetic by emphasizing his limitations and the narrowness of his outlook in general, rather than presenting him as a hardened racist. Marcel is just another frightened human being, who works hard and takes no risks in order to assure both economic and emotional security. It is the exposure to a strange land with undefined parameters that elicits his hostile criticism. On a realistic level, his racist attitude arises from fear of two well-documented threats: economic and sexual competition. The economic crisis that followed World War II had forced Marcel to dispense with intermediaries, and to try and sell his fabrics directly to the Arabs. For the first time, he must deal with Arabs in the small towns of the interior, and to be successful he must deal with them as equals. Also for the first time, perhaps, he must speak Arabic. In the city, where French is the language of the dominant class, he can assert that dominance with his perfect mastery of that language. Now he finds the roles reversed, and the Arab has the upper hand because of his linguistic fluency. Marcel resents the Arabs' haughtiness, and his own position of suppliant: "He became irritable, raised his voice, laughed awkwardly, he seemed like a woman who is trying to be attractive and is unsure of herself." His manhood is put in doubt, and his response is to make scornful comments to Janine about Arab conceit. The final insult is administered by the magnificent Arab who crosses the town square and almost walks over Marcel's case of samples. "They think they can get away with anything nowadays," remarks Marcel. Even Arab cooking is inferior: "*We* know how to cook"; the French rendering of the emphatic "we" (*nous autres*) underlines the otherness Marcel feels in a predominantly Arab town.

Marcel does not actually voice his fears for Janine's security, yet her reaction to the strange environment is physical. "Adulterous" may seem an extreme epithet in view of the reality of Janine's experience, but she is disloyal to the structure of the little world she lives in with her husband, to their marriage. She feels drawn toward the autonomy of these people of the interior, who seem not to depend on material comforts or possessions for their well-being. Janine is encumbered by overweight, luggage, a complaining husband, a heavy meal, the years of conjugality: in the oasis town, people display a freedom and independence such as she enjoyed in her youth. The Arabs do not even seem to notice her existence: "She found that even when they were dressed in rags, they had a proud demeanor, which was not the case with the Arabs in their home town." The Arabs in the coastal towns depend on the Europeans for a living, and therefore adopt a more servile attitude, but here in the interior the French presence is minimal—pork served in the hotel restaurant, and a military decoration on the chest of the old Arab waiter. Out in the desert, the nomads are sovereign.

Hostility or serene indifference greet the French couple, both inside and outside the town. The local people and their landscape are at one in their autonomy vis-à-vis the strangers. All is cold and hard; even Janine's experience of physical union with the world is like a cold flood rather than a warm glow, as she leans against the stone parapet of the fortress. But Janine's fear is stronger than her yearning for freedom, and she returns to the warmth of her husband "as her safest haven."

The impression of physical weight that Camus evokes in his portrayal of these characters makes them real and tangible people, what E. M. Forster would call "round" characters rather than the somewhat abstract characters of *The Plague*. Marcel and Janine are among Camus's most successful fictional creations: they are creations of flesh and blood rather than the stereotypical image of the *pied-noir*. Marcel may represent the reactionary racist European in Algeria, yet at the same time he is just a man, beset by the fear of death, loneliness and poverty like any other. Camus's old Algiers friend, Charles Poncet, suggested that, living in Paris as he did, "Camus may have felt more of a duty to defend the interests of the *pied-noir* against the unanimous hostility of the French left." Camus certainly wanted to dissipate the "image d'Epinal" disseminated by some of the French press, which portrayed Algeria as a colony "inhabited by a million *colons* with whips and cigars, riding around in Cadillacs."

"The Adulterous Woman" does not defend the interests of the *pied-noir,* but rather reveals the extent to which fear inspires scorn and hostility. Marcel and Janine are quite literally out of their element in central Algeria: they need the definition of a coastline to feel secure, for the desert is as limitless as the ocean; the prevailing imagery of the descriptive passages is drawn from the open sea. Even in their home town, the couple no longer goes to the beach, but exists in an ever more restricted area: "The years had passed in the shadowy light they maintained with the shutters half-closed." It is only a half-life, and what characterizes both the conjugal relationship and Janine's experience in the desert is sterility. The story suggests that the couple has no future, only a precarious present. Janine's encounter with the desert makes her newly aware of the vastness of space and time, into which the Arabs seem to fit while she remains excluded, unable to read "the obscure signs of a strange writing whose meaning had to be deciphered."

Camus's attitude to the Algerian situation at this point is revealed as more humanistic than political. Marcel's opinions are obviously distasteful, yet Camus mitigated them in order to make the character more universal. The two sides are not black and white, and a solution does not lie in the eviction or enslavement of one party in the dispute. And yet in this story as in "The Guest," the characters are not really at home in the country they regard as their own.

In "The Adulterous Woman" a hostile natural environment is handled with equanimity by the Arabs, while the Europeans are acutely uncomfortable. A sandstorm is blowing, a "mineral mist" surrounds the bus on which Janine and her husband are traveling. A few palm trees seem to be "cut out of metal," and Janine's dream of a desert of soft sand is disappointed: "The desert was not like that, but was only stone, stone everywhere, in the sky that was still overcast with the dust of the stone, cold and rasping." In the jolting bus, the Arabs "looked as though they were asleep, wrapped up in their burnoose. Some had tucked up their feet on the seat and swayed more than the others with the movement of the vehicle. . . . The passengers . . . had sailed in silence through a kind of pale night." Janine notices that "despite their voluminous garments, they seemed to have plenty of room on the seats which were only just wide enough for her and her husband." She and Marcel are impeded by their clothes and their baggage, but "all these people from the South apparently traveled empty-handed."

Only when Janine stops all movement can she begin to understand the desert and its people. "For a long time, a few men had been traveling without respite over the dry earth, scraped to the bone, of this unbounded land, men who had no possessions but were no man's slave, wretched but free lords of a strange kingdom." The scene recalls the end of *Crime and Punishment,* where Raskolnikov sees the nomads across the river from his prison. For a moment Janine shares this accord, but she is brought back to reality by her husband. "She felt too tall, too solid, and too white for this world she had just entered." She is a misfit in the landscape.

So too is Daru, the protagonist of "The Guest." The ambiguity of the title word, *l'hôte,* meaning both "guest" and "host," and of which meaning should be applied to which character, is resolved by the landscape. Paul Fortier has shown how the landscape and its changing aspects offer an interpretation of historical events and of moral values ("Décor"). Daru believes himself in harmony with the natural world around him. But it is an illusion. The sun is dominant during the drought, "the plateaus charred month after month, the earth gradually shrivelling, literally scorched." The snowfall represents a brief reprieve, a temporary truce before hostility is renewed. When the sun shines again, Daru feels a kind of exaltation, but it is as if the sun were in league with the rocks against him, quickly drying out the puddles of melting snow and returning the landscape to its former rockiness. Now the sun becomes destructive, and "began to devour his brow . . . sweat trickled down it."

The physical attack portends the human violence with which the teacher is threatened on his return to the school. The wind "lurking" around the school building parallels the activities of the rebels who are following his movements. And the precise location of Daru's school, on an isolated plateau, an intermediate stage between the coastal plain and the mountains, reflects the moral stance of neutrality and isolation maintained by the schoolteacher (Paul Fortier, *Une Lecture de Camus*). The Arab prisoner, as Fortier points out, resembles the desert, "his skin sunburnt but slightly discolored by the cold." He fears what the Frenchmen may do to him, but he does not fear the desert. Of course in reality the natural world is hostile to the Arabs too: Daru is well aware that "in the desert, all men, both he and his guest, were nothing." But Camus's landscapes are never innocent. A welcoming environment can become inimical and can inflict pain and even death on the unwary individual.

In all Camus's works, it is the mineral element of the world that proves hostile to mankind. The Algerian sun, which has such a positive and beneficent influence on the bronzed young bodies on the Mediterranean beach, can at times be deadly. It is portrayed as metallic in its destructive role in the short stories (Marcia Weis, *The Lyrical Essays of Albert Camus*).

This is also the case in other texts. In *A Happy Death,* for example, Mersault falls asleep in the afternoon sun: "Now the sun struck with ever swifter blows on every stone on the path. . . . The slopes were rocky and full of flint. . . . The entire mountain vibrated beneath the light and the crickets, the heat increased and besieged them beneath their oak tree. Patrice . . . could feel in his stomach the dull blows of the mountain, like a woman in labor." When Mersault wakes and begins his descent, he faints; the French *syncope* denotes a break in rhythm, a break that is repeated during Mersault's last swim before the onset of his fatal relapse, when the harmonious movements of his body in the warm water are abruptly thrown out of gear by a sudden cold current: "He had to stop, his teeth chattering and his movements un-coordinated [*désaccordés*]." In contrast to this disharmony, Camus portrays the Arabs who appear riding donkeys, against a background of luxuriant and fruitful vegetation: "The paths were still embroidered with prickly pear, olive and jujube trees." The series of long vowel sounds in the French text contributes to the feeling of relaxed, smooth, and rhythmic movement.

A similar juxtaposition occurs in *The Stranger.* When Meursault is walking on the beach at noon, both sun and sea become metallic: "each rapier of light," "an ocean of boiling metal," "the light splashed on the steel and it was like a long sparkling blade," "the cymbals of the sun," "the dazzling blade," "this burning sword." The reality of the knife is indistinguishable from the sun's rays and the light reflected off the sea. And in Meursault's hand is the gun, modern man's contribution to deadly metallic objects. In direct contrast to this portrait of physical disarray, of jangling nerves and assaulted senses, Camus depicts the Arabs, who experience none of this hostility. They are lying in the shade beside a little spring: "They seemed quite calm and almost contented. Our coming changed nothing." One of the Arabs plays a flute, and the impression of harmony is accentuated by the movement of the Arabs' bodies, which "slipped [*coulés*] behind the rock": it is as if they were absorbed into the landscape. Even in the unnatural surroundings of the prison, the Arab prisoners communicate with their visitors in a gentle murmur, while the Europeans have to shout to make themselves heard.

The opinions Camus expressed in a political context are apparently contradicted by the fictional worlds of these short stories. Camus opposed independence because it would lead to the expulsion of his own people. Yet the European characters he places in an Algerian setting are uncomfortable strangers in a country they regard as theirs. In "The Guest," for example, despite the sympathetic portrayal of characters, it is clear that Daru's position is untenable. Warm human bonds between individuals are not enough to assure a peaceful settlement of struggle in the political arena.

Daru fits in with Albert Memmi's portrait of the left-wing colonizer. He "refuses to become a part of his group of fellow citizens. At the same time it is impossible for him to identify his future with that of the colonized. Politically, who is he? Is he not an expression of himself, of a negligible force in the varied conflicts within colonialism?" (*The Colonizer*). Daru has isolated himself from his fellow Europeans, and lives alone on a barren plateau in the foothills. As a schoolteacher he is obviously committed to the welfare and education of his pupils, and sympathetic towards their impoverished and ill-nourished condition. He feels at home: "Daru had been born there. Anywhere else he felt an exile." In earlier versions of the manuscript, Daru was a disenchanted businessman from the coast, who had given up his old life and become a teacher. In the final version, Camus stresses Daru's roots in this harsh landscape; yet his origins continue to separate him from the indigenous population: "Faced with this wretchedness [Daru], who lived almost like a monk in this isolated school, yet was happy with the little he had and with this simple life, had felt like a lord." Colonialist rule is symbolized by the drawing on the school blackboard of the four rivers of France: the local schoolchildren follow the same curriculum as children in metropolitan France, even though it may be irrelevant to their culture and their needs. The colonial administration uses the schools as distribution centers for emergency supplies of food during the drought, so that children have to come to school to receive their allocation. Daru is thus placed in the position of an overlord, separate from "that army of ragged ghosts." The word *army* evokes a sense of hostility and violence which runs through the whole narrative and explodes across the map of France at the end of the story.

The advent of Balducci and his Arab prisoner brings the reality of the current situation into Daru's monastic retreat, brings movement into a static world, and forces him to take a position. "Commitment comes like a guest who does not want to leave" (Peter Cryle, *Bilan Critique*). It is his failure to choose in a positive way that leaves him helpless to affect the course of events. His attitude toward Balducci and the Arab is entirely laudable: Balducci is a tough but sympathetic Corsican who dislikes mistreating an Arab, but who believes in discipline, while the Arab, despite his act of violence, is nevertheless a man who deserves to be treated with human dignity. By refusing to take the Arab to prison, Daru offends Balducci personally; by allowing the Arab a choice he does not understand, he alienates himself from the local people. His actions are misunderstood by the groups represented by the two individuals, just as Daru fails to recognize the political reality behind those two people.

On a personal level, ambiguity and humanitarian instincts are possible; but on a political level, actions cannot bear any nuance without being misconstrued. Thus the colonial administration will view Daru's refusal as a treacherous act, while the Arabs interpret the result of his inaction as a betrayal too: "You have handed over our brother. You will pay." The words "hand over" recall mockingly Daru's thrice-repeated "I will not hand him over"; Camus obviously had some biblical references in mind, for in an earlier version of the story, the teacher's name is Pierre (Peter), and at one time he considered "Cain" as a title. Daru's future in Algeria is precarious, and the use of the pluperfect in the final sentence bears out this sense of finality. "Daru looked at the sky, the plateau, and beyond it the invisible landscape that stretched out to the sea. In this vast country he had loved so much, he was alone." The reference to the sea indicates the direction in which Daru will now have to travel, into his exile.

The individual's viewpoint cannot be reduced to a single vision, and yet circumstances often demand it. By refusing to commit himself to one side or the other, Daru loses all. He deplores the Arab's resigned decision to accept his fate, and yet his own indecisiveness allows him also to be swept away by events; he is no better than the Arab at choosing his own future. The text clearly shows that Daru's behavior is understandable but sterile. In a polarized situation, one must choose between black and white and put aside all the shades of gray that intervene, if one is to have any impact on the situation.

The criticisms leveled at Camus during the late 1950s dealt mainly with his unwillingness to ignore the gray nuances: in a situation where two hostile *groups* were involved, *individuals* would surge into view and temper the objective evaluation with a visceral sympathy. Like his character Daru, Camus became "suspect to the nationalists of both sides. I am blamed by one side for not being sufficiently . . . patriotic. For the other side, I'm too much so" (Robert Mallet, quoted in Herbert Lottman, *Albert Camus: A Biography*).

There is no doubt that Camus suffered intense anguish over his role in the Algerian tragedy. When an old Algerian friend asked him why he had accepted the necessity of violence during the Resistance but rejected it with respect to the Moslem independence movement, his response reveals what Daru ignored—an awareness of his fundamental identity: "It's true that I wasn't shocked by resistance to the Nazis, because I was French and my country was occupied. I should [*devrais*] accept the Algerian resistance, but I'm French."

Camus's reaction to the political struggle was never objective, but was colored by fear for the safety of his family in Algiers as well as by the pressure of more reactionary views within his family in France. After the failure of his mission in 1956, his participation in events was limited to private action to help individuals. He knew that he was going against the tide of his time; decisions were being made on a national rather than a local level. "All the power of science today is aimed at strengthening the state. Not one scholar has thought of directing his research towards the defense of the individual. But that is where a freemasonary would have some meaning."

"The Silent Men" depicts another aspect of the ambiguity of political action, and of the way in which it can divide men rather than unite them. The artisans in this story are the people Camus knew in his youth, and remind us of the men in *The Wrong Side and the Right Side,* old before their time, remembering with nostalgia the sunlit beaches and freedom of their youth. This is no romantic portrayal of the worker: physical fatigue and a sense of hopelessness in a dying trade are the predominant sentiments of Yvars and his co-workers.

In the conflict between boss and workers, there are no winners. The shopowner, who is depicted as honest and sympathetic, cannot afford to raise wages because the cooperage business is in crisis. The workers, humiliated by the failure of their strike and the lack of union support for their cause, decide to remain silent in the presence of their boss. Benevolent though he may be, he cannot understand what life is like for the poor, and they are unable to communicate it to him. Their own solidarity cuts across racial lines; the conflict is centered on the relationship between employer and employees. No one seems to have conceived of it in terms of "class" conflict: like Daru, they relate to each other as people rather than as representatives of a social or political reality.

Their action, however limited, is an assertion of human dignity rather than political revolt. Hence their evident confusion when faced with the ill-ness of the boss's daughter; they suppress their feelings of common humanity in the face of the scandal of the death of a child, but they are not happy about it. They cannot formulate ideas on the complex issues involved, and so they cling stubbornly to the one decision they have made, to remain silent, even at the expense of a vital part of their humanity.

In this story Camus shows through the complexities and ambiguities of a particular situation how irrelevant political theory can be. Politics itself must be ambiguous if it is to take account of reality. "The Silent Men" portrays people struggling for economic survival, ignorant of the wider theoretical application of their dilemma.

"The Guest" also demonstrates an individual situation, but one in which the hero chooses not to be part of a group. It reveals the failure of a stand that refuses total commitment to either side. "The Renegade," on the other hand, affirms the dangers inherent in such a commitment.

Paradoxically, this story's subtitle, "A Confused Mind," contradicts the world in which the renegade functions, although the form of the story, a frenzied monologue, does bear witness to a crazed mind. The renegade's progression in life, however, follows a straight and determined line: from a sickly and depressed childhood, he plans a course of action that will lead directly to the exercise of power. "Powerful, yes, that was the word that I constantly rolled on my tongue, I dreamed of absolute power, the kind that brings people to their knees." Thus the seminary is merely a means to an end, the theft from the bursary in Algiers a necessary step in the direction of the attainment of his dream. But on arrival in Taghâsa, the city of salt in the desert (again the hostile mineral element), he discovers that instead of wielding power, he must become a slave. The distinct line of his own progression is halted, for the world of Taghâsa is overwhelming in its geometric patterns, and its stark setting of black and white. The renegade's dream of power comes to an abrupt end in a cell of salt. He no longer has any control over the situation, because his potential power lay in the propagation of the word, and he is now speechless, for his captors have cut out his tongue. Physical force reigns in Taghâsa, and the renegade embraces his new servitude with delirious passion. "The maddest passion of the twentieth century: slavery." The renegade's conversion fits in with Camus's definition of the aim of Russian Communism—"the exaltation of the executioner by his victims."

Taghâsa is the perfect example of the totalitarian state: symmetry and efficient organization imposed by violence rather than by reasonable persuasion, absolute values suggested by the stark contrast of black on white, and the sterility of the world of salt. Only when the renegade leaves the city to lie in wait for the French missionary do any colors reappear in the landscape, or the lines lose their rigid angles.

The renegade can be seen as an example of the modern intellectual in search of ideological absolutes; when one fails, another takes its place (Victor Brombert, The Intellectual Hero). Certainly he is willing to accept any tyranny in order to attain the "kingdom" he envisages. But the major thrust of the narrative is to show how violence, when used as a means to what may be a laudable end, becomes a way of life. The violence implicit in the renegade's dream of power is camouflaged by the explicit mission of the conversion of a ferocious people to Christianity. But when violence is used to convert the potential conqueror to slave, it is received with a pathological pleasure, and the renegade can conceive of no other means of action when threatened by the arrival of a new missionary. Thus violence is not limited to the attainment of a certain goal, but pervades the whole landscape, the human mind, and the verbal expression of the confused workings of that mind.

It is significant that the renegade was regarded as a young man of limited intelligence, unsure of himself or his capabilities. "Order, an order . . . yes, I have always wanted order." The order of the Church is replaced by the more powerful order of violence: "the city of order, in fact, right angles, square rooms, inflexible men." Camus's comment on Rebatet and Morgan is relevant here too: "Universal definition of Fascism: having no character, they found themselves a doctrine." And that doctrine requires total submission and loss of liberty. "Truth is square, heavy, dense, it will not tolerate nuance."

The title of the story obviously refers to the narrator's treachery to his Church when he adopts the pagan religion of his captors. But he had already betrayed the ideals of that Church before leaving France. He is a colonialist who has swallowed the myth that conquest is justified by the need to "save the souls of the infidel," a myth that disguises a lust for power. This disguise proves no match for the rulers of Taghâsa: the renegade betrays the myth too, and "goes native." He is a renegade in both the religious and political senses of the word. His mind is confused because he has no moral values on which to base his decisions. It is the attraction of power that provides his only motivation.

There are obvious links between "The Renegade" and *The Fall*, both in form and content. The renegade realizes Clamence's dream of tyranny, and his text is also monologue, but this time there is no interlocutor, for the words are never formed. Speech is totally suppressed in favor of violent gesture. The inhabitants of Taghâsa are also silent men, but this is the silence of certainty rather than that of doubt. The only sound uttered by the renegade is the repeated "râ râ" of his tongueless mouth. A striking image in Camus's 1956 "Appeal for a Civilian Truce" in Algiers suggests that the renegade represents the course of history when men accept cruelty and inhumanity with a passive fatalism. Then history "repeats itself, like a bleeding mouth that spews out only a furious stuttering."

The theme of violence, which relates to the political level of interpretation, also reiterates the problems of writing. The last sentence of the story, which is the only one outside quotation marks, refers to the "garrulous slave," an extraordinarily harsh portrait of the writer, particularly since his "words" communicate nothing. The mouthful of salt is the final assertion of the sterility of his endeavor.

"The Renegade" marks the low point in Camus's view of his art, and probably coincides with the period around 1954 when, in a letter to René Char, he confessed that he was "literally vitriolized by doubt." The last two stories in the collection, however, are more optimistic. "Jonas, or the Artist at Work" deals with the conflicting demands of the world and the artist's need for solitude. The ironic tone is reminiscent of *The Fall*, but the pain it hides is less intense and distanced by the benevolent attitude of the narrator.

A considerable number of details relate to Camus's own experience, from the description of the apartment to the problem of organizing his work and family life. "The fight to the finish between me and my children is over, with the children the winners," Camus wrote to Grenier in 1949. "I no longer work at home, but try to do so in my office at the NRF, with the door locked and the telephone off the hook. The victors now occupy all the conquered territory and behave like all conquerors, cynically." In "Jonas," the bantering tone of the satire of Parisian life gradually gives way to a more somber note as Jonas's vocation is threatened, first by his own lack of responsibility, then by the invasion of friends, critics, and hangers-on. The opening line of "Jonas" states simply that he "believed in his star" but he allows other aspects of his life to take precedence. He tries escape from the apartment, but wine and women provide no inspiration. He must find the solution within the confines of the apartment, and each new attempt involves a rearrangement of the space available (Peter Cryle, "The Written Painting and the Painted Word in 'Jonas'"). Like that other artist, Grand, he must continually start again without altering the basic structure of the givens, reorganize within limits. The words *recommencer* and *organisation* recur constantly in the text.

Just as Jonah chose to neglect the dictates of God, so Jonas allows the exigencies of his "star" to be swamped by the demands of outside influences. He enjoys the adulation of disciples, even though he realizes that he is merely a fashion; these admirers showed an interest "in painting when they could just as easily have been mad about the English royal family or gourmet restaurants." The ironic juxtaposition suggests Camus's modesty with regard to his estimate of the importance of the artist.

Jonas's ultimate solution is to build a loft, making use of the excess height of the apartment, where he can be alone while still retaining at least aural contact with his family. The only evidence we have of Jonas's activity is his subsequent physical collapse and the canvas with one word, *solitaire* or *solidaire*, perhaps both. The loft, a compromise comparable to Clamence's *malconfort*, is not an ideal situation but a possible balance between two absolutes. The reader can only imagine Jonas's anguish before the blank white canvas: his retreat and self-discipline do not lead to the creation of a work of art, but at least he has succeeded in conceptualizing the problem, and will recover his health.

The ironic tone and the relatively optimistic ending—Jonas can begin again—reveal an upswing in Camus's vision of his work. His conclusions about the role of the artist are not new: he needs the inspiration of the world of men as well as the solitary cell to be creative; his duty is a double one, and the balance must be constantly reassessed and reasserted.

Jonah defied God's orders because they seemed arbitrary. Jonas ignores the demands of his star, which also requires obedience to certain laws and structures, like the celestial body it resembles. The tyranny of art is compared to that of the Old Testament God: it must be recognized as such before the artist can evolve his admittedly ambiguous response to its dictates, and avoid the sterility that total submission or irresponsibility produces.

The idea of organization over anarchy is evident in the last story in the collection, "The Growing Stone." In the earlier stories, sterility is linked with the desert, parched earth, dust. In "The Growing Stone" the ambiance is suffused with water, an element that encourages fertility, but left unmanaged it leads to decay, rotting overcrowded vegetation, and muddy roads. The hero d'Arrast is an engineer, and it is in this story that the rules of a person's profession are most closely integrated with the human and social demands to which that person responds.

Although the setting of the story is quite specific, and is based on Camus's personal experiences during his visit to South America in 1949, the main character, d'Arrast, is not developed in depth. Indeed, during the initial scenes of the story, he is referred to simply as "the man" (l'homme), and the reader's only impression is that of a gentle giant. Even when some details are filled in, the engineer's past remains mysterious. In contrast to Marcel and Janine, and to Daru, who cling to their past, d'Arrast has closed it off, leaving the future open and uncertain.

His current role is to build a dam that will prevent seasonal flooding in the small town of Iguape. The notables who gather at the club to welcome the French engineer typify the petty colonial elite, benevolent and paternalistic toward the local populace, obsequious and gushing toward the foreign visitor. The judicial system is a parody: the judge is an effusive dandy, the chief of police a drunken lout who bullies d'Arrast until put in his place by the judge, at which point he assumes the air of "a child who has been caught out," and "sidles out like a dunce in trouble." To d'Arrast's dismay, the judge insists that he select a suitable punishment for the transgressor: he eventually succeeds in persuading the judge to forget the matter, but in the meantime the chief of police remains in the ridiculous situation of being in his own jail.

D'Arrast is welcomed by the local people, and he feels a greater affinity with them than with the notables. But a barrier remains: he cannot share the simple faith of the ship's cook, and during the celebrations for Saint George he is rejected as a stranger: "They don't want you to stay now." D'Arrast accepts his dismissal: "I don't know how to dance," he tells Socrate, his driver.

D'Arrast's position is like that of Daru. He has rejected his roots in the European aristocracy as well as the new regime of policemen and shopkeepers, but he has not found a new place for himself. "Over there, in Europe, it was shame and anger. Here, exile or solitude." He is a man without an identity. The notables look on him as one of themselves, and so the native people view him with suspicion or indifference. In this he is like Meursault, who had to be considered an enemy by the Arab on the beach. It will need a striking gesture to overturn the assumptions of the people of Iguape.

During the religious procession d'Arrast is invited to join the town notables on a balcony of the judge's house facing the church: the significance of the position of the ruling class is evident. But d'Arrast goes down among the people to look for the cook, who is staggering under the rock he has sworn to carry to the church. D'Arrast has to go against the tide to reach the cook: "He had to struggle against the joyful crowd, the candle bearers, the offended penitents. Slowly but surely, bearing all his weight against the human tide, he opened up a path." When he finds the cook, he sees that the man's companions keep replacing the rock every time he stumbles. Again d'Arrast defies the will of the people: ignoring the cries of "to the church, to the church," he turns to the left and carries the stone down to the slums instead. His gesture is not understood immediately; he has defied the oppressive rule of the Church just as he defied an unjust system of power that states that "punishment is necessary."

There is certainly a link between d'Arrast and the figure of Christ, but it would be an exaggeration to view him as a personification of Christ. Camus uses the word *resurrection* rather than *reappearance* or *resurgence* to describe the figure of d'Arrast in the car's blinking headlights. Like the statue of Christ that floated upstream to the town of Iguape, d'Arrast goes against the tide. But Christ is appropriated by the notables, and incorporated into the system of oppression and submission: d'Arrast refuses to be annexed by the ruling elite, and so perhaps he, rather than Meursault, can be considered the only Christ we deserve. A similar opposition exists between the two stones. "The real growing stone is not the one in the grotto, an object of selfish superstitions and false hopes . . . [but] the one that symbolizes a friendship . . . between two people. On the stone is founded not the Church of God, but the community of men" (Monique Crochet, *Les Mythes dans l'oeuvre de Camus*).

Of all the characters in *Exile and the Kingdom*, d'Arrast is the only one of heroic stature. But he resists the role: he has left a position of social prominence in Europe, he rejects the power offered him by the judge, and the stone he carries to the slums puts out the fire in the middle of the hut, an anti-Promethean gesture. Once more we are back with the stone of Sisyphus, "but this time two men have carried it together" (Hazel Barnes, *The Literature of Possibility*). Sisyphus accepted his daily task because he so loved life, and it is "life beginning anew" that reveals to d'Arrast the possibility of creating a kingdom in the midst of exile.

D'Arrast is a man who can change the order of this small world: not only can he tame the natural world by controlling the river, but he can also change a system of power in human society. The poor people of the town are treated as children by the Church and State that rule them. D'Arrast shows them the way to independence, symbolically by carrying the rock to the poorest hovel, realistically by providing work on the dam project. He acts not according to the dictates of an abstract ideology, but in response to an instinctive human compassion. It is his *body* that shows him the way. The final words, "Sit down with us," justify d'Arrast's joy; the stranger is invited to join the group. The underlying inference is that a process of emancipation can be achieved by peaceful means, for the dominant imagery of the story has none of the violence of "The Guest" or "The Renegade"; the flowing of water, which permeates the text, water that d'Arrast will direct to make it serve these people rather than dominate them, denotes a peaceful transition over time.

This was Camus's dream for Algeria: "I love [Algeria] as a Frenchman who loves Arabs, and wants them to be at home in Algeria without himself having to feel a stranger there because of that" (Mallet, quoted in Lottman). But it harked back to a period when federation of some kind was still a viable policy. The situation depicted in "The Growing Stone" is still relatively simple because it takes place prior to the awakening of political consciousness among the masses, and d'Arrast is the first man to rebel against the status quo. He illustrates Camus's conception of true freemasonry: by aiding an individual he can influence a community. Once violent means are introduced, however, human beings lose their liberty, both of speech and action. "The Renegade" offers an explanation of Camus's public silence on Algeria after 1958. In a situation where violence is the order of the day, the word has no power for good. The cutting out of the renegade's tongue removes all hope of achieving his mission through reasonable dialogue. It is left to the

French army to impose control by force, making a mockery of the Christian message.

The stories of *Exile and the Kingdom* reveal the impasse in which Camus found himself with regard to the Algerian situation. His existence as a writer depended on his identity as a Frenchman, yet his experience as an Algerian made liberty his foremost social ideal. There was no political solution to his personal dilemma. Had he lived, he would doubtless have accepted the inevitable tide of events, just as Daru did. But his vision of the trends in society, of the triumph of violence over dialogue, of the state over the individual, is now generally recognized as a relevant indictment of the modern world.

Chronology

1913   Albert Camus born in Algeria, November 7.

1914   Father dies in Battle of the Marne, World War I.

1918–30   Educated at grade school and the lycée in Algiers.

1930   Study of philosophy at University of Algiers is interrupted by first serious attack of tuberculosis.

1933–34   First marriage, ending in divorce.

1934–35   Brief membership in Communist party.

1935   Active in Théâtre du Travail (later *Théâtre de l'Equipe*); production of *La Révolté dans les Asturies* (*The Revolt in Asturia*), of which he is part author.

1936   Receives degree in philosophy.

1937   *L'Envers et l'endroit* (*Betwixt and Between*) published.

1938   Reporter for the *Alger Républicain*. *Noces* (*Nuptials*) published.

1940   Marries Francine Faure; returns to Algeria in January, 1941.

1942   *The Stranger* (*L'Etranger*) published. Joins French Resistance movement; edits clandestine newspaper *Combat*.

1943   Publication of *The Myth of Sisyphus* (*Le Mythe de Sisyphe*); becomes an editor at Gallimard in Paris.

1944   Production of *The Misunderstanding* (*Le Malentendu*). Meets Jean-Paul Sartre.

1945   Production of *Caligula*.

1946–47   Lecture tour of the United States.

1947   *The Plague* (*La Peste*).

1948   Production of *State of Siege* (*L'Etat de siège*).

1949   Lecture tour of South America; production of *The Just Assass-ins* (*Les Justes*).

1949–51   New attacks of tuberculosis.

1951   Publication of *The Rebel* (*L'Homme révolté*) leads to quarrel and eventual break with Jean-Paul Sartre.

1956   *The Fall* (*La Chute*); production of *Requiem for a Nun,* adapted from Faulkner.

1957   Receives Nobel Prize. Publication of *Exile and the Kingdom* (*L'Exil et le royaume*).

1958   Production of *The Possessed* (*Les Possédés*), adapted from Dostoevsky.

1959   Appointed director of the new state-supported experimental theater.

1960   Camus dies in an automobile accident, January 4.

Contributors

HAROLD BLOOM, Sterling Professor of the Humanities at Yale University, is the author of *The Anxiety of Influence, Poetry and Repression,* and many other volumes of literary criticism. His forthcoming study, *Freud: Transference and Authority,* attempts a full-scale reading of all of Freud's major writings. A MacArthur Prize Fellow, he is general editor of five series of literary criticism published by Chelsea House. During 1987–88, he served as Charles Eliot Norton Professor of Poetry at Harvard University.

VICTOR BROMBERT is Henry Putnam Professor of Comparative Literature and Romance Languages at Princeton University. He is the author of *The Intellectual Hero, Victor Hugo and the Visionary World,* and *The Novels of Flaubert.*

ROGER SHATTUCK has written extensively on Proust and other modern French authors. His books include *Banquet Years: The Origins of the Avant-Garde in France, 1885 to World War One, The Forbidden Experiment: The Story of the Wild Boy of Aveyron, Marcel Proust,* and *Proust's Binoculars.*

PAUL DE MAN was, until his death in 1983, Sterling Professor of Comparative Literature at Yale University. He is the author of *Blindness and Insight, Allegories of Reading, Figural Language in Rousseau, Nietzsche, Rilke, and Proust,* and *The Rhetoric of Romanticism.* Posthumous collections of his work include *The Resistance to Theory, Aesthetic Ideology,* and *Fugitive Essays.*

JACQUES GUICHARNAUD is Benjamin F. Barge Professor of French at Yale University and the author of a major study of Molière. His books include *Twentieth Century French Theater* and *Raymond Queneau.*

E. FREEMAN is Lecturer in French at the University of Bristol.

DONALD LAZERE teaches in the Department of English at California Polytechnic State University, San Luis Obispo. He is the author of *The Unique*

Creation of Albert Camus and editor of *American Media and Mass Culture: Left Perspectives.*

RENÉ GIRARD is Andrew B. Hammond Professor of French Language and Literature at Stanford University. His works include *Deceit, Desire and the Novel, Violence and the Sacred,* and *To Double Business Bound.*

PATRICK McCARTHY is the author of *Celine: A Biography,* as well as his biography of Camus.

DAVID R. ELLISON is Dean of Studies at Mount Holyoke College. *The Reading of Proust* is his first book.

ENGLISH SHOWALTER, JR., teaches in the Department of French at Rutgers University. He is the author of *The Evolution of the French Novel, 1641–1782* and *Exiles and Strangers: A Reading of Camus's* Exile and the Kingdom.

SUSAN TARROW teaches in the Department of Romance Studies at Cornell University.

Bibliography

Abraham, C. "*Caligula:* Drama of Revolt or Drama of Deception?" *Modern Drama* 5 (1963): 451–53.

Aho, James. "Suffering, Redemption and Violence: Albert Camus and the Sociology of Violence." *Rendezvous* 9, no. 1–2 (1974): 51–62.

Aiken, Henry David. "The Revolt against Ideology." *Commentary* 37 (April 1964): 29–39.

Aron, Raymond. *The Opium of the Intellectuals.* New York: Norton, 1962.

Barchilon, José. "A Study of Camus's Mythopoeic Tale, *The Fall,* with Some Comments about the Origin of Esthetic Feelings." *Journal of the American Psychoanalytic Association* 19 (1971): 193–240.

Barnes, Hazel. *The Literature of Possibility: A Study in Humanistic Existentialism.* New York: Tavistock, 1959.

Barthes, Roland. *Writing Degree Zero.* Translated by Annette Lavers and Colin Smith. New York: Hill & Wang, 1968.

Beauvoir, Simone de. *Force of Circumstance.* Translated by Richard Howard. New York: Putnam, 1965.

Beebe, Maurice. "Criticism of Albert Camus: A Selected Checklist of Studies in English." *Modern Fiction Studies* 10 (1964): 303–14.

Bersani, Leo. *Balzac to Beckett: Center and Circumstance in French Fiction.* New York: Oxford University Press, 1970.

Bertocci, Angelo. "Camus's *La Peste* and the Absurd." *Romanic Review* 49 (1958): 33–41.

Bittner, William. "The Death of Camus." *The Atlantic Monthly* 207 (February 1961): 85–88.

Braun, Lev. *Witness of Decline: Albert Camus, Moralist of the Absurd.* Rutherford, N.J.: Fairleigh Dickinson University Press, 1974.

Brée, Germaine. "Albert Camus et le 'Théâtre de l'Equipe.'" *The French Review* 22 (1948–49): 225–29.

———. *Camus.* New Brunswick, N.J.: Rutgers University Press, 1961.

———. *Camus and Sartre, Crisis and Commitment.* New York: Delta, 1972.

———, ed. *Camus: A Collection of Critical Essays.* Englewood Cliffs, N.J.: Prentice-Hall, 1962.

Brée, Germaine, and Margaret Guiton. *The French Novel from Gide to Camus.* New York: Harcourt, Brace & World, 1962.

Brustein, Robert. "Nihilism on Broadway." *The New Republic,* 29 February 1960. Reprinted in *Seasons of Discontent.* New York: Simon and Schuster, 1965.

Burnier, Michel. *Choice of Action: The French Existentialists on the Political Front Line.* New York: Random House, 1968.

Carruth, Hayden. *After the Stranger: Imaginary Dialogues with Camus.* New York: Macmillan, 1965.

Caute, David. *The Illusion: An Essay on Politics, Theatre, and the Novel.* New York: Harper & Row, 1971.

Champigny, Robert. *A Pagan Hero: An Interpretation of Meursault in Camus'* The Stranger. Philadelphia: University of Pennsylvania Press, 1969.

Church, D. M. "*Le Malentendu:* Search for Modern Tragedy." *French Studies* 20 (1966): 33–46.

Claire, Thomas. "Landscape and Religious Imagery in Camus's 'La Pierre qui pousse.'" *Studies in Short Fiction* 13 (1976): 321–29.

Cohn, Robert Greer. "Sartre-Camus Resartus." *Yale French Studies* 30 (1962–63): 73–77.

Couch, J. P. "Camus' Dramatic Adaptations and Translations." *The French Review* 33 (1959–60): 27–36.

Cox, Harvey. *The Secular City.* New York: Macmillan, 1965.

Cranston, Maurice. "Albert Camus." *Encounter* 28 (February 1967): 43–55.

Cruickshank, John. *Albert Camus and the Literature of Revolt.* London: Oxford University Press, 1959.

———. "The Art of Allegory in *La Peste.*" *Symposium* 9 (1957): 61–74.

———. *The Novelist as Philosopher.* London: Oxford University Press, 1962.

Curtis, Jerry L. "Alienation and the Foreigner in *Exile and the Kingdom.*" *French Literature Series* 2 (1975): 127–38.

———. "Structure and Space in Camus's *Jonas.*" *Modern Fiction Studies* 22 (1976–77): 571–76.

Davis, Richard Gorham. "Exploration into the Guilt of Man." Review of *The Fall. New York Times Book Review,* 17 February 1957.

———. "Faith for an Age without Faith." Review of *Exile and the Kingdom. New York Times Book Review,* 9 March 1958.

Doubrovsky, Serge. "The Ethics of Albert Camus." *Preuves* 116 (October 1960): 39–49.

Driver, Tom F. "Superior Suicide." *Christian Century* 23 (1960): 352–54.

Engelberg, Edward. *The Unknown Distance: From Consciousness to Conscience, Goethe to Camus.* Cambridge, Mass.: Harvard University Press, 1972.

Falk, Eugene. *Types of Thematic Structure: The Nature and Function of Motifs in Gide, Camus, and Sartre.* Chicago: University of Chicago Press, 1967.

Feibleman, James K. "Camus and the Passion of Humanism." *The Kenyon Review* 25 (1963): 281–92.

Feurlicht, Ignace. "Camus's *L'Etranger* Reconsidered." *PMLA* 27 (1963): 606–21.

Fiedler, Leslie A. "The Pope and the Prophet." *Commentary* 21 (February 1956): 190–95.

Fitch, Brian. "Camus' Desert Hieroglyphics." *Proceedings of the Comparative Literature Symposium* 8 (1975): 117–31.

Fontinell, Eugene. "A Tribute to Camus: Recent Studies of His Work." *Cross Currents* 10 (1960): 283–89.

Fowlie, Wallace. *Dionysus in Paris: A Guide to Contemporary French Theater*. New York: Meridian, 1960.

Freeman, E. "Camus' Brechtian Apprenticeship in the Theatre." *Forum for Modern Language Studies* 4 (1968): 285–98.

——. "Camus, Suetonius, and the Caligula Myth." *Symposium* 24 (1970): 230–42.

——. "*Les Justes*—Modern Tragedy or Old-Fashioned Melodrama?" *Modern Language Quarterly* 31 (1970): 78–91.

Frohock, Wilbur M. *Style and Temper: Studies in French Fiction, 1925–1961*. Cambridge, Mass.: Harvard University Press, 1967.

Gale, John. "Does America Know *The Stranger*? A Reappraisal of a Translation." *Modern Fiction Studies* 20 (1974): 139–47.

Geha, Richard, Jr. "Albert Camus: Another Wish for Death." *Psychoanalytic Review* 54 (1967): 106–22.

Glicksberg, Charles Irving. *The Tragic Vision in Twentieth-Century Literature*. Carbondale: Southern Illinois University Press, 1963.

Goodhand, R. H. "The Omphalus and the Phoenix: Symbolism of the Center in Camus' 'La pierre qui pousse.' " *Studies in Short Fiction* 21 (1984): 117–26.

Grobe, Edwin P. "The Psychological Structure of Camus's *L'Hôte*." *The French Review* 40 (1966): 357–76.

——. "Tarrou's Confession: The Ethical Force of the Past Definite." *The French Review* 39 (1966): 550–58.

Hackel, Sergei. "Raskolnikov through the Looking-Glass: Dostoevsky and Camus's *L'Etranger*," *Contemporary Literature* 9 (1968): 189–209.

Haggis, D. R. *Albert Camus:* La Peste. London: Edward Arnold, 1962.

Haig, Stirling. "The Epilogue of *Crime and Punishment* and Camus's *La Femme Adultère*." *Comparative Literature Studies* 3 (1966): 445–49.

Hanna, T. *The Thought and Art of Albert Camus*. Chicago: Henry Regnery, 1958.

Hartman, Geoffrey H. "Camus and Malraux: The Common Ground." In *Beyond Formalism: Literary Essays, 1958–1970*. New Haven: Yale University Press, 1970.

Hassan, Ihab. *The Dismemberment of Orpheus*. New York: Oxford University Press, 1971.

Hochberg, Herbert. "Albert Camus and the Ethic of Absurdity." *Ethics* 75 (1964–65): 87–102.

Hoffman, Stanley, et al. "Homage to Camus." *The Massachusetts Review* 1 (1960): 212–14.

Howarth, W. D. "History in the Theatre: The French and English Traditions." *Trivium* 1 (1966): 151–68.

Hoy, Peter C. *Camus in English*. Paris: Les Lettres Modernes, 1971.

Joiner, Lawrence D. "Camus's *Le Renégat*: Identity Denied." *Studies in Short Fiction* 13 (1976): 37–41.

——. "Camus's *The Renegade*: A Quest for Sexual Identity." *Research Studies* 45 (1977): 171–76.

——. "Reverie and Silence in *Le Renégat*." *Romance Notes* 16 (1975): 262–67.

Jones, R. "Camus and the Aphorism: *L'Exil et le royaume*." *The Modern Language Review* 78 (1983): 308–18.

Kamber, Gerald. "The Allegory of the Names in *L'Etranger*." *Modern Language Quarterly* 22 (1961): 292–301.

Kauffman, Walter. *Religion from Tolstoy to Camus.* New York: Harper, 1964.

Kazin, Alfred. "Condemned Man." *Reporter,* 16 February 1961, 54–58. Reprinted in *Contemporaries,* 291–95. Boston: Little, Brown, 1962.

Kennedy, Ellen Conroy. "Camus at His Sources." *The Kenyon Review* 31 (1969): 122–27.

King, Adele. *Camus.* London: Oliver & Boyd, 1964.

Knopf, Blanche. "Albert Camus in the Sun." *The Atlantic Monthly* 207 (February 1961): 77–79, 84.

Koestler, Arthur. *The Yogi and the Commissar.* New York: Macmillan, 1945.

Koppenhaver, Allen J. "*The Fall* and After: Albert Camus and Arthur Miller." *Modern Drama* 9 (1966): 206–9.

Krieger, Murray. *The Tragic Vision.* New York: Holt, Rinehart & Winston, 1960.

Lamont, Rosette. "The Anti-Bourgeois." *The French Review* 34 (1960–61): 445–53.

Lazere, Donald. *The Unique Creation of Albert Camus.* New Haven: Yale University Press, 1973.

Lebesque, Morvan. *Portrait of Camus.* New York: Herder & Herder, 1971.

Lehan, Richard Daniel. "Camus' American Affinities." *Symposium* 13 (1959): 255–70.

———. "Camus and Hemingway." *Wisconsin Studies in Contemporary Literature* 1, no. 2 (Spring–Summer 1960): 37–48.

Leites, Nathan. "*The Stranger.*" In *Art and Psychoanalysis,* edited by William Phillips, 247–67. New York: Meridian, 1963.

Lewis, R. W. B. *The Picaresque Saint: Representative Figures in Contemporary Fiction.* Philadelphia: Lippincott, 1959.

Lottman, Herbert R. *Albert Camus: A Biography.* Garden City, N.Y.: Doubleday, 1979.

Luppe, Robert. *Albert Camus.* London: Merlin, 1966.

McCarthy, Patrick. *Camus: A Critical Study of His Life and Work.* London: Hamish Hamilton, 1982.

Macksey, Richard. "The Artist in the Labyrinth: Design or *Dasein.*" *MLN* 77 (1962): 239–56.

McPheeters, D. W. "Camus' Translations of Lope and Calderon." *Symposium* 12 (1958): 52–64.

Madden, David. "Ambiguity in Albert Camus's *The Fall.*" *Modern Fiction Studies* 12 (1966–67): 46–72.

Malraux, André. *Anti-Memoirs.* New York: Holt, Rinehart & Winston, 1968.

Maquet, Albert. *Albert Camus: The Invincible Summer.* New York: George Braziller, 1958.

Mason, Haydn T. "Voltaire and Camus." *Romanic Review* 59 (1968): 198–212.

Maurois, André. *From Proust to Camus.* Garden City, N.Y.: Doubleday, 1968.

Memmi, Albert. *The Colonizer and the Colonized.* Boston: Beacon Press, 1967.

Merton, Thomas. *Albert Camus's The Plague: Introduction and Commentary.* New York: Seabury Press, 1968.

———. "Camus's Journals of the Plague Years." *The Sewanee Review* 75 (1967): 717–30.

———. "The Other Side of Despair: Notes on Christian Existentialism." *Critic* 24, no. 2 (October–November 1965): 13–23.

Merwin, W. S. "Through the Blur of Pain." Review of *Exile and the Kingdom. The Nation,* 16 August 1958, 74–75.

Miles, O. Thomas. "Three Authors in Search of a Character." *Personalist* 46 (1965): 65–72.

Miller, Stephen. "The Posthumous Victory of Albert Camus." *Commentary* 70 (November 1980): 53–58.

The Minnesota Review 4, no. 3 (Spring 1964). Special Camus issue.

Modern Fiction Studies 10, no. 3 (Autumn 1964). Special Camus issue.

Moeller, Charles. "Albert Camus: The Question of Hope." *Cross Currents* 8 (1958): 172–84.

Moore, Harry T. *Twentieth-Century French Literature.* Carbondale: Southern Illinois University Press, 1966.

Moses, Edwin. "Functional Complexity: The Narrative Techniques of *The Plague.*" *Modern Fiction Studies* 20 (1974): 419–29.

Murchland, Bernard G. "Albert Camus: Rebel." *Catholic World* 188 (1958–59): 308–14.

———. "Between Solitude and Solidarity." *Commonweal* 23 (October 1970): 91–95.

Nadeau, Maurice. *The French Novel since the War.* London: Methuen, 1967.

Neilson, Frank. "The Plague: Camus's Pro-Fascist Allegory." *Literature and Ideology* no. 15 (1973): 17–26.

North, R. J. *Myth in the Modern French Theatre.* Keele, England: University of Keele Publications, 1962.

O'Brien, Conor Cruise. *Albert Camus of Europe and Africa.* New York: Viking Press, 1970.

O'Brien, Justin. "Camus' Lyrical and Critical Essays." *Columbia Forum* 12 (1969): 32–33.

———. *The French Literary Horizon.* New Brunswick, N.J.: Rutgers University Press, 1967.

Onimus, Jean. *Albert Camus and Christianity.* Tuscaloosa: University of Alabama Press, 1965.

Parker, E. *Albert Camus: The Artist in the Arena.* Madison: University of Wisconsin Press, 1965.

Parsell, D. B. "Aspects of Comedy in Camus's *Le Malentendu.*" *Symposium* 37 (1983–1984): 302–17.

Pasco, A. H. "'And seated ye shall fall': Some Lexical Markers in Camus's 'Jonas.'" *Modern Fiction Studies* 28 (1982): 240–42.

Petersen, Carol. *Albert Camus.* New York: Ungar, 1969.

Peyre, Henri. *French Novelists of Today.* New York: Oxford University Press, 1967.

Podhoretz, Norman. "Solitary or Solidary?" Review of *Exile and the Kingdom. The New Yorker,* 29 March 1958, 115–22.

Pollmann, Lew. *Sartre and Camus: The Literature of Existence.* New York: Ungar, 1970.

Porter, L. M. "From Chronicle to Novel: Artistic Elaboration in Camus's *La Peste.*" *Modern Fiction Studies* 28 (1982–83): 589–98.

Proix, Robert, ed. *Albert Camus and the Men of the Stone.* San Francisco: Stauffacher/Greenwood Press, 1971.

Quilliot, Roger. *The Sea and Prisons: A Commentary on the Life and Thought of Albert Camus.* University: University of Alabama Press, 1970.

Reck, Rima Drell. "Albert Camus: The Artist and His Time." *Modern Language Quarterly* 23 (1962): 129–34.

———. *Literature and Responsibility: The French Novelist in the Twentieth Century.* Baton Rouge: Louisiana State University Press, 1969.

Redfern, W. D. "Camus and Confusion." *Symposium* 20 (1966): 329–42.

Rhein, Phillip H. *Albert Camus.* New York: Twayne, 1969.

Rizzuto, Anthony. *Camus' Imperial Vision.* Carbondale: Southern Illinois University Press, 1981.

Robbe-Grillet, Alain. *For a New Novel.* New York: Grove Press, 1965.

Rocks, James E. "Camus Reads Defoe: *A Journal of the Plague Year* as a Source of *The Plague.*" *Tulane Studies in English* 15 (1967): 81–87.

Roeming, Robert F. *Camus: A Bibliography.* Madison: University of Wisconsin Press, 1968.

Rooke, Constance. "Camus's 'The Guest.'" *Studies in Short Fiction* 14 (1977): 78–81.

Rossi, Louis. "Albert Camus: The Plague of Absurdity." *The Kenyon Review* 20 (1958): 399–422.

Roudiez, Leon. "Camus and *Moby Dick.*" *Symposium* 15 (1961): 30–40.

———. "Strangers in Melville and Camus." *The French Review* 31 (1957–58): 217–26.

Rysten, Felix S. A. *False Prophets in the Fiction of Camus, Dostoevsky, Melville, and Others.* Coral Gables, Fla.: University of Miami Press, 1972.

Sarraute, Nathalie. *The Age of Suspicion: Essays on the Novel.* New York: George Braziller, 1963.

Sartre, Jean-Paul. "Camus' *The Outsider.*" In *Situations.* Translated by Benita Eisler. New York: George Braziller, 1965.

Savage, E. B. "Masks and Mummeries in *Enrico IV* and *Caligula.*" *Modern Drama* 6 (1964): 397–401.

Scott, N. A. *Albert Camus.* London: Bowes & Bowes, 1962.

———, ed. *The Unquiet Vision: Mirrors of Man in Existentialism.* New York: World Publishing, 1969.

Sebba, Helen. "Stuart Gilbert's Meursault: A Strange 'Stranger.'" *Contemporary Literature* 13 (1972): 334–40.

Seltzer, Leon F. "Camus's Absurd and the World of Melville's Confidence-Man." *PMLA* 82 (1967): 14–27.

Showalter, English. "Camus's Mysterious Guests: A Note on the Value of Ambiguity." *Studies in Short Fiction* 4 (1966): 348–50.

———. *Exiles and Strangers: A Reading of Camus's* Exile and the Kingdom. Columbus: Ohio State University Press, 1984.

Solotaroff, Theodore. "Camus's Portable Pedestal." *The New Republic,* 21 December 1968, 27–30.

Somers, Paul P., Jr. "Camus *Si,* Sartre *No;* or, The Delightful M. Meursault." *The French Review* 42 (1968–69): 693–700.

Sonnenfeld, A. "Albert Camus as Dramatist: The Sources of His Failure." *Tulane Drama Review* 5 (June 1961): 106–23.

Sontag, Susan. "Camus' Notebooks." *New York Review of Books,* 26 September 1963, 1–3.

Spector, Robert Donald. "Albert Camus, 1913–1969: A Final Interview." *Venture* 3, no. 4 (Spring–Summer 1960): 26–38.

Sperber, Michael. "Camus' *The Fall:* The Icarus Complex." *American Imago* 26 (1969): 269–80.

Stamm, Julian. "Camus' *Stranger:* His Act of Violence." *American Imago* 26 (1969): 281–90.

Starobinski, Jean. "Albert Camus and the Plague." *CIBA Symposium* 10, no. 2 (1962): 62–70.

Sterling, Elwyn F. "A Story of Cain: Another Look at *L'Hôte.*" *The French Review* 54 (1980–81): 524–29.

Strauss, W. A. "*Caligula:* Ancient Sources and Modern Parallels." *Comparative Literature* 3 (1951): 160–73.

Suther, Judith D., ed. *Essays on Camus' Exile and the Kingdom.* University, Miss.: Romance Monographs, 1980.

Symposium 24, no. 3 (Fall 1970). Special Camus issue.

Thody, Philip. *Albert Camus: A Study of His Work.* New York: Macmillan, 1957.

———. *Albert Camus 1913–1960.* London: Hamish Hamilton, 1961.

Trahan, Elizabeth. "Clamence vs. Dostoevsky: An Approach to *La Chute.*" *Comparative Literature* 18 (1966): 337–50.

Trilling, Lionel. "*The Guest:* Commentary." In *The Experience of Literature,* 370–72. New York: Holt, Rinehart & Winston, 1967.

Ullman, Stephen. *The Image in the Modern French Novel: Gide, Alain-Fournier, Proust, Camus.* Cambridge: Cambridge University Press, 1960.

Updike, John. "In Praise of the Blind, Black God." *New Yorker,* 21 October 1972, 157–67.

Venture 3, no. 4 (Spring–Summer 1960). Special Camus issue.

Viggiani, C. A. "Albert Camus in 1936: The Beginnings of a Career." *Symposium* 12 (1958): 7–18.

———. "Camus' *L'Etranger.*" *PMLA* 71 (1956): 865–87.

Virtanen, R. "Camus' *Le Malentendu* and Some Analogues." *Comparative Literature* 10 (1958): 232–40.

Wagner, C. Roland. "The Silence of *The Stranger.*" *Modern Fiction Studies* 16 (1970): 27–40.

Walker, I. H. "Camus, Plotinus, and Patrie: The Remaking of a Myth." *Modern Language Review* 77 (1982): 829–39.

———. "The Composition of *Caligula.*" *Symposium* 20 (1966): 263–77.

Weis, Marcia. *The Lyrical Essays of Albert Camus.* Ottawa: Editions Namman de Sherbrooke, 1976.

West, Paul. "Albert Camus and the Aesthetic Tradition." In *New World Writing,* 80–91. New York: New American Library, 1958.

Widmer, Kingsley. *The Literary Rebel.* Carbondale: Southern Illinois University Press, 1965.

Willhoite, Fred H., Jr. *Beyond Nihilism: Albert Camus' Contribution to Political Thought.* Baton Rouge: Louisiana State University Press, 1968.

Williams, Raymond. *Modern Tragedy.* Stanford: Stanford University Press, 1966.

Womack, William R., and F. S. Heck. "A Note on Camus's *The Guest*." *International Fiction Review* 2 (1975): 163–65.

Yale French Studies 25 (Spring 1960). Special Camus issue.

Zants, Emily. "Camus's Deserts and Their Allies, Kingdoms of the Stranger." *Symposium* 17 (1963): 30–41.

Zyla, Wolodymyr T., and Wendell M. Aycock, eds. *Albert Camus's Literary Milieu: Arid Lands*. Proceedings of the Comparative Literature Symposium (Texas Tech) 8. Lubbock: Texas Tech Press, 1976.

Acknowledgments

" Le Renégat' or the Terror of the Absolute" by Victor Brombert from *The Intellectual Hero: Studies in the French Novel 1880–1955* by Victor Brombert, © 1961 by Victor Brombert. Reprinted by permission.

"Two Inside Narratives: *Billy Budd* and *L'Etranger*" by Roger Shattuck from *Texas Studies in Literature and Language* 4, no. 3 (Autumn 1962), © 1962 by the University of Texas Press. Reprinted by permission.

"The Mask of Albert Camus: *Notebooks 1942–1951*" (originally entitled "The Mask of Albert Camus") by Paul de Man from *The New York Review of Books 5* no. 10, © 1965 by Nyrev, Inc. Reprinted by permission of *The New York Review of Books*.

"Man and His Acts: Jean-Paul Satre and Albert Camus" by Jacques Guicharnaud from *Modern French Theatre from Giraudoux to Genet* by Jacques Guicharnaud, © 1967 by Yale University Press. Reprinted by permission.

"*Caligula*" by E. Freeman from *The Theatre of Albert Camus: A Critical Study* by E. Freeman, © 1971 by Methuen & Co. Reprinted by permission.

"*The Myth* and *The Rebel*: Diversity and Unity" by Donald Lazere from *The Unique Creation of Albert Camus* by Donald Lazere, © 1973 by Yale University Press. Reprinted by permission of the author.

"Camus's Stranger Retried" by René Girard from *To Double Business Bound: Essays on Literature, Mimesis and Anthropology* by René Girard, © 1978 by The Johns Hopkins University Press. Reprinted by permission.

"*The Plague*" (originally entitled "Of Plagues, Cold Wars, Tedium, Revolts and Quarrels") by Patrick McCarthy from *Camus* by Patrick McCarthy, © 1982 by Patrick McCarthy. Reprinted by permission of the author and Random House.

"The Rhetoric of Dizziness: *La Chute*" (originally entitled "Camus and the Rhetoric of Dizziness: *La Chute*") by David R. Ellison from *Contemporary Literature* 24, no. 3 (Fall 1983), © 1983 by The University of Wisconsin Press. Reprinted by permission.

" 'The Growing Stone': Reconciliation and Conclusion" by English Showalter, Jr., from *Exiles and Strangers: A Reading of Camus's* Exile and the Kingdom by

English Showalter, Jr., © 1984 the Ohio State University Press. Reprinted by permission.

"Exile from the Kingdon" by Susan Tarrow from *Exile from the Kingdom: A Political Reading of Albert Camus* by Susan Tarrow, © 1985 by The University of Alabama Press. Reprinted by permission.

Index